A New Pattern for a Tired World

Books by Louis Bromfield

A MODERN HERO	NIGHT IN BOMBAY
TWENTY-FOUR HOURS	WILD IS THE RIVER
AWAKE AND REHEARSE	UNTIL THE DAY BREAK
THE STRANGE CASE OF MISS ANNIE	MRS. PARKINGTON
SPRAGG	WHAT BECAME OF ANNA BOLTON
A GOOD WOMAN	THE WORLD WE LIVE IN
EARLY AUTUMN	PLEASANT VALLEY
POSSESSION	A FEW BRASS TACKS
THE GREEN BAY TREE	KENNY
THE FARM	COLORADO
HERE TODAY AND GONE TOMORROW	MALABAR FARM
THE MAN WHO HAD EVERYTHING	THE WILD COUNTRY
THE RAINS CAME	OUT OF THE EARTH
IT TAKES ALL KINDS	MR. SMITH

A NEW PATTERN FOR A TIRED WORLD

A NEW PATTERN

for

A TIRED WORLD

by

LOUIS BROMFIELD

HARPER & BROTHERS, PUBLISHERS

New York

Contents

Marked While Engaged in the Lost Art of Reading

1. LIBERALISM

Blaming the other fellow is sterile diplomacy; it is much more important to make a new start.

TOM DRIBERG, British Labor M. P. in *Time* Magazine

It is also false that, to be liberal, we must see *government* as the sole agent of advance. Has not the initiative and genius of one man—George Washington Carver—done at least as much for the "progress and reform" of the South as the government's ballyhooed TVA? Do we disbelieve in "progress and reform" simply because we trust the spontaneous energies of free men, and distrust Washington?

E. MERRILL ROOT, "Are the 'Liberals' Liberal?,"
Human Events, September 23, 1953

True liberalism is found not in striving to spread bureaucracy, but in striving to set bounds to it. True liberalism seeks all legitimate freedom, in the confident belief that without freedom, all other blessings are vain. Liberalism is a force truly of the spirit coming from a realization that economic freedom cannot be sacrificed if political freedom is to be preserved.

HERBERT HOOVER, from an address at Case Institute of
Technology, Cleveland, Ohio, April 11, 1953

Is there an open season for treason, as there is for deer hunting and trout fishing? This question is posed by Mrs. Eleanor Roosevelt. According to an A.P. dispatch from Seattle, she deplored the "furore" over the White case, as she once deplored the exposure of her friends, Alger Hiss and Lauchlin Currie. Mrs. Roosevelt is quoted as adding that a change has occurred in the nation's "moral climate," "placing the case of White in a different perspective from 1946." The vast majority of Americans, one suspects, would be inclined to paraphrase a saying of Calvin Coolidge in this connection. There is no right to commit treason and espionage, or to abuse governmental office to advance the interests of a foreign power, under any circumstances, *in any year, at any time.*

THE FREEMAN, an editorial

The new mood of social science is little different from that of the conservative critics of the nineteenth century, except that now the intellectuals attribute the gloom to their own lostness. The mood is mixed with sad contrition.

NEW LEADER

It is not entirely fanciful to regard sex as being to the individual what power is to the collectivity. We are all familiar with the miseries and abnormalities of those who try to escape from the harsh realities of the flesh into fantasies of idealized love. Similar miseries and abnormalities are liable to result from a like attempt to escape from the harsh realities of power into fantasies of political idealism.

MALCOLM MUGGERIDGE in *Time* Magazine

The American State is a peculiar organism, unlike anything in modern Europe or in the ancient world.

JAMES BRYCE in *The American Commonwealth*

To one who advised him to set up a democracy in Sparta, "Pray," said Lycurgus, "do you first set up a democracy in your own house."

LYCURGUS in Plutarch's *Apothegms of Kings and Great Commanders*

2. WORLD AID

There is no such thing as foreign relations in the abstract.

GEORGE F. KENNAN

This is in some aspects an age of "Tout comprendre c'est tout pardonner." Gone are the inflexible laws of political morality applied or, at any rate, expounded by people like Gladstone or Broadbent. Gone is the belief in the intrinsic desirability and applicability of the principles of the British Constitution; gone is the old belief in the universal applicability of the doctrines of the Rights of Man. We are historical relativists. We understand that it is absurd to expect Russia to evolve in the direction of Anglo-Saxon representative government; we can see that the People's Democracies are just what the doctor ordered, that the Mao regime in China is perhaps a little rough, a little careless of objective truth, but nevertheless that may be, probably is, the way that true freedom will come to China. Every society can find its own way to salvation, and it is stupidity or arrogance to expect the political and social evolution of the world to be based on universally accepted principles and practices. Each nation can go to heaven or hell in its own way and, who knows? the destinations in either case will be much the same. We can take the long view and see the historical accidents and necessities that justify departures from what our fathers would have thought the norms of political wisdom and morality.

There is one exception to this law of universal toleration; one country that is not allowed to go its own way; one whose eccentricities are unforgivable, one whose eccentric practices call not for understanding but condemnation. That country is, needless to say, the United States.

> D. W. Brogan, from "America's Way: Action without
> Doctrine," *Manchester Guardian Weekly*, October 29, 1953

America's China policy seems to us neither idealistic nor realistic. How can there be idealism in friendship with a regime (Chiang Kai-shek's) which corruptly squandered the billions of dollars generously given to it? What realism is there in refusing to understand that such a regime can never regain power in China? That China's actual, effective government is the Communist government in Peking? And that the more vigorously Peking is boycotted by the West the more closely Peking will be tied up with Moscow?

> Tom Driberg, British Labor M. P. in *Time* Magazine

"I hope the Korean situation does not wind up in an anticlimax which finds Syngman Rhee at any sort of odds with either the UN or Washington . . . The UN and U.S. interest in driving the communists to the Manchurian borders obviously involves vastly more than extending the status of the South Korean Republic. It involves the total fate of Asia and must be handled as such."

> The late U.S. Senator Arthur Vandenberg in a letter dated
> October 24, 1950 (Quoted by Demaree Bess in the *Saturday
> Evening Post*)

In Asia, China is the key to the trouble. Had America provided early aid to Chiang and a Yangtse TVA, instead of pressing for a Communist coalition, not only would a historical balance have been found to Japan but a historically pro-American power would have been placed on those frontiers where the Soviet population is least numerous and where the strategic links to Great Russia are weakest. It is an additional irony that the precise opposite of this has come about, partly because Franklin Roosevelt preferred to scuttle Chiang (the erstwhile "gallant fighter against Fascism") for the *beaux yeux* of Generalissimo Stalin, and partly because Chiang was confronted with intrigues against him by American writers and American generals such as Stilwell. The fire of propaganda about "Chiang, the corrupt fascist" later spread to Britain, and here it received additional encouragement from capitalist traders who hoped that China would "break up." Where Borodin failed, this worked.

GEORGE CATLIN in The New Leader

While we've had casualties and it's been a terrifically expensive thing, in blood and treasure both, in the two wars, the real fighting and the greatest destruction has been in Europe. The people over there want to be free and maintain their kind of society, but they're getting awfully tired of being used as the battleground of the world.

What caused the trouble was that we were interested in punishing our enemies and we had a war psychosis—whatever you want to call it—and we didn't realize that what had happened is that Japan and Germany had dropped out as world powers and left a power vacuum, so to speak, with no understanding and no peace settlement. We had no understanding with the Russians and, with this radical difference in our philosophies on how a human society should be operated, we were left in a very dangerous position in the world. No one thought until after the unconditional surrender of Germany, "Well, what are you going to do with the German people?"

CHARLES E. WILSON, Secretary of Defense (quoted in *U.S. News and World Report*, November 13, 1953

Will that part of the world which Stalin conquers with our war planes and our tanks be consecrated to freedom? Or, after a Russian victory with our aid, must we step in with our armies to impose the four freedoms on millions of people 10,000 miles away who have never known either freedom from want or freedom from terrorism?

The late U.S. Senator ROBERT A. TAFT

Just set down the names of the countries that have been receiving economic and military aid from the United States, either in alphabetical order or by continents and regions. Then what do you get? Certainly nothing you can imagine to be a table of essential political ingredients for a free world. It looks more like a queue, with at least one thing in common, namely, an appetite for American dollars. What is the bond of ideas between Burma or Siam on one side of the world and Belgium or Scandinavia on the other side? It is not even anti-Communist. A great deal of it is neutral, like India, and some of it teeters on the fence, saying, "Dollars, dollars, lest we fall into the hands of the Communists."

GARET GARRETT in *Human Events*, November 11, 1953

. . . we should now propose: (1) the withdrawal of all foreign troops from Germany and immediate free all-German elections, both under the supervision of the UN; (2) resumption of negotiations on the Austrian peace treaty on the basis of the near-complete "long draft";

and (3) a new Locarno-type treaty to guarantee the united Germany against aggression and to guarantee the rest of Europe against a resurgence of German militarism. Such proposals will place the burden for action on the Kremlin; further procrastination will only bring new political defeats for democracy in Europe.

New Leader, editorial

Since the end of World War Two, every man, woman and child in the United States has contributed $256 to foreign aid. That is the startling total of our efforts to combat the spread of "stomach" Communism in Europe and Asia.

What, in the long run, has all this money accomplished? Is Italy today less threatened by Communism than five years ago? Has Japan been able to create a stable economy? Is India, or Indonesia, immune to Communist infiltration and agitation? The answer is that the spread of Communism has neither been stopped nor seriously impaired. Because of the patchwork fashion of our foreign aid program most of these economic efforts have canceled each other out. An almost totally neglected reason behind this failure is the basic problem of overpopulation.

We have exported food and farm tools to the starving millions in Europe and the Far East. Yet at the same time we have introduced modern welfare methods which have tremendously increased the number of hungry mouths to be fed. In a tragically shortsighted and wasteful manner we have created a vicious circle, a situation which reminds one of those chi-chi Hollywood sitting rooms; a charming log fire is burning while the air conditioner goes full blast.

The Eisenhower Administration must further rethink and replan America's foreign aid program. A change in attitude is needed first. Until now, talk has always been about shortages—of food, land, medical facilities, dollars, tools, and so on. It has rarely been admitted that in some places there are simply too many people for all the other things to go around—and that the United States can't supply all that is considered lacking.

Population policies have not kept up with scientific and industrial advances. Today's developments demand a maximum of goods and services, of educational and cultural facilities for each human being—not just the creation of a maximum number of human beings. American aid, to be fully effective, must be so applied that it encourages the well-being of individuals rather than the growth of a faceless, ever-increasing mass. Otherwise individual dignity, the great democratic ideal of this age, stands in danger of being swamped by subsidized, constantly mounting, and inevitably underprivileged populations.

MARTIN EBON in *The Freeman*

Of all the curious attitudes—pragmatism, statism, One-Worldism, etc. —that shape the thinking of today's "liberal" sophisticate, one attitude is especially bubbleheaded; it is the attitude that government sovereignty reigns supreme over economic law as well as political law. The government, it is held, can suspend or even repeal the law of supply and demand. The dangers of inflation are strictly storybook. We must recognize inflation as a better way of life. Glorious deficit finance is here to stay. . . .

Two types of this economic vacuumism dog us. One is sweeping, the other subtle. Both varieties are evident in the 83rd Congress, which will reconvene this January 4. The sweeping variety could be detected in the stock catch phrases of the social salvationists testifying for their fat give-away bills: "at all costs" or "at any price" should this or that welfare measure be enacted. Yet it is reasonable to ask, would not "any price"—say the price of freedom or the price of economic stability—be too high?

Senator Symington (D., Mo.) put forth a variety of this sweeping disregard of mere economics when he said: "You can't stop a Soviet bomber with a balanced budget." Would the Senator then argue that you can stop a Soviet bomber with an unbalanced budget? Such a Hobson's choice—atomic attack or deficit finance—is designed to ride herd over stubborn economic complications.

WILLIAM H. PETERSON in *Human Events*, November 18, 1953

Observe good faith and justice toward all nations; cultivate peace and harmony with all.

Europe has a set of primary interests, which to us have none, or a very remote relation. Hence she must be engaged in frequent controversies, the causes of which are essentially foreign to our concerns. Hence, therefore, it must be unwise for us to implicate ourselves, by artificial ties, in the ordinary vicissitudes of her politics, or the ordinary combinations and collisions of her friendships and enmities. . . .

GEORGE WASHINGTON in his Farewell Address

3. MILITARISM

Radford's forthcoming address will propound a second challenging "feeler."

Again by adroit implication, as in the case of his spectacular suggestion regarding the anti-Red struggle in Indochina, Radford will oppose cutting military spending in the next fiscal year.

ROBERT S. ALLEN in syndicated column, Dec. 1, 1953

For God's sake, do not drag me into another war! I am worn down and worn out with crusading and defending Europe and protecting mankind: I *must* think a little for myself.

I am sorry for the Spaniards—I am sorry for the Greeks—I deplore the fate of the Jews; the people of the Sandwich Islands are groaning under the most detestable tyranny. Bagdad is oppressed; I do not like the present state of the Delta.

Am I to fight for all these people? The world is bursting with sin and sorrow. Am I to be champion of the Decalogue and to be eternally raising fleets and armies to make all men good and happy? We have just done saving Europe and I am afraid the consequences will be that we shall cut each other's throats.

> SIDNEY SMITH to Lady Grey (1765). Quoted from *Unconditional Hatred* by Capt. Russell Grenfell, British Royal Navy

Senators supporting the Air Force budget cuts picked up some useful information during the recent hearings. Example: the Air Force had $2,500,000,000 it hadn't even been able to put under contract. All told, the Defense Department has $99,000,000,000 in unspent appropriations.

> NEWSWEEK, August 3, 1953

The Joint Chiefs of Staff, all able men and patriots, are in an exceedingly unenviable position. As they proceed with their much-advertised "new look" at defense planning and defense spending, they find themselves painfully squeezed between an irresistible force and an immovable object.

The irresistible force is the revolution in warfare ushered in by the vast technological advances of the last decade. The immovable object is the immense resistance to basic change, the vested interest in things as they are, in all three of the services. . . .

The Weapon System Evaluation Board has never passed on the value of the Navy's supercarriers, simply because to do so would touch off a tremendous inter-service row. Indeed, the board now refuses to pass on any "controversial" weapons whatsoever, for fear of rows. This is a measure of the power of resistance to change within the services.

Under the circumstances, it is not surprising that the new Joint Chiefs' famous "new look" is beginning to look more and more like a decision to carry on about as before. This is perhaps inevitable, while the new chiefs, and their newly appointed civilian superiors are coming to grips with the tremendous problems which confront them. But in the long run, carrying on as before may prove a dangerous expedient in the age of the revolution in warfare.

> STEWART ALSOP in the New York *Herald Tribune*

It is all very well for General Omar Bradley to say that air attack on the homelands of America or Russia would be difficult by means of "the big, long-haul planes coming across the icecap," but that, "if war were thrust upon us, from bases in the territories of our allies we could strike at the vitals of Communist power." That was a catastrophic remark when heard by Parisians or Londoners who, it seems, are to man the front for a policy settled elsewhere. They won't do it. They will see America to hell first. It is doubtful if the NATO agreement is worth the paper it is written on, since it produces the illusion of a security which does not exist.

GEORGE CATLIN in the *New Leader*

TOKYO, Oct. 31 (AP)—Rearmament-minded Japanese Saturday labeled as "a fantastic target" the 325,000 to 350,000-man army agreed upon by American and Japanese diplomats in Washington.

"An army of more than 300,000 men can be raised only on a conscription basis," said a logistics colonel in Japan's 110,000-man national safety force. "And I do not think the public is in a mood to revive conscription for some years to come."

The colonel added that the Japanese plan of expanding the present safety force to 180,000 in three to five years is the "maximum we can hope for."

ASSOCIATED PRESS DISPATCH

[NOTE: Japan is at present "protected" by a *conscripted* army of *Americans* plus military installations, costing hundreds of millions each year—all this in addition to the heavy toll in lives, matériel and money taken by the Korean fiasco a short distance away.]

Through force of circumstance, the British have had to face the realities of modern warfare. They cannot afford the luxury of pretending that the three main elements of defense—air, land and sea—can each play an equal role. They are compelled to rely on new concepts rather than on standing armies which can never match the Red Army. Although traditionally a sea power, the British have accepted the fact that Russia cannot be blockaded and have therefore drastically curtailed naval expenditures. Their air force has become the "first line of defense" in the ocean of the sky.

The British have given up trying to satisfy all their generals and admirals and the loyal alumni of the two original sister services. How long can we in the United States afford to stake our destiny on service loyalties rather than on strategic realities?

C. LESTER WALKER in the *Readers Digest*

During the years of the Marshall Plan—now Harold Stassen's Foreign Operations Administration—we provided foreign aid of all sorts. In addition, "Point Four" projects of "technical aid for underdeveloped territories" mushroomed in the Near and Far East. The armed forces have always engaged in little-publicized welfare efforts of their own. And, through the United Nations technical aid program, additional millions of taxpayers' money have been going into remote Asian villages and other "target areas."

Nobody really knows just what has been done by all these overlapping programs, agencies, and projects. The phrase "technical aid" sounds sufficiently solid to cloak the helter-skelter creations of global bureaucracies. Results were what might be expected. The U.N.'s Economic and Social Council admitted last year, in a 400-page survey, that postwar world food production increased "significantly less" than the globe's population.

If foreign aid had been successful in long-range terms, food production might have increased more rapidly than population. The exact opposite has happened. Obviously, the best will in the world, and the biggest dollar appropriations, are no substitute for a properly thought-out program.

MARTIN EBON in *The Freeman*

As a boy, Georgi Malenkov excelled in mathematics and hoped to be an engineer. His Supreme Soviet speech, announcing that the Kremlin had the hydrogen bomb, reflects his precise, calculating approach. As he looked at the world situation (mounting rebellion at home, a popular American will to aid that rebellion, the complete political collapse of Western Europe from cold-war fatigue), Malenkov must have thought: "What can I do or say to alter these trends—to prop up the Communist movement, to frighten the American advocates of liberation, to make Western Europe even more eager for peace at any price?" The H-bomb announcement cost Malenkov nothing and will serve all three purposes.

Most certainly, Malenkov's statement was, as Edward Crankshaw put it, a "carefully prepared climax to an elaborately contrived session of the Supreme Soviet, the chief purpose of which was plainly to divert public attention from the internal crisis of the regime." Nevertheless, it would be foolish to pretend that it will not, indeed, spur Western Europe's pressure for appeasement and, at the same time, confuse the hot-and-cold liberationists of the Eisenhower regime (hot in November 1952, glacial in June 1953).

It matters not one whit whether Malenkov has the bomb or not; if he doesn't have it now, he will have it later. The political reality is that most of the world thinks he has it now. And because this means that the thought of global war is more than ever abhorred, it also means that the present U.S. policy of security *through stockpiles and military alliances is hopelessly outdated.* The Stockholm Peace Appeal, capitalizing on the natural revulsion against Hiroshima; the war in Korea, showing that no mortal dared unleash the A-bomb when retaliation was possible, and now the Malenkov announcement have combined to render the bomb impotent as a guarantee of anyone's security. Because the use of the bomb by either side means sure annihilation for both, the world now looks for political solutions.

NEW LEADER, editorial

If you decide to fight for survival, you may want more emphasis on civil defense, radar, interceptors with ability to deliver our own H bombs rather than too much emphasis on land armies.

HON. STYLES BRIDGES, U.S. Senator

With new technologies and new strategic concepts developing, there is every reason to suppose that defense spending and the number of troops stationed abroad can be substantially cut. But new technologies and new strategies will not alone suffice.

The administrators in Washington will also have to resist the pressure-groups, foreign and domestic, the professional doom-criers and perhaps most of all the stand-patters who cry heresy at any proposed deviation from the static-defense policies of the recent past. That resistance will require courage, clarity and candor.

WALL STREET JOURNAL, editorial

When the new Administration's searchlight was turned upon our global commitments, they proved to be even more formidable than had been suspected. Our foreign obligations—military, political, economic and welfare—had piled up so fast and so high that most experts agreed the burden upon the American people was becoming intolerable. The most dangerous feature of these obligations was not the original outlay which they had required but the enormous upkeep costs which they had imposed. For example, American military installations had been set up in forty-nine foreign countries, and were the costliest per man ever devised; moreover, there was a strong tendency to regard them all as more or less permanent.

DEMAREE BESS in the *Saturday Evening Post*

It is quite possible that the U.S.S.R. has been able to produce in limited quantity a crude sort of atomic bomb which can be detonated from a tower. That the Soviets possess in large quantity workable atomic bombs which can be delivered by long-range aircraft or guided missiles is less certain. There can be no quarrel with the school which holds it would be dangerously foolish to assume that the Russians do not have any atomic weapon. However, we are doing ourselves irreparable damage in the war of diplomatic maneuver by playing up Soviet strength in the hope of keeping defense expenditures popular at home and among our allies. The public must learn to meet the Soviet threat without alarmist shots in the arm. Every time we talk up Soviet strength we weaken our own position and the resistance to Communism of the already faint-hearted neutralists in Europe and Asia.

THE FREEMAN, September 21, 1953

Those European clashes, which were not confined to East Germany, but extended to other satellites, demonstrated beyond any further doubt the weaknesses in the outer reaches of the postwar Soviet Empire which had hitherto been only suspected. Obviously Moscow could no longer make confident plans depending upon the European satellite armies which had absorbed so much of her effort and attention since 1945.

DEMAREE BESS in the *Saturday Evening Post*

. . . it seems to us that certain fundamental principles are clear and have long been clear.

One is that it doesn't take six U.S. divisions to deter the Soviets from overrunning West Europe. If any external pressure at all can be said to deter them, it is the warning written into the Atlantic pact that an attack upon West Europe will be regarded by the U.S. as an attack upon itself. For that deterrent to operate, it is not necessary even to have token U.S. forces in Europe (except, for the time being, in Germany, not yet part of NATO). It is necessary only for the Soviets to know it—and they do.

Speaking of deterrents, a second principle is that the presence of large numbers of U.S. troops in Europe deters the Europeans from doing as much as they could for their own defense. Without those troops, or with fewer of them, the Europeans would very quickly mobilize enough forces to defend themselves.

WALL STREET JOURNAL, editorial

We need versatile military forces, competent both for offense and for defense. This poses grave problems of allotting matériel, money, men, and attention. The balancing of the branches of our military services may require enlarging present budgets; if achieved within present budgets it most certainly would require some drastic reallocations of funds within the government as a whole. In seeking a balanced military force, we must also squarely face the effects of additional expenditures on our economy; we recognize the hazard of spending ourselves into bank-ruptcy.

> JAMES R. KILLIAN, JR., President, Massachusetts Institute of Technology and A. G. HILL, Director of the Lincoln Laboratory, in the *Atlantic Monthly*

Three years of fighting in Korea has fully confirmed the unemotional analysis of American military strategists, made long before the 1950 communist attack, that present-day Korea is a military liability and not an asset to the United States. This Asian peninsula, considered so strategically vital half a century ago that Russia, China and Japan fought two wars for its possession, has been rendered strategically insignificant by the development of the bombing airplane. Today the same Japanese strategists who once attached so much value to Korea can be indifferent to its fate; airfields in adjacent Siberia and Manchuria offer just as much of a threat to Japan as any Korean airfields could do. On the other hand, Russia and China no longer need to be greatly concerned about Korea unless an aggressive anticommunist government emerges there on their land frontiers. Moreover, it is an unfortunate fact that the communist bloc, due entirely to geography, can dominate Korea much more cheaply and easily than any anticommunists. If an agreement is again reached for the withdrawal of all foreign troops from Korea, Russian and Chinese soldiers will still stand directly on her indefensible borders, but the anticommunist forces can be no closer than Japan, isolated across the turbulent waters of the Sea of Japan.

> DEMAREE BESS in the *Saturday Evening Post*

To want the French to go on fighting the Vietminh Army and also to want complete independence is not more contradictory perhaps than to want the Vietnamese to refuse a distant dependence on Moscow and accept a less distant one on Paris.

> MANCHESTER GUARDIAN WEEKLY

. . . resolute men and women, rooted to this earth and fighting on and for their portion of it, remain the *final* determinant.

> GENERAL MATTHEW RIDGWAY in address at Lafayette College

Now you have more than 40 countries, in four continents, to whose defense the United States is committed either directly by treaty and pact or morally by implication of its foreign policy. Their total population is more than one billion, and that is practically one-half of the entire human race—to be defended by 160 million Americans. And to a very large proportion of that half of the human race the kind of freedom we think we are talking about is totally unknown.

And still do you know what the free world is? Or where it is? Or what it will fight for? Will it fight for the security of the United States?

GARET GARRET in *Human Events*, November 11, 1953

The statement has been given currency that a few scientists, naïve in the ways of military operations, have promised complete security from an air attack. This is rubbish. No informed and competent scientists who have considered the problem have concluded that a perfect defense is possible or probable. They hold the view that our present low defense capabilities can be improved manyfold. We have the technical resources to accomplish this if they are mobilized and put to use. It is this improvement that scientists advocate, not the building of a perfect system with all the astronomical numbers that this implies. The estimated percentage of invading planes which can be shot down once we have some of the improvements now under development is secret information. It is not 100 per cent, or even 95 per cent, but it is a great gain over our existing powers of attrition. Let no one be under the misapprehension that a perfect air defense is technically or economically feasible.

JAMES R. KILLIAN, JR., President, Massachusetts Institute of Technology and A. G. HILL, Director of the Lincoln Laboratory, in the *Atlantic Monthly*

A Korea unified by force at a high cost in American lives would still be at the mercy of her communist neighbors except insofar as the United States was prepared to defend her.

DEMAREE BESS in the *Saturday Evening Post*

There never was a war that was not inward; I must
fight till I have conquered in myself what causes war. . . .

MARIANNE MOORE from "In Distrust of Merit"

In this connection, it is interesting to remember that the failures and weaknesses of the league were often attributed to the fact that its membership did not include the U.S. and Russia (except for a few years in the thirties). Yet both the U.S. and the Soviet Union are charter members of the U.N. and this fact has not made any visible contribution to world peace and harmony. It is always dangerous to overestimate what formal institutions can achieve in the absence of common conception of law, justice and morality.

WILLIAM HENRY CHAMBERLAIN

The all-out United Nationalists threaten that if the U.N. should break down, then the United States would be "isolated." They are suffering from semantic delusions. If the U.N. should vanish overnight, the United States would be not one millimeter more or less isolated than today. Friendship and enmity among nations did not begin or end with the United Nations. Whether the U.N. flourishes, flounders, or dies, allies will continue to be allies, the indifferent will remain indifferent, and our enemies will still be against us. The Republic of Korea is not a U.N. member, but her troops and ours together carried the brunt of a terrible war. India is a U.N. member, but no Indian soldiers fought alongside ours in Korea, while Indian diplomats sabotaged our interests. The Soviet Union supplied and directed the fight against us, and the Soviet Union is an honored member of the United Nations.

The Secretary of State put his finger on the fundamental absurdity of the United Nations as at present constituted. We have set up an organization for the alleged purpose of preventing war and aggression, and we have included in its inner command the power that is carrying on perpetual war and aggression. We have put the top criminal on the Police Commission.

THE FREEMAN

5. GENERAL

Perhaps democracy, which seeks comfort, is by nature incapable of understanding the dynamics of power, which may account for the brevity of almost all democratic regimes in history. Indeed, one can readily imagine a situation in which whoever dominates the world will continue to dominate it for an indefinite future—not for pacifist but for technological reasons. The regime imposed on the shoulders of mankind could endure as long as Rome's, because, whether feared or hated or both, no one in the atomic age will decide to pay the brutal costs of overthrowing it. The next two decades are pregnant with the lasting shape of the future.

GEORGE CATLIN in the *New Leader*

In view of the subsequent behavior of General de Gaulle, Americans who became emotional about him in 1943 must feel rather sheepish today; and that may likewise prove true of Americans who have waxed emotional about Doctor Rhee. The truth is, as history has often shown, that emotions are seldom a sound basis for international relations; the most effective bonds between nations are those constructed of mutual self-interests.

DEMAREE BESS in the *Saturday Evening Post*

In the same way the American innocent abroad will see in Europe a distorted image of America. He will see in religion a unifying, pacifying force as it is, on the whole, in America, not, as it often is, say, in France or Italy, a dividing force. He will underestimate the influence of doctrine and see in the palimpsests of European history picturesque backgrounds to modern problems instead of seeing in them the proof visible, in Rome or in Paris or in Berlin, of the fact that human societies are subject to mortality and that history which in America creates confidence in American destiny may well in Europe breed a sense of despair or resignation to the possibility, the probability, of total disaster.

> D. W. BROGAN in "America's Way; Action Without Doctrine," *Manchester Guardian Weekly*, October 29, 1953

The Soviet leaders want Western Europe in order to strengthen their war potential in relation to the U.S. If Soviet Russia gains control over the German, French and Belgian coal, iron and steel production, then she will have come close to the production capacity of the U.S. That's the real aim.

The Soviet Union sees only one real enemy on the face of the earth —the U.S. And Soviet leaders are really convinced that, one day, there will be a clash, whether it be at a conference table or in another way.

But even if the clash occurs at a conference table the Soviet Union's chances for a favorable solution would be much better if this immense war potential were in Russian hands. That's how I see the whole problem of the world.

Any guarantee from us would not interest Soviet Russia much, but it would "save face." That's important to them. Nobody wants to attack them after all. With an offer of a guarantee they would not be forced to confess that they were bluffing, that they really wanted to make peace because things were going badly for them internally. Since they have talked so much about peace, why not tell them they are not threatened, why not offer it to them in black and white?

. . . if the data given by Khrushchev [Nikita S. Khrushchev, member of the ruling Presidium of Soviet Russia] are correct we must assume that agricultural production in Russia is really down to that of 1928. You know that the population of the Soviet Union has increased since that time by about 50 million people. That means there is about one third more people to feed with the same amount of food. That's a terrible situation. If it is not remedied soon, the Soviet Union faces the threat of really big internal troubles.

If then Russia gets a promise of financial aid to develop her internal resources, and if she need not fear attack, then I believe the moment will have come to negotiate with a reasonable chance of success. There is a great deal of fear in the Soviet attitude. It is not fear of Germany, but of being attacked by the U.S.

Thinking it over you get the impression that, in this world, the words "fight," "war" and "struggle" dominate everything, not the word "peace." But men need peace, peace for Europe and the entire world, so that this burden can be taken from men's backs. We need true peace for Europe and the world so that men can learn again to think in peaceful terms, can build and enjoy life again.

KONRAD ADENAUER, Chancellor of the Federal Republic of
Germany in *U.S. News and World
Report*, November 13, 1953

Bad as our international economic policies have been in some respects, those of most European and Asian countries have been incomparably worse. Their exchange controls, artificial currency valuations, bilateralism, import quotas, license requirements, and direct prohibitions, not to speak of their network of internal restrictions, have done far more to throttle two-way trade than the American tariff barrier.

The greatest barrier to a free flow of international trade today, in brief, is not American economic isolationism but European economic isolationism and Asian economic isolationism. That most of Europe, following more isolationist policies than at any time since the seventeenth century, should have succeeded in turning the isolationist charge primarily against us, is certainly not the least remarkable example of the Alice-in-Wonderland ideological climate of the present age.

HENRY HAZLITT in *Newsweek*

The so-called "dollar shortage" that has plagued the world since the end of World War Two is a striking example of the far-ranging consequences that can flow from the neglect of simple economic truths. The "dollar shortage" is said to result from "fundamental structural maladjustments" and to require extensive American aid to foreign countries. It has led to the proliferation of complicated systems of direct controls over transactions involving foreign exchange in one country after another; yet these controls have been powerless to prevent the frequent recurrence of the difficulties that led to their imposition. So far, 1953 is the first odd postwar year that Great Britain, the one-time international banker of the world, has not experienced a dramatic foreign exchange crisis. International conference has followed international conference, and yet the "dollar" problem persists.

This certainly appears a complicated and intractable problem. Yet its fundamental cause and cure are alike simple: the dollar shortage is a result of governmentally controlled and rigid exchange rates; if exchange rates were freed from control and allowed to find their own levels in a free market, as the Canadian dollar now does, the dollar shortage would evaporate overnight. The need to conserve dollars would no longer serve as an excuse for exchange controls, import and export quotas, and the rest of that complicated paraphernalia of modern mercantilism. On the other hand, so long as exchange rates continue to be determined by governmental fiat, and to be held rigid except for occasional devaluations or appreciations, there is almost no hope for the successful elimination of direct controls over international trade. Future attempts at liberalization of trade, however numerous and high-sounding the international agreements which they produce, will be doomed to the resounding failure that has marked the noble experiments of recent years.

MILTON FRIEDMAN in *The Freeman*

If the countries of the world would follow Canada's example, they could remove at one blow all import restrictions and export subsidies, all restrictions on capital flows, all discriminatory measures, without fear that a dollar shortage would arise. Freedom of foreign trade from restrictions would promote greater freedom of internal trade as well, and the one would reinforce the other in increasing the efficiency and productivity of the world as a whole and each nation separately. Experiments in this direction promise dividends every bit as rich and remarkable as have been produced in various countries—notably Germany—by experiments in freeing domestic economies.

MILTON FRIEDMAN in *The Freeman*

Every nation has the government it deserves.

AROUET DE VOLTAIRE

International affairs is a field in which the pursuit of knowledge without understanding is peculiarly pointless and useless.

GEORGE F. KENNAN, in an address before the Alumni of
Princeton University, February, 1953

I want to tell you, Socialists, that I have studied your philosophy, read your works upon economics . . . studied your standard works both in English and German. . . . I have heard your orators and watched the work of your movement, the world over. I have kept close watch upon your doctrines for thirty years; have been closely associated with many of you and know how you think and what you propose. I know too what you have up your sleeves. And I want to say that I am entirely at variance with your philosophy. Economically you are unsound; socially you are wrong; industrially you are an impossibility.

SAMUEL GOMPERS, late President of the
American Federation of Labor

Author's Note

This is a book about many things which concern us all. When I use the word "all" I mean not only citizens of the U.S. but British, Chinese, Indians, the people of Latin America, indeed mankind everywhere in the world. In times of confusion and violence such as these, such a book cannot be either a mild one or a tactful one, designed to spare the feelings of those here and there who have found themselves either through ambition or accident, in positions of great authority in which they have failed or at best made only mediocre contributions toward the peace, welfare and future stability of the world. Nor can it be unviolent and appeasing toward many of the radical ideas or the utopianism which have confused so many issues, produced so many destructive values and caused so much suffering and tragedy.

Whatever is set forth in these pages I have deeply felt, both as an American who has had long experience in many countries and known many of the figures who have molded the tragic outline of our times, and as a true internationalist with no feeling or prejudice regarding race, creed, color or nationality. Some of the ideas expounded meet with the agreement—even to the point of profound conviction—of many individuals in positions of great experience, power and authority who, through the circumstances of their situation, cannot either state them openly or espouse them, however much they may believe in their soundness and truth. In times such as these when sensation races sensation in the pages of the press, and the significance of events and the shape of the immediate future change almost from day to day, it is impossible to write a *current* book. The author has attempted no such thing; whatever is written here is considered in the light, not of immediate topical events, but of the long-range future which is so difficult to separate from the violent and transitory emotions and happenings recorded in day-to-day journalism.

Much of the material is controversial, but if controversy means the stimulation of thought and ideas, so much the better. It is only thus that the citizens of a republic may protect themselves from the evils threatening them from within their borders as well as those which threaten from beyond.

L. B.
Malabar Farm
1953

A New Pattern for a Tired World

I

Government by Propaganda and Pressure

1

It is unnecessary to destroy the Western capitalist nations in war. They will spend themselves into total destruction.

NIKOLAI LENIN

HISTORY will doubtless regard this age not only as one of vast wars, disorders and revolutions but also as the Age of Propaganda, of the press agent, the lobbyist, the public relations man, the demagogue and the Cominform. The average citizen in every nation and most of all in the U.S. is bombarded constantly by propaganda and press releases designed to cloud his judgment, appeal to his prejudices, fill him with deliberate misinformation for a calculated purpose, and generally sell him down the river.

Government during the past generation has become itself one of the greatest propagandists, all the way from the professional elements in the armed services, who hire thousands of press agents at taxpayers' expense to sell their own particular bill of goods, down to the smallest bureau which sends out mimeographed sheets concerning the wonderful humanitarian work it is doing and how indispensable this work is to the welfare of the nation and the world, and above all how indispensable it is for the political party in power to be continued in office. One of the great evils of bureaucracy is that it tends increasingly to become self-perpetuating at the expense of the country. The armed forces represent our greatest bureaucracy and our most powerful all-pervading lobby.

Propaganda has seeped into the news columns of great, powerful

1

and respected newspapers which once would have held such a pattern of behavior in contempt. Once objective journalists have turned their reports from Washington or Paris or Moscow into subtle editorial commentaries slanted this way or that, sometimes with the approval of the editors and employers and sometimes not— sometimes indeed without even any perception upon their part. Often enough it has been done so subtly, that the editor or employer was and is wholly unaware of what is being done. (The simplest way is to quote from people and speeches selectively, choosing statements and comments which slant the story completely but conceal the motive and permit the reporter to escape detection, responsibility or criticism.) The news release, "leak," propaganda, "buildup," "trial balloon" technique during the past twenty years has become the very essence of "government by crisis," a technique at which the armed forces have become the most expert practitioners and one which is practiced by politicians, zealots, cranks and even officials high in public office.

It is done very largely by creating public terror of elements and events which are vast, and frequently indefinable, which cannot be pinned down and analyzed. Perhaps the worst offenders, save for unscrupulous politicians, are the cloud of columnists and commentators who became eloquent and even hysterical in their fears and alarms. And of course the politicians and the journalists who dash from country to country on three-day visits with notebook in hand to return home and write, in book or press or magazine, "authentic" accounts of profound and world-shattering conditions and events which cannot possibly be understood or properly interpreted save upon a basis of profound and detailed knowledge and long, intelligent study. This is one of the evils of rapid travel in a shrunken world.

The phrases "from an authoritative source" and "from indisputably reliable sources" appear over and over again in propaganda bulletins, press releases and in the reports of columnists and correspondents working out of Washington. Such phrases cover everything, from the operations of the secret Communist propagandist through carefully calculated "leaks" and the propaganda of the armed forces "public relations" officers to the irresponsible and imaginative workings of the columnist's and correspondent's mind. They are indispensable to the process of wish fulfillment, as they permit any journalist to set forth as a fact what he hopes will happen. In the hometown newspaper the gullible editor, entertained lavishly from time to time by generals, bureaucrats and politicians while they scare the daylights out of him, frequently follows the lead and presently there is built up a wave of alarm, apprehension, misunderstanding and actual terror which induces in the average citizen the malleability necessary to the achievement of the purposes and the ambitions of some individual or group of individuals or bureau high in government or in the armed forces.

The brass of the armed forces has long been adept at this technique. Everyone remembers the tired, mysterious submarine, which used to make its annual appearance off the coasts of the United States on the eve of debate in Congress on an armed forces appropriations bill. Now we have familiar and almost as addled reports of vast and overwhelming armaments being built up in Soviet Russia. It is notable that in all the fear propaganda about the advances in bomb construction in Russia, not once has any *fact* been revealed as to the source of information or as to where *the* bomb (apparently one was enough for propaganda purposes) was exploded. It is obvious that if such facts exist there is no reason why the sources of information and the factual details should not be fully revealed to the American people. Indeed, the moral obligation of the generals and the politicians, under a government of the people, is definitely to reveal *everything* save peak security factors regarding such reports to the people themselves.

This factor made especially disquieting to any thoughtful person the expressed doubt of ex-President Truman that the Russians had *any* atomic bombs. Presumably the President of the United States and the Civilian Commander-in-Chief of the Army should know *all* the facts, or else all government becomes meaningless and merely an instrument of irresponsible militarist propaganda. The only other logical implications are that the military forces have taken us over completely and have excluded even their Commander-in-Chief from obligatory and vital information, that an ex-President is guilty of mischievous manipulation of grave and even tragic information, or that the Russians very possibly do *not* have workable, transportable, effective bombs. One fact not to be overlooked is that despite efforts to confuse and blur the whole question an atomic or hydrogen explosion is quite different from a practical, workable and transportable bomb. In any case, the people of the U.S. are victims of typical propaganda manipulation of facts and information.

In Washington there was a great scandal concerning the "five per centers" who distributed mink coats, deep freezers and at times gifts of a more negotiable nature, in return for privileges and favors for clients from persons high in government and even in the White House, but no outcry was ever raised concerning the journalistic "five per centers" whose behavior is more subtle but more immoral and infinitely more dangerous to the welfare of the nation and the responsible operation of government by the people. These were and are the journalists who make a deal with government officials and bureaus, high or low, under which, in return for "leaks" and secret information, they agree openly or tacitly to make propaganda for the individual or for the ambitions and purposes of the individual, or, as the case may be, the Pentagon or even an obscure bureau.

This bargaining is very common practice and well known to those on the inside in Washington, so well known indeed that such tie-ups in many cases have become outwardly as respectable and recognized as long-established marriages. Most of the mysterious "leaks," which occasionally scandalize a few congressmen and government officials, are consistently in this "five per center" category of journalists in which not mink coats and quick freezers but the printed word, propaganda and favors, are the currency of bribery.

In all of this, of course, the people of the United States are the victims. It is notable that some of these journalistic "five per centers" have been the loudest in their denunciations of such characters as Maragon and Vaughan, overlooking in themselves a lack of ethics and morality greater and more dangerous than that of the crass and obvious little "five per centers" or political chiselers.

It is not surprising that in all this cloud of intrigue, irresponsibility, lying and humbug the poor victim—the average citizen—is left confused and frightened and at times disgusted, never knowing whom to trust or quite where to turn to discover from his own government even the simplest elements of fact and truth. In the stupendous and complex events of our times, it is very nearly impossible for the average citizen to keep informed and, in many cases, even an education in our schools and universities has left him almost wholly innocent and *un*informed concerning the basic facts of geography, race, economics and the simpler facts of history in relation to the events taking place in our times. Frequently he is helpless, and at the mercy of the unethical and the unscrupulous. The passion of partisanship in our times has not tended toward objectivity, better understanding or greater truth, and unfortunately there is a whole generation now of age which has never known anything but distortion, propaganda, government by crisis and slanted journalism— a generation, curiously enough, which in reaction turns cynical, conservative and even reactionary simply as a means of defense against such disreputable tactics.

2

A nation constantly thinking of War and preparing for War is certain to get War since in the end the concentration of expenditure, energies and mind can only explode in conflict.

VON CLAUSEWITZ

It is not impossible that history will also regard the period of which I write as the Age of the Big Lie in which bureaucracy and propaganda took over the functions of informed representative government and created calamity for the world. In one sense all this corruption represents a victory over representative government by the very enemies with which the free nations found themselves confronted in the terrible struggles of our times.

The Big Lie was the invention of Goebbels and Ribbentrop, of Hitler and Mussolini, of Stalin and the Kremlin. In the end the technique of the Big Lie has never been successful. It failed in Germany, in Italy, and it is rapidly failing in Russia itself, with the talk of a "workers' Paradise" and the shooting down of workers. Unfortunately it has corrupted the free governments in almost exact ratio to the degree in which free government has become "big government" and bureaucracy has flourished. In some instances the corruption has reached a point at which the confidence of the people in their own governments has become undermined.

This is not the least of the evil results of contact with the forces of corruption. It is corruption of a singularly evil sort, far worse than the ordinary venal corruption of bribes and cheating, for it is subtle and is sometimes not perceptible until the disease is already far advanced.

The inventors of the Big Lie technique and its most skillful practitioners from Goebbels onward have always stipulated that the Lie must be a big one, so big in fact that its very preposterousness gives it the weight of belief and the false face of truth. And, of course, it must be reiterated again and again—even as certain elements began, *before* cease-fire negotiations were realized in Korea and in the face of every possible sign of weakness and disintegration in Soviet Russia, to open all guns in press releases and from "reliable sources," to create a propaganda against peace and for more and more forced military service and arms appropriations. Over and over again the warnings "that we must not relax," "that we must maintain huge armaments and armies for the defense of the free world" were repeated in interviews from interested generals and in the writing of captive "five per center" columnists and correspondents.

The difficulty, and one of the great flaws of "the scare technique," is that it must constantly be cultivated so that it will increasingly create alarm and even terror, that it must operate like a snowball steadily gaining momentum and size and weight until in the end whole nations and peoples are crushed and subjected by it. It must be established that those who oppose or even question the propaganda or the Big Lie will be forced to appear unpatriotic and disloyal, or vicious reactionaries and "enemies of the people."

It was exactly in this fashion that Goebbels and his staff were able to change the very psychology of the German people and render them malleable, helpless and the victims of disaster. It is the same technique constantly employed by the men in the Kremlin to keep the Russian people docile and in terror of all the rest of the world. And it is notable that the "scare technique" and its practitioners in this country have given the greatest aid to their fellow practitioners on the opposite side of the Iron Curtain by giving, through their utterances, substance and belief to the insistent Kremlin cry that all Americans are warmongers and seek only war and the subjugation and destruction of Russia and the Russian people. It is only necessary to print verbatim in *Pravda, Izvestia* or the *Red Star* some of the major utterances of certain politicians, generals and columnists to give substance and truth before the Russian people and indeed the world to the accusation of "warmongering" in the United States. One cannot resist the suspicion that if these elements of our society, together with those who interfere in the affairs of peoples everywhere in the world (always "for their own good"), would only relax their hysteria or calculation and be honest, the world would make rapid and impressive strides in the direction of peace.

In addition to the practitioners among the politicians, generals and captive journalists, there is another element, perhaps more dangerous, which also espouses the scare technique. These are the Americans suffering from what might best be described as "a Messiah complex," who feel a compulsion to save the world and constantly to meddle in the affairs of other peoples and nations, regardless of whether, as is more and more the case, this interference is actually resented.

The Messiah complex is peculiarly an Anglo-Saxon disease which at times can border upon the ecstatic and the psychopathic. It existed strongly among the English people who sent missionaries everywhere in the world although they took care to have them accompanied by traders. In the United States we are inclined to send the missionaries, unaccompanied however by traders, and to spread money and welfare broadcast in return for no material rewards whatever and frequently with small benefits or none at all to the *great masses* of the people in the nations we are supposed to be aiding.

3

If the young men of this day are to be trained to look clearly and intelligently on American foreign relations, the teaching to which they are subjected must be stern and uncompromising. It must be founded in humility and renunciation of easy effects. It must exclude all that is Pollyannish and superficial. It must reject utopianism and every form of idealism not rooted in an honest and unsparing recognition of the nature of man. It must be free from the tyranny of slogans, fashionable words and semantic taboos. It must proceed from a recognition that the understanding of this subject can never be more simply acquired than the understanding of its basic component, which is man himself.

GEORGE F. KENNAN

I have heard it said by more than one foreigner that we are the only nation in the world that exhibits all the annoying traits and practices of imperialism without asking for any of the rewards of imperialism. The mere machinery of imperialism, with all its implied and actual interferences, is in itself annoying. When no actual exploitation accompanies the outward appearance, puzzlement and annoyance on the part of the recipients are the result, and finally resentment and even hatred. As one Brazilian put it, "We don't understand what goes on. You pour money into the country wholesale with all the accompaniments of waste, stupidity and folly in the apparent assumption that you can buy anything you like including our friendship and self-respect and pride and even progress. That makes us think you are damned fools. Then you insult us by telling us that you do this because we are a backward nation."

Back of all this of course lies a perhaps commendable impulse on the part of a very few politicians and people to bring the same standards of living and welfare which exist in the United States to the other countries of the world, but it is covered and its charitable aspect obscured and canceled out by a certain sanctimonious condescension in which large phrases such as "world responsibility" and the "necessity of defending the free world" are freely cast about. Often enough one hears the comment, "Why do other peoples dislike and hate us? Why, when we are pouring money into Italy and France, does the Communist Party continue to thrive and even to increase?" Let me suggest that this is fundamentally not the fault of the Italian or French people *en masse*, but of our own policies and the methods of putting them into operation.

There are very sound and fairly uncomplicated reasons why this is so, reasons which are gone into later in this book, but there is also involved the hurt pride of whole peoples possessed of a much longer and richer history and culture and civilization than that of the United States. There is too a constant and steady resentment of the very smugness of the American attitude (at least of our State Department) and in general of those who harp continuously on our "world responsibility," and of the reiteration of the fact that the material living standards of the United States are the *only* values to be considered and that we can and *must* confer these benefits, along with something known vaguely as "Democracy," willy-nilly upon other peoples whether they want them or not, our government paying for the process out of the earnings of the average taxpaying American citizen.

One cannot resist asking, as does many an intelligent and wise foreigner, "Who conferred this 'responsibility for the world' upon the American government and by implication upon the American people? Was it God? Or just this missionary group with a Messiah complex? Or who? Or what?" One can scarcely put the whole burden of the responsibility upon God for a task which to any thinking child is obviously impossible and can only end in immense confusion and possible disaster, not only to ourselves but to a large part of the world which we attempt to manage and make subject to our dictation.

This same sanctimonious group with the Messiah complex is by no means as scrupulous in its methods nor as reverent of Truth as its holy attitude might imply. It freely participates in the scare technique and the propaganda of the Big Lie. The selling of the United Nations to the American people was upon this basis. The argument was that we all want peace and that if we do not have a United Nations we shall have *only* war—an argument which is obviously spurious and is scarcely supported by the bitter tragedy-farce of "police action" by the United Nations in Korea and the prospect growing out of the proposed Korean protectorate status of only more and more wars and misery. The common utterance one heard (and hears less and less) that the United Nations was "the one hope for world peace" is obvious nonsense regarding an organization which concerns itself only with politics and ignores economics. The proof of its failure has already been established by the fact that in any really major or violent crisis, negotiations by-pass the United Nations altogether and are undertaken between the major nations or among groups of nations. The North Atlantic Alliance is no more than an old-fashioned "power" alliance by one group of U.N. members against another group of U.N. members. Where indeed does this leave the avowed purposes of an organization set up to establish world peace, government and order? The issue cannot be argued save on the basis of hypocrisy, ignorance, or deliberate self-deception.

The fact is that twenty years of government "from crisis to crisis," many of them contrived, accompanied by the fear technique, missionary zeal and at times the propaganda of the Big Lie, broke for a time at least the very spirit of the American people and came near to reducing them like the German and Russian peoples to utter bovine subjection to a combination of big government, bureaucracy and militarism.

The growing technique of secrecy in government actions and decisions, justified originally on the score of war conditions, has tended more and more to exclude the American people, and even their representatives in Congress, from any actual participation in government and in foreign policy, and has transferred action and policy into the hands of appointed or career bureaucrats without direct responsibility to the people. Moreover, it has given to the chief executive, in violation of the Constitution, the power to make certain treaties, under the name of "executive agreements," with foreign nations and even to make war (as in the case of Korea) without the sanction or even the knowledge of the people and their representatives in Congress.

In this respect we have again, in the process of fighting the Fascist and Communist enemies of representative government, taken over many attributes of the enemy himself, a process which is not new in history from the time of Rome and Carthage onward. Such a process is the accompaniment to domination of government by the military forces in every case. It conforms exactly to the "gradualist" pattern under which free peoples in Europe have been taken over by Nazi, Fascist and Communist bureaucracies and dictatorships.

This process has reduced the weaker ones among our people to a condition of mute acquiescence or downright terror. The secrecy surrounding the tragic decisions of Yalta, Teheran and Potsdam, the by-passing of the Constitution by a President in plunging us into the third greatest war in our history under the hypocritical pretense that it was a United Nations "police action," the policies and regulations of secrecy which many bureaus of government sought and obtained under the Truman Administration, are all very clear and historical evidence of how near, under various disguises, a combination of propaganda, the Big Lie, bureaucracy and militarism has come to destroying the whole fundamental concept of free representative government by the people.

With respect to the bureaucracy and the military powers, we have by no means as yet wholly escaped the danger. Indeed, even history may never reveal how narrowly we escaped complete domination by militarism, if indeed we are as yet entirely free of this greatest of all perils to all free peoples. The assumption induced in the American people, by the same old propaganda tactics, that the blight of conscription must be perpetuated as a permanent necessity is only one step in the sacrifice of our freedoms to military domination and ambition for power and prestige, and one step backward from freedom and the realization of a decent peaceful life, which is the ultimate goal of any civilized government.[1] The continuation of conscription can only be maintained by constant and energetic propaganda designed to create fear and by the use of constant misrepresentation of fact and the use of the Big Lie technique. Here for a third time is an example of corruption by the methods of the very enemy we have been fighting. On the civilian side and under existing conditions we remain at the mercy of any President, who is actually able to make war at any time or to commit us secretly to every sort of compromising agreement. Under such conditions our fate and that of a large part of the world depend wholly upon the honesty, decency, knowledge, intelligence and general character of any Presi-

[1] These references are to notes in a separate section following the text.

dent, good or bad, informed or ignorant—a condition which is perilous indeed. The assertion frequently heard, that this is not so, is completely nullified by fact itself. It has already been proven within this
decade at Yalta, at Teheran, in Korea and elsewhere. All this is a long
way indeed from the fundamental fact of all representative government as the servant of the people and not its master and very close
to the practice of all Nazi-Fascist, Communist principle. It is also
a long way from the ideals of true representative government which
our Utopians seek perpetually (and under such conditions with
hypocrisy) to impose upon other nations.

The Big Lie technique is very largely responsible for the fact that
we live perpetually in a state that is neither war nor peace but one
in which, as in that created by the Big Brother dictator in George
Orwell's *1984*, "war is peace and peace is war." For a parallel, almost
exact, of many of the propaganda conditions actually existing today
in a broader sense, we need go little further than the Orwell book. A
state in which war is peace and peace is war is obviously the perfect
climate for the generals and admirals. In it they manage to keep the
prestige they acquire in time of war together with the immense
appropriations and power, and they are able to infiltrate all departments of government and to commit and maintain vast extravagances,
and actually to create obstacles to the realization of peace, either
deliberately or through the medieval concepts which frequently
afflict the typical military mind.

In producing this climate in which war is peace and peace is war,
constant propaganda and the technique of terror and the Big Lie are
indispensable, a fact which accounts largely for the veritable army
of press agents and public relations officers maintained as an army
within an army by the professional element of our armed forces.

None of this is exaggeration. One has only to observe the presence
and influence of the generals everywhere in our government today
and the ways in which they dominate the lives of all of us, from

necessitating vast taxes of which military appropriations consume at the present time by far the greater part, to conscripting resentful young men for military service and perhaps death and mutilation in forty-nine countries of the world.

Not only is this determination of the military powers and their friends to maintain compulsory military service indefinitely the first step in the violation of our liberties and an indignity to the young men who are compelled to waste two of the most important years of their lives in military service, but it has serious economic aspects as well. For it deprives the nation of the creative abilities and the capacity to produce more wealth and more purchasing power of three millions and a half young men every two years. Moreover, it piles up vast military expenses which, if removed or even reduced, would permit the nation to balance its budget, do away with disastrous deficit spending and reduce taxes which have approached the point of becoming confiscatory. Military domination of any government or people throughout history has in time always brought to that nation not only economic ruin but the steady and increasing distortion of moral principles followed by war and ruin. Domination by the military can lead to a diversionary war just as surely as the policies of dictatorship, although the progress of such a course, step by step, may not be so clear. There is no reason to suppose that history will alter its record upon the basis that we are different from any other people.[2]

So long as such conditions continue and the public fails to revolt, we are bound to live in a constant state of alarms, threats and crisis, in constant danger of war and in a distorted and wasteful economic climate which can in the end only be disastrous. It is a situation and a condition which gives substantial and at times complete truth to the Kremlin accusations of "warmongering." It blocks all possibility of conference and negotiation and the opening of the congested channels of trade, food, raw materials, markets, exchange of goods and other economic factors which lie at the very root of nearly all the troubles of the world. Today our policies and actions are determined and guided by a strange mixture of hazy impractical idealism and of militarism promoted by a campaign of calculated fear. This is an aspect of our national behavior and policies recognized as a cause for alarm long ago by the experienced Churchill, in many ways the greatest and wisest realistic statesman of our times.

It is doubtful that the world will make much progress toward real peace and genuine prosperity so long as nations and international relations are subject to constant intervention and at times domination by the professional military caste or so long as vital decisions and policies are influenced, controlled or kept from the people by military men or *appointed* bureaucrats or bureaus which have no direct responsibility to the people. It is exactly by this process of gradual encroachment, of obscure, concealed and indirect authority, without corresponding responsibility, by the technique of crisis and terror, concealment and secrecy that the liberal or mildly socialistic governments of central Europe were translated gradually into bureaucratic and oligarchic Nazi or Communist dictatorships in which the people themselves had less and less direction, force and authority in government, and truth and fact became distorted into the psychological atmosphere of a nightmare and all freedoms became lost.

4

Is it not a fact that the General Staff and the President and his advisors rushed into a war which they had already won (with Japan)—in which the enemy had already made overtures of peace—and without the decency of adequate warning reduced two of his cities to rubble and struck, not terror, but the most agonizing death into the hearts of their populations, several hundred thousand of them at a stroke? Did Machiavelli, the cool, the rational, the goal-pursuing, ever contemplate such a wanton and exuberant employment of crime?

THE FREEMAN, August 10, 1953

In a country so large as the United States in which no one party has as yet been able to take over government entirely, such a *complete* transformation as took place in many smaller European nations is unlikely. Nevertheless the conditions I have been describing can paralyze the functioning of representative government. The atmosphere of perpetual crisis and emergency in which we have been living constantly for nearly a generation is as explosive and as dangerous as can be insofar as the possibility of war is concerned. Its dangers affect not only this country but nearly every other nation of the world, a fact of which they are becoming aware and with an increasing sense of alarm. Nothing is more dangerous than for a single nation to assume that it has world responsibility thrust upon its shoulders and then to behave in a domineering, unpredictable and irresponsible fashion, which is exactly what we have been doing. Great Britain in the heyday of the Empire believed, at least partly, in Rudyard Kipling's absurd and pretentious slogan of "the white man's burden" but it did not behave in the muddled and meddling fashion which characterizes our own absurd and pretentious policy of "world responsibility." Our own behavior smacks more of the "race superiority" absurdities which twice brought disaster to the German people—under Kaiser Wilhelm II and under Adolf Hitler. In both disasters the military through the "General Staff" played an activating role.

This same atmosphere of alarm and confusion leads to many a reactionary conception and plan with roots in the military concepts of Napoleon or the political concepts of Metternich and Palmerston. Add to this the naïveté, ignorance of history, of economics and even of the real conditions of the changed and changing world in which we live, which characterizes many of the officials high in our government, and the situation becomes charged with desperate and explosive danger. If ever there was a time when the world and this nation needed the kind of politician and statesman with which Britain was once blessed and has now largely lost—the politician-statesman who was trained and educated for his role—the time is now.

In our foreign policy we continue to approach the future not in the terms of general wisdom learned from experience, fact and history itself but in specialized patterns of the past which have become almost wholly obsolete. It is as if we had consciously and constantly rejected the substance and retained the skeleton; as if we had almost deliberately chosen the methods, the maneuvers, the conceptions of the immediate past that led directly to World Wars I and II and eventually to the dreadful and tragic blunder of Korea, while ignoring economic and sociological factors in a world revolution which are stronger than any nation, or any armament, or military forces or any ideology. Add to this the pattern of crisis-to-crisis government, propaganda, foggy and sentimental idealism and the Big Lie, and the confusion becomes monstrous—a confusion which not only reduces the average American citizen to despair but bewilders all the other nations of the world.

Somewhere, at some time, and the sooner the better, the world and in particular the United States must arrive at wholly new conceptions of economic and international relations. We must come to think in terms of the incredibly changed world in which we live, in terms that bear some resemblance to the truth and reality of that world and which include the fact that, more and more, economics— trade, food, population, markets and raw materials—lie at the very root of all the troubles of the world today. These problems cannot be solved by the wholesale bestowal and distribution of American wealth, in the old-fashioned concept of Lady Bountiful passing from cottage to cottage with her basket well laden with the luxuries of the Castle. They cannot be solved by the arbitrary bestowal or imposition of political "democracy" with the touch of a fairy wand, or by brutal assault of tanks and guns upon peoples who have little conception or understanding of or even words in their languages for democracy, freedom, liberty and human dignity, and whose greatest concern is merely to keep alive, to find enough to eat even for one day and to find each day shelter from the weather.[3]

Political concepts and ideologies do not create economic concepts but arise *from* economic unbalance and wrongs. Democracy, in any of its hazy countless sometimes phony forms, cannot flourish or even be maintained in an atmosphere of misery, starvation, illiteracy and ignorance. It cannot simply because these things in themselves infect and destroy the very structure of government by the people and leave the people the victims of the first dictator-general, demagogue, criminal or psychopath to come along and take over power while victimizing the people in the process by persuading them that he alone can solve troubles which essentially are not political at all but material and economic.[4]

If we are to create a new world or a world in which there can be permanent peace and welfare and freedom from the evil burdens of perpetual wars, militarism and military influences, there must come into being new concepts in terms of scalding realities and truths accepted by peoples generally throughout the world.

5

International affairs is not a science. And there is no understanding of international affairs that does not embrace understanding of the human individual.

Only if these principles are observed will we be able to free ourselves from the strain of utopianism that has been present in the teaching of international affairs in our country in recent decades. By this I mean teaching that portrays incorrectly the nature of our world environment and our relation to it and encourages students to disregard the urgent real requirements of international life in favor of the cultivation of artificial and impractical visions of world betterment. This argument about the philosophy of our approach to our problems of foreign relations is one that has been agitating our academic communities intensely in recent months. I am myself a partisan in the dispute. I shall only say here that further exposure to the bitter realities of the practice of international relations in a place where these realities are about as bitter as they can conceivably be, has strengthened my conviction that the shortcomings in the teaching of international affairs, and primarily the leanings toward shallow and utopian interpretations, represent, in their ultimate effect, an important limitation of our ability to handle ourselves effectively in world affairs.

GEORGE F. KENNAN in an address before the
Princeton Alumni Association, February, 1953

There has been much degradation in our time of such once honorable words as "liberal" and "freedom" and "democracy" and "idealism" and many others. They have been used carelessly and frequently as tools of corruption, conspiracy, treason and mere sloppy thinking and aimless missionary zeal. Some of the defilement has come from the evil forces of conspiracy represented by the Nazis, the Fascists and the Communists but much of it has come too from the sentimentalists and the gushing reformers who simply by-pass fact and reality in warm and ecstatic enjoyment and appreciation of their own goodness and virtue. And in by-passing the realities they merely defeat their own occasionally commendable, declared purposes and bring confusion and misery to an already suffering world. Nothing is so dangerous as a superficial, illogical, uninformed reformer and "idealist." He who deals with facts builds a solid structure which will endure; he who deals with dreams of a world as it ought to be or as he would like it to become overnight, only builds a ramshackle structure on sand, which inevitably must fall of its own weight of folly and superficiality, bringing with its fall new confusions and disasters.

Whatever of government, of science, of ethics and morals, of civilization, man has been able to achieve, he has attained the hard way with much suffering and the realization, sooner or later, that he must deal first of all and eternally with reality and truth. Utopia is perhaps a pleasant exercise, like a poem written in a child's exercise book; however, the progress of humanity was never achieved by such pleasant exercises but rather by the careful consideration of all the immense difficulties, physical and spiritual, which confront man and are in essence a part of him. It was achieved by the slow construction, block by block, of an edifice based upon man's limitations as well as his virtues. At the very foundation lie the sound and solid rocks of truth, logic and reality, the power to regard all these honestly, solidly and objectively, and above all, to realize that the wrongs, the maladjustments, the wars, the revolutions and the oppressions of our times are not the results of ideologies or highfalutin words, phrases, declarations and charters, good or evil, but arise from questions of population, raw materials, markets and a general free exchange of food and goods.

It was a common and popular assumption that World War II was made by the Nazis, the Fascists and the Nationalists of Japan, by Hitler and by Mussolini. There is little truth in such an assumption, beyond the fact that these forces triggered the explosion. The Nazis, the Fascists, the dictators, even in Russia, were and are merely the political manifestations of much deeper severe economic maladjustments.

In reality *all* the major powers were responsible for World Wars I and II, including ourselves. Political and military alliances and maneuverings are not only futile in the face of the maladjustments just mentioned but induce and augment essentially *artificial* strains and tensions. These in turn become explosive and destructive both to peace and to economic agreements which might otherwise serve to establish enduring peace and prosperity. This conception of world affairs based upon the idea of military and political alliances rather than economic agreement is the essential and tragic fault of the military mind. It lies at the root of the futility and potential menace of the U.N., which functions upon a basis of old-fashioned political and military alliances and operations while ignoring the fundamental stresses of economics, population, food and trade. This factor makes the propaganda, both of the generals and of the U.N., doubly sinister and dangerous to the peace of the world. Both are respectively and essentially the quintessence of militarism and power politics, which precipitated if not caused every war for more than two centuries.

II

The Failure of a Policy

1

One of our fundamental mistakes was our well-meant effort to "assume world leadership." . . . Our effort to decide European policy ourselves, and particularly our effort to push Europe into defending itself more than it thinks it needs to, has merely been resented, and has led to much of the anti-American feeling that now exists. Our real role in Europe was not to lead there, but to follow . . . literally to offer to "back it up." What we should have said is something like this—"You and we may not agree regarding the extent of the danger of a Soviet attack. We'll leave that to you to decide. But if you fellows will pledge to support each other, we will pledge to come to your defense in the event of any attack which you yourselves decide to repel by armed forces. Otherwise we won't try to interfere in your affairs or tell you what to do."

THE FREEMAN, September 7, 1953

SOME fifteen years ago there was developed through the leadership of Sumner Welles, Under Secretary of State in Washington, something known as "The Good Neighbor Policy." Its purpose was for this country to co-operate with the Latin-American nations of the Western Hemisphere in the development of natural wealth and resources as well as industrial and agricultural knowledge, and to promote in general an atmosphere of family friendliness in the whole of the Western Hemisphere. The unspoken, underlying and deeply important purpose of this farsighted and statesmanlike program was economic *co-operation* in the Western Hemisphere followed eventually and perhaps remotely by economic and possibly political union throughout the rich and enormous area. History may possibly value this policy as the most potentially important concept of American foreign policy in our time and the soundest as a foundation stone of *genuine* world peace and prosperity.

Almost before the program had a chance to be established, the United States entered World War II and the energies and leadership which should have been employed in its development were absorbed in the gigantic war effort. This was unfortunate but perhaps inevitable, although the general neglect of the Latin-American nations and their interests need never have reached the depths it finally attained under the Truman Administration.

However, it was not the war effort alone which brought a premature end to the policy. There were other influences as well, among them a President, Franklin D. Roosevelt, whose sympathies and traditional background were European and, in particular, British. For the past seven or eight years, until the inauguration of President Eisenhower, this same trend toward European, and in particular British interests, and a wholesale neglect and blundering in the directions of Asia and South America, has been accentuated by the influence of a Secretary of State, Dean Acheson, whose sympathies were far more European, and far more sharply British even than those of President Roosevelt. Insofar as our foreign policy was concerned this Secretary was actually President of the U.S.

It has been said many times by important and knowledgeable people that Secretary of State Acheson was the best Foreign Minister Great Britain has had in the last generation. His influence upon our foreign policy was doubly great since he exerted a powerful fascination over the rather muddled and ill-prepared man who, by political accident, became President of the United States. Acheson, a literate lawyer who dressed and looked like a European, exerted over President Truman what appears to have been a virtually hypnotic influence. Acheson, in the eyes of Truman, could do no wrong, and with a stubbornness which increased in exact ratio to the opposition and criticism directed at his Secretary of State, Truman defended and supported, even to the final point of serious political damage to himself, every act and policy, good, bad or confused, of Mr. Acheson.[1]

Under Truman and Acheson, the American foreign policy was almost entirely centered upon a tired and bankrupt Europe to the neglect both of Asia and the Latin-American nations. Our tactics and policies in Asia ended with the tragic loss of China's friendship and support. Relations with the Latin-American nations, even with Brazil, which has persistently, and at times in the face of snubs, maintained a close friendship with the United States, were largely ignored. The American taxpayer sacrificed billions of dollars, given outright t\ re-establish European economy, restore the old colonial empires whi·h cannot be restored, and build European defenses against the ran.·hackle Soviet Empire.

The buildup of European industrial production could not in any direct economic fashion benefit to any great degree a nation such as the United States which is by far the greatest industrial producer among the nations in the world. It could only benefit the United States by eventually taking the financial responsibility for Europe off the shoulders of the average American citizen and taxpayer—and this benefit was in fact only a theory and a hope which even today remains a rather forlorn one, for reasons which are becoming increasingly apparent.

Over a period of years this policy has cost the American people many thousands of dollars per family. Its results remain increasingly dubious, in a world in which the very foundations of the wealth and power of the once great European nations—colonies and empires—are disintegrating or have disappeared.

The whole pattern—and it is an intricate and immensely complicated one—of the policies and procedures and acts of the Truman-Acheson alliance has not yet been explained or even revealed and it may never be, since the confusion was so enormous and so many elements were involved—the inexperience and even ignorance of ex-President Truman, his occasional vindictiveness, his limited political vision and his peculiar, intense, almost psychopathic loyalties and friendships, regardless of the ethical or moral or intellectual qualities of the persons concerned. Beyond this lay the European and especially British affiliations and sympathies of Acheson and the resentment which these created in many parts of the nation, particularly in the South and the Middle West. This resentment reacted against Truman and increased the opposition which largely repudiated him and most of his policies in the elections of 1952.

But still further and beyond these elements were other factors which have never been explored, the roots of which extend far back into the Roosevelt Administration. Notable among these is the whole strange story of the infiltration into government of actual Communists and countless "liberals" who espoused not the pattern of Jeffersonian and French Revolution liberalism, but the dubious reactionary archaic "radicalism" of the Marxian philosophy. That these elements exerted a very great influence and were responsible indirectly and at times directly for many facets of the hidden and still undisclosed activities of the Roosevelt and the Truman-Acheson Administrations, both at home and abroad, is beyond dispute even in the half-born history of our times. They were everywhere in government, boring, operating, influencing, molding policies, making propaganda, destroying records and in general augmenting a confusion which operated to the damage of American and even European interests and almost wholly in favor of the interests of Marxian Communism and of Soviet Russian imperialism. They have also complicated enormously the task of future historians.[2]

The general effect of these incredibly intricate influences, like that of much of the military propaganda coming from the Pentagon and the Truman chiefs of staff, was to stress the immense power and threat of Russia (a strongly debatable attitude) while at the same time operating paradoxically so that this same Russian power would benefit. The ramifications of these partly planned and partly unplanned and muddled operations have not even begun to be unraveled. The extent to which they involved people of extreme importance and the extent to which these same people of importance co-operated willingly and consciously or merely as dupes still remains very largely a mystery. As Rebecca West expressed it in her brilliant articles concerning Jowett's criticism of the Hiss trial, "Somewhere someone high in government has not yet taken off his false beard." It may never come off, partly because certain individuals have been able until now to conceal or disguise not only motives but actions, partly because other individuals are being sheltered and protected even now from the results of their follies by persons in high authority, and partly because so many of those involved were merely muddled and emotional dupes who really did not understand their own motives and still less the disastrous effects of their actions.

And there are other elements, such as the role of Supreme Court Justice Felix Frankfurter as constant adviser to important people through the Roosevelt and Truman Administrations. Although doubtless well intentioned in his "liberal" ideas, the fact is that he taught at Harvard and introduced into positions of great authority in Washington a number of young men whose influence in our government was at least mischievous and in some cases produced tragic results for themselves and for others, including the whole people of the U.S. Among these were Lee Pressman, who admitted under oath that most of the time he worked in government in Washington he was a member of the Communist Party, and Alger Hiss, now in prison for perjury, after a trial which clearly indicated the deeper charge of treason which could not be prosecuted.[3] And there were others, less prominent, as well as all of those who in turn found their way into positions of confidence and high responsibility through the intervention of these once "bright young men." Through some of these disciples, as has been clearly shown by a Senatorial Investigations Committee, there was created a whole network of Communists and fellow travelers who hired each other, managed to place each other in offices of great authority and in general to infiltrate every department of the American government.[4]

In all of this there is no intent to bring accusations. These facts from the record are mentioned merely to demonstrate how intricate, muddled, involved and complicated are the influences and intrigues which have affected our foreign policies during a period of crisis in world affairs, when we found ourselves saddled with an immense world prestige but no great experience, and with an administration of dubious quality still riddled by prejudices and influences whose roots extended far into the past and even into the quagmire of European and Communist intrigue and influences.

Not all the Congressional hearings in the world nor all the criminal court proceedings will ever succeed in unraveling this extraordinary tangle of intrigue, emotion, self-conscious virtue and martyrdom, stupidity, duplicity and dupery, vicious personal ambition, passion for power and common treason. Nor probably will history ever record the degree to which the American people were duped or the degree to which this extraordinary Roosevelt-Truman-Acheson Administration and set of circumstances misrepresented their will and sense of ethics, especially in the realm of "foreign policy." Even upon the basis of the partly revealed record, the period was an extraordinary and tragic one not only for the U.S. but for the world, and the chain of events stemming from that period is by no means finished.

Much of the complicated mess also involved a kind of ineptness which bordered upon stupidity, of incompetence in both military and diplomatic circles. The extraordinary absence of memory in General George Marshall at the time of the Pearl Harbor crisis, his record in the Chinese débacle, his questionable tactics in his dealings with Congress over the number of American conscripts sent to Europe after the war, and above all his statement, uttered almost with pride, that "he had never voted and did not expect to vote in the coming election," all argue curious qualities of mind which do not support President Truman's eulogy that "General

Marshall is the greatest living American." General Marshall was not alone in the administration so far as general ineptness was concerned. The tragedy is that very frequently ineptness and stupidity in our government served the purposes of self-seeking nations who were indifferent to our welfare, as well as the purposes of our enemies, quite as much as if there had been deliberate intrigue and plotting with such a definite aim in mind. Whatever the motivation, the results were disastrous and we have not yet finished with them.

In the whole complex picture the evidence is abundant and clear that neither foreign policies, whether blunders or successes, nor history is entirely the result of wisdom or sober thought and reflection or objective and informed tactics and planning. Rather they are formed largely from a web of influences, friendships, prejudices, emotions, tradition, stupidities, internal politics, and sometimes deliberately villainous and criminal actions. Perhaps at no time in all history has there been so clear a record and picture of this theory or fact as during the past ten years or more of American history, which is indeed, in these times, very largely a history of the world as well.

The only clear fact which emerges is that during the Truman-Acheson period Asia was largely neglected and Latin America abandoned for the sake of a policy which concentrated upon the salvation and rehabilitation of Europe and the colonial empires, which cannot be rehabilitated. Neither are they of any real and lasting importance as a defense against Soviet Russia, unless they unite economically, militarily and eventually in political federation and, above all, display a will to regard their own problems with realism untouched by illusions and dreams of a wealth and a power which can never possibly be theirs again in the old imperial sense, or perhaps indeed in any other sense.

The prime purpose of this Acheson-Truman policy was an effort to bolster up the fortunes of the United Kingdom and the dream of Laborites and Tories alike that Britain will once again be a rich, important and really powerful nation, rather than a smallish part of a federation of commonwealths, each potentially or in reality richer and more powerful than the mother country and held to her by weakening ties which are more sentimental than economic, political or realistic.

Such a rehabilitation of British power, wealth and prestige could only come about through the most intricate and villainous of international political intrigues which would put this country and Russia into a war ending in the paralysis and collapse of both and the conquest and subjection by Britain of new world colonies, markets and sources of raw materials—a possibility which is altogether inconceivable.

Beyond this general and impossible policy, itself vague and nebulous, of rehabilitating Europe and primarily Britain, there has been no apparent policy of any kind but that of action from crisis to crisis and of improvising from day to day, while neglecting both Asia and Latin America.

2

We are fighting the wrong war (Korea), at the wrong place, at the wrong time and with the wrong enemy.

GENERAL OMAR BRADLEY

The very best evidence of this curious neglect and muddle and ineptness is the factual record of our behavior in the Korean crisis. The crisis itself was created by Acheson and Truman who withdrew all troops and then secretly sent out instructions to our foreign representatives to take the attitude that we should regard the loss of Korea and Formosa as unimportant—a fact for the record which was *forced* out of Acheson at a Congressional hearing and still stands as an evidence of his ineptness and his attitude toward the American people, whose servant he was.

If a battalion of American troops had been left in Korea, it is highly improbable that Soviet Russia through the false front of Korean Reds and Chinese "volunteers" would have moved in. When

Russia eventually stirred up trouble by second-hand aggression, Truman and Acheson were the first to send in troops and engage us in the vast tragedy and expense of an undeclared war hypocritically called a "United Nations police action," a "police action" in which we have supplied more than ninety-five per cent of the cost in money, material and, most tragic of all, casualties, prisoners and deaths. We have, in large part as a result of this, been saddled with the conscription of millions of unfortunate young Americans, the vast expense of military installations scattered over all the world, armed forces totaling three and a half million young men—all for a policy which in the end *cannot* succeed and which Britain actually opposes as a handicap to her trade and her already tottering economy. For what is to become of Korea, lying in the midst of Russia, China and Japan, even if we succeed in saving her from occupation and establish there a free republic? Wars today are won by economics and food as well as by guns, and vastly overpopulated, half-starving nations, with abysmally low living standards, do not wait for conquest by economics nor to abide by "suggestions" from the U.N. It is the choice between starving and killing, and it is in these terms, both economic and realistic, that we must consider a world in violent revolution if we are to establish a stable and consistent policy based upon something more solid and enduring than mere sentimentality or day-by-day improvisation.

The attempt to preserve the complete independence of the Korean people can only be sustained by burdening the American people with the *perpetual* occupation and protection of Korea and by creating an Asiatic Balkan condition and the constant threat of a third world war with China, Russia or eventually even Japan.

Dean Acheson, despite the fact that he is regarded as a statesman by many who confuse a smooth manner and a black homburg with astuteness and diplomatic talent, has, like General Marshall, a talent for inept remarks. His policy and methods are best illustrated by the remark he made when he was questioned by newspapermen regarding his plans in reaction to the Red seizure of the Chinese government. It was, "We shall wait until the dust has settled." Surely this is on a par with the ineptness of his remark about "turning his back on Alger Hiss." The former is important because it seems to epitomize the foreign policy of the Truman-Acheson Administration, and because it implies helplessness, lack of imagination and initiative and even stupidity and a lack of any direction whatever. One can condone or even admire Acheson's loyalty to Hiss as a private citizen, but in the exalted role of Secretary of State it was as inept as it was politically calamitous.

Meanwhile, as our President and State Department ignored hard facts or improvised from day to day elsewhere in the world, billions in money were poured into Europe, millions of tons of valuable natural resources (vital precious and unrenewable wealth far more valuable to our permanent economy than mere money) were scattered around the world in the form of war materials made of copper, zinc, iron and other industrially precious metals and representing many labor hours and much ingenuity. American youth has been conscripted and sent all over the world for longer periods of military service than exist in European countries, and thousands of young Americans have been killed. And these things have been done in the name of a policy that is bound to fail. For the world is in violent revolution everywhere against the old pattern whereby over-populated small European nations rose to great imperial and colonial wealth and power on the economically prostrate backs of less fortunate, less advanced and more helpless nations.

3

Whoever would understand foreign affairs, therefore, cannot and will not do it solely by understanding the intricacies of tariffs or the various classifications of treaties or the ways in which the United Nations Charter differs from the Covenant of the League of Nations or the techniques of sampling mass opinion. International affairs are primarily a matter of the behavior of governments. But the behavior of govern-

ments is in turn a matter of the behavior of individual man in the political context, and of the workings of all those basic impulses—national feeling, charity, ambition, fear, jealousy, egotism and group attachment—which are the stuff of his behavior in the community of other men.

Whoever does not understand these things will never understand what is taking place in the inter-relationships of nations. And he will not learn them from courses that purport to deal with international affairs alone. He will learn them, rather, from those things which have been recognized for thousands of years as the essentials of humanistic study; from history and from the more subtle and revealing expressions of man's nature that go by the names of art and literature.

GEORGE F. KENNAN in an address before the
Alumni of Princeton University, February, 1953

This world in turmoil has been called a sick world, but I have no doubt that in every period of revolution and change the world has been called sick. So the Greek world must have been called sick after Pericles and the Roman after Marcus Aurelius. The monks who saw the Dark Ages change into feudalism probably saw little improvement and wagged their heads in alarm as they worked over their illuminated manuscripts. And so Don Quixote found a sick, mad world in the mirror of himself. And so the Victorian British capitalists and the American Robber Barons of the nineteenth century found what was merely a changing and progressing world, a sick and tormented one. A world is always sick to those whose interests and plans are thwarted by opposition or change.

It is odd today that the phenomenon known as the "intellectual" is the one who finds our world a sick one. It is among the "intellectuals" that we have found the leading betrayers of our times, the Don Quixotes who see only themselves in the mirror. In such times as these when human experience, common sense and thoughtful action are all-important, the "intellectual" with his remoteness and his specialized manner of life and communication, becomes useless and even a burden to mankind.

But perhaps we had best define the word "intellectual" as it is used here and in common parlance at the present time. He is perhaps a man isolated and out of balance in the Greek sense, who thinks too much and lives too little in the market-place conditions, a fact which renders him both abnormal and unhealthy, and in a world in crisis, where common sense and common experience are of great value, even dangerous. Very often he is a specialist in some field, who cannot see the forest for the trees, who moves down his own small blind alley believing that in that blind alley, which represents his own concentrated effort, lies the secret to salvation of the universe. Frequently he is like the cranks who write letters to the press saying that if all of us stood on our heads each morning or walked barefoot through the grass, mankind's sorrows would all disappear and we should have peace. He is a man detached and isolated from his fellow men, from the smell of flowers, the taste of rich, good food, the delights of the warm bed and of unself-conscious sensuality. In many ways he is a man under a curse. Almost never is he a man of action, almost never is he actually creative although he may be as analytical as any medical student scraping flesh bit by bit to bare the nerves of a corpse in a morgue. His psychic reactions are those of mingled defense and braggadocio, of a defensive superiority arising very frequently from a cloudy sense of his own abnormality and loneliness. Frequently he is devoured by internal bitterness which manifests itself in strange diets, in puritanical denials, in mortifications of the flesh and not infrequently in treason and the betrayal of those things which ordinary men hold real and fundamental—such things as loyalties, warmth and even creation itself. Of such stuff was Schopenhauer made and Nietzsche, and in our time, Alger Hiss, Nunn-May, Pontecorvo, and still another, Klaus Fuchs. He moves round and round within the narrow, deformed bowl of his own society, enclosed and restricted within the limits of those who he considers can or wish to understand him, and talks on his own lofty, chilly, curious and limited level.

The political opinions of such men, as shown by the political and economic utterances of some physicists and many of the other specialists of our times, become often enough merely ludicrous when they are not actually dangerous. Such abnormal characters as Bruno Pontecorvo, Klaus Fuchs and Allan Nunn-May and even Joliot-Curie all exhibit a strange distorted psychology. They are gifted with a capacity for intense and intellectual thought on the one hand and handicapped by childishness on the other. They have played a great role in the evil as well as the scientific development and advances of our times and for nearly a generation they have exerted at times a dangerous influence in the politics of the U.S. and of European nations. No one questions their contributions to the advance of science and no one reproaches them for the evil uses to which some of their discoveries have been put, but they belong no more in government than do the military men. Jefferson was aware of this when he wrote, in a letter to a friend in England, "The sum total of the common sense of the common man is the greatest and soundest force on earth"—as indeed the Cominform is beginning to find out in all parts of the earth.

It is possible that the corruption of the evil politician is less dangerous in government than the intervention and power of the kind of intellectual I am describing, who frequently possesses an inhuman, unbalanced and even distorted point of view regarding all the facts and relationships of human living and government, and who seldom if ever represents or understands the problems, trials, worries and yearnings of the great bulk of the human race. Because of this, he is frequently willing to risk the betrayal and ruin of other men merely to prove a point or experiment or theory. Perhaps last of all our citizens, including even the corrupt politician, should he be permitted participation or responsibility in government, because all too often, divorced from all common passions and yearnings, he is as an individual, not quite human.

None of this is to imply that good brains are not essential to government, but merely to assert that the specialized intellectual in any field, from teaching through physics to philosophy, does not belong in government and in politics, however brilliant he may be in his own field. The mere fact of specialization is a limiting and even a crippling element. Politics and government are primarily and emphatically fields in which practical common sense and human experience in terms of one's fellow men are of immense importance. This is a fact long recognized in Britain, a nation which has a finer record of statesmen and trained politicians than probably any other throughout history. In the overspecialization which is the greatest defect of our American education, we produce more and more lopsided intellectuals who cannot distinguish the parts from the whole, either in dealing with the universe or in the affairs of their fellow men. We produce far too many scholars who, as it was well put by Sir Albert Howard, go on learning more and more about less and less. I think no sensible citizen would deprecate the accomplishments of our great physicists and chemists or of such philosophers as Emerson and William James, but it is doubtful how effective, how sound or how beneficial the influence of any of these men would be or would have been in government or in politics, especially in any role having executive authority.

The tendency during the past twenty years has been more and more to place in positions of great authority, and, frequently in fields which have nothing to do with their particular specialization, men of intellectual distinction, either academic or scientific. In virtually every case, such appointments (none of these men were ever elected by popular vote) have resulted in disappointment and even blundering and near disaster. As advisers, perhaps yes, but neither as executives nor administrators nor as framers of law.

In characteristic humbleness, the plain people have accepted such appointments and such authority in the immediate past but there is rising evidence that their common sense is asserting itself even through the ballot box in the conviction that these men do not belong in government, regardless of the brilliance of their personal and specialized achievements.

Moreover, there lies behind the achievements of many of these specialized intellectuals the dark shadow of the scientific materialism which in the U.S. as in Soviet Russia has tended more and more to obscure spiritual, religious, cultural and even practical human values. Yet these values, fundamentally, are perhaps more important to civilization and humanity and the actual growth of mankind than the internal combustion engine, the atomic bomb, the electric light or the Einstein theory. The intellectual in government tends to measure government, law and progress in terms of formulas and slide rules, a method which is best demonstrated by the Soviet government with results which are patently appalling.

There exist throughout history great leaders who have molded the course of mankind—such men as Julius Caesar, Voltaire, Napoleon, Thomas Jefferson, William Pitt and others. They were men of great intelligence, of wide knowledge and interest in almost every field of human endeavor. They possessed, primarily, a great and lively interest in the human race itself and all of them were in one way or another excellent politicians. Because of their knowledge, experience and interest they helped to direct the whole course of history and human progress. Not one of them was an academician or a specialist. They were primarily human and decidedly men of the world and of action.

In addition to the specialized intellectual, there are many who *fancy* themselves as "intellectuals" but who lack the power to think out anything to the end. These intellectuals in quotes are pretentious fellows for whom a little knowledge is a dangerous thing, educated frequently enough beyond their intelligence. They are likely to regard themselves as saviors of mankind. They are touched with the smugness of those half-thinkers who believe they know better than mankind itself what it needs. They have a taste for martyrdom but when faced by the prospect, fold up and leave actual martyrdom in the realm of imaginary conversation. ("I said to him and he said to me.") Thus they live partially at least and perpetually in the dream world of Walter Mitty. They speak of MAN and LABOR and

RACE, without even understanding these things, but rarely of *a* man or *a* woman. They turn the personal tragedies of the individual or the oppression of a minority into vulgar and often heartless propaganda. They are rather sloppy perfectionists in their ideals and dreams but rarely so in practice. From time to time, like women in menopause, they experience hot flashes all over at the spectacle of their own virtue and humanity. They are the kind who, like the tired housewife watching Barbara Stanwyck in the movies, "enjoy a good cry now and then." They belong to every sort of humanitarian committee operated by some shrewd "executive secretary" who makes his living thus and a good living it is. "A sick world" is their favorite phrase. They are vindictive and emotional and as confused as any oversexed adolescent girl. They have a fancy for intrigue and politics but no talent for it and persistently find themselves hoist on their own petard. A good many of them are skim-milk Machiavellis. They vastly underestimate both the virtues and powers of the common sense which Jefferson and Franklin so admired. Unlike the true intellectual who seldom mixes in vulgar politics, these individuals are always plunging neck deep in the mire and then complaining bitterly that somehow their white samite garments have become muddied. (See all those who have dabbled with Communism.) They have confused and muddled our times and have done their best to sicken the world. They constitute the great majority of those who, before an investigating committee, take refuge in the Fifth Amendment. During the early days of the New Deal they descended upon Washington like a plague of locusts.

Europe once had a word for them—the "Intelligentsia"—but this word has become as dated and old-fashioned as the hobble skirt or "Vera and the Nihilists." In this country, these fringe intellectuals appropriated to themselves a beautiful, an almost holy word, to which they had no right. This word was "liberal," with a long and honorable history dating from Voltaire, with its roots in the French Revolution and the burning assertion of the rights of man and the individual and the subservience of the state to man's own virtues, genius and dignity as an individual. As the Russians debased the meaning of that loose word "democracy" so these fringe intellectuals, by appropriating the word "liberal," confused and debased its meaning, and in general befuddled all issues.

Their "liberalism" was not based upon the doctrines of Liberty, Equality and Fraternity but upon the sour and bitter doctrines of Marx, who elevated the state and the oligarchy and the bureaucracy above the rights of any individual or all individuals. In Europe from Kerensky onward they were the betrayers of the people. They were the weak, indecisive, unprepared, unskillful and unwise elements who opened the door in Czechoslovakia, in Hungary, in Poland and elsewhere and held it open for the aggressive, unscrupulous and dynamic Communists to take over. In turn, these tinpot Machiavellis were the first to be liquidated by their "friends," the Communists, who held them in contempt.[5]

For a long period, there was no label for them save the misapplied one of "liberal"; then during the elections of 1952, a word arose spontaneously out of the people themselves, as such words emerge in time of need into the richness and flexibility of the golden English language. There was a need for the word and it came into existence. The word was "egghead."

I doubt that we shall ever discover who first used the descriptive word, but it provided a satisfying image with Martian overtones; overnight it became popular and universally employed. It freed that noble word "liberal" from its long and soiled bondage and gave it once more a semblance of its true and honorable meaning. Today the word "egghead" is a part of the language and if the editors of the next revised dictionary need a definition they might well use the description indicated above.

4

This much, then, must be said in defense of the delinquent liberals. The edge of their passion for freedom had been growing blunter for decades before the rise of totalitarianism put their loyalties to a test. It is not only freedom that they betray, however, in apologizing for the Soviet tyranny, or pussyfooting about it, or blackening America so savagely that Russia shines in unspoken contrast. They are betraying civilization itself. They are lending a hand in the destruction of its basic values, promoting a return march in every phase of human progress. Reinstitution of slavery, revival of torture, star chamber proceedings, execution without trial, disruption of families, deportation of nations, massacre of communities, corruption of science, art, philosophy, history, tearing down of the standards of truth, justice, mercy, the dignity and the rights of man—even his right to martyrdom—everything that had been won in the long struggle up from savagery and barbarism. . . . This too may be advanced in defense of the delinquent liberals—they are the victims of a swindle which nothing in past history had prepared them to detect.

MAX EASTMAN in *The Freeman*

The "eggheads" infested Washington for nearly a generation. They ranged from the professor of a freshwater college thrust overnight into a position of vast authority to the small town lawyer who had always been regarded by his fellow citizens as "a little queer" and who turned up suddenly issuing bulletins and ukases written in a strange language which would have delighted Swift. The language was promptly given a Swiftian name, "gobbledygook" —another word that came into being because it was needed to describe something for which there was until then no word and which, fortunately, until the emergence into prominence of the bureaucrat, had had no existence.

The "eggheads" muddled the China problem; they sometimes set back a solution of race problems in certain areas by many years. They could not hold liquor at cocktail parties and talked far more than they should have talked. They brought in other hordes of little "eggheads" to fill up the countless bureaus and commissions they invented to confound confusion still further. Until, at last, the American people in their common sense became aware of them and the nation was liberated. They were in essence the very apotheosis of pretentious and sloppy mediocrity. Their effect has been tragic, perhaps most of all in our foreign policy.

Many of them have been eliminated and even discredited, but some still remain in many offices, clinging like children in a tantrum to their comfortable and expensive armchairs. They cry out "Persecution" and "Graft" and "Steal" and "Patronage" but no one listens. The period of the plague and the fashion for "eggheads" has come to an end all the way from Hiss and Lattimore down to the little fellows with soiled shirts and thick glasses who fancied themselves as Marxian Machiavellis. It is unfortunate but inevitable that the reaction against them brought into prominence elements equally muddled and destructive at the opposite end of the spectrum.

They were the bane of our age. They confused and muddled whatever they touched. They are responsible for much tragedy at home and in the world. They gave and took bad advice. They are very much a part of the history of our State Department and foreign policy during the years of the China disaster, the Korean War, the infiltration of Communists into the government; they are part of the whole picture of corruption and confusion and disgrace which afflicted our government for a period of more than ten years. It is unfortunate that they cannot be ignored, wiped off the page and forgotten. They have left a blot across the pages of the history of our times. As spiritual by-blows of Lord Keynes they had their fingers up to their elbows in the pie of Bretton Woods, of Dumbarton Oaks, of the United Nations, of Yalta. As with Hiss and Lattimore, they held high positions and sometimes their treacherous or ignorant or emotionally foolish counsel was acted upon.

The defeat of the Democratic Party in 1953 was largely attributed to the resentment of the American people over Korea, corruption and Communism, but in reality it reflected as well the revolt of the Common People against the presence and influence in government of the "intellectual" and the "egghead." I do not mean the Common People in the sense of Henry Wallace's "Common Man." That phrase was the very embodiment of the "egghead," intellectual attitude—a large, cloudy and amorphous concept like "mankind" and "world responsibility" or "proletarian," that carried at the same time intimations of superciliousness and superficiality and even condescension toward the ordinary citizen. The Revolt of the Common People is a revolt of the farmer, the real estate broker, the filling station operator, the average professional man, the skilled industrial worker—indeed of the greatest part of the middle class of which the large majority of our citizenry are members and which is the very backbone of our economy and shared wealth as well as the principal champion of our liberties. The word "proletariat," one of the worn and pompous phrases of Communist and egghead propaganda, is meaningless in the U.S.

5

The lesson of Korea, and, indeed, of the whole eight years of U.N. activity is that this organization is miscast when it is placed in the role of an agency for opposing aggression. In the U.N. membership are potential aggressors, neutrals and many states which are unable to take any significant part in modern warfare because of poverty and economic backwardness. With its Tower of Babel of divided counsels it is the worst conceivable organization for military operations.

WILLIAM HENRY CHAMBERLAIN

The world in which we live is a world in turmoil if you wish, but not a sick world. It is a world in which things happen more rapidly than ever before in history, a world in which London lies only twenty hours from Australia on the bottom of the earth, in which I have had lunch in São Paulo, dinner in Lima, breakfast in Miami and been home for tea in Ohio. It is a world in which everything has become shrunken, where nations once as far apart as Atlantis and Cathay are uneasy neighbors. It is a world in which nations, peoples and individuals can talk to each other within a second or two, in which appointed bureaucrats with power but no direct responsibility become all-powerful and ambassadors sink to the level of office boys. It is a world in which the crackling radio hourly brings new ideas of freedom or rebellion, of resentment and discontent, into huts and kraals, yurts and bazaars in remote mountains, deserts and jungles. But worst of all it is a world wholly muddled by time lags and immense variations of living standards, literacy and political experience, and by traditions long dead which will not lie down as a self-respecting corpse should do.

Part of this world still lies in the Middle Ages or beyond, yet it has electric light and radios and planes fly overhead. In part of it we attempt to force independence and democracy (which is a luxury that must be earned rather than either given or imposed by a loud-mouthed sergeant) upon peoples who cannot read or write and have no words in their languages for freedom, democracy, liberty or human dignity. In India millions were "freed" from the British Empire who had never heard of it and did not know what it was. It is a world in which Communists whisper to jungle pygmies that they are oppressed and that Stalin or Malenkov or some other remote medieval tyrant will "free" them, a world in which psychopaths intrigue and become tyrants raised to great power by the stresses arising from economic and sociological injustices and maladjustments.

In short it is a world which will have to work out its own problems the hard way, which has been the method employed by the human race since its beginning in steaming swamps. The tough, the shrewd, the dynamic, sometimes the fortunate and lucky, will survive and dominate, under the fundamental law of the universe. It is a world in which leadership, knowledge, wisdom, statesmanship are desperately needed and in which these elements are scarce indeed. It is a world in which leaders should try to see the whole problem rather than its separate parts, to work out frictions and problems upon a sensible basis and not upon such tragic, irresponsible formulas as the "unconditional surrender" forced upon the Germans or the impossible "protection" doctrine given the Koreans. Above all it is a world in which there will be no peace and no prosperity and no advance of civilization or in science (save on the present barbaric basis of use for wars) until leaders and people stop living and planning policies from crisis to crisis, and observe long-range reality and hard fact, until they cease to live and direct all their activities in terms of politics and militarism rather than the very basic human realities of food and economics.

6

Will the President be impressed instead by historical evidence that Russian expansion westward, which has spurted out periodically for centuries, sooner or later overreaches itself and can then be pushed back? Recent events have confirmed the European view that the Soviet Empire is more precariously spread out than ever before, and that Stalin's restless successors in the Kremlin are uneasily aware that their European outposts are shaky.

DEMAREE BESS in the *Saturday Evening Post*

Beyond the confusion of historical time lags and the mechanical shrinking of the world lies the muddling of the Utopians who perpetually hitch up the cart before the horse and wonder that the operation does not work. The hard fact is that the world is not yet ready for world government. It is ready for co-operation and unification into workable economic and cultural and political units constantly growing in size and prosperity, nutrition, exchange of goods and raw materials and foods. Forcing the emetic of a United Nations, conceived wholly on a political basis with reformatory overtones, down the throat of the world while ignoring economics, raw materials, markets and food, can only cause the patient, as might be expected, to vomit. Nor is the perpetual agitation of the warmongers, common alike to Russia, to the United States and to Britain and to Europe, anything but a wretched and sinister drive toward disaster in terms of arms and warfare which solves absolutely nothing.

Worst of all perhaps is the absurd doctrine espoused by generals, admirals and some hysterical newspaper columnists and editors, that the United States must draft its young men, spend billions on equipment and aid, waste its precious natural resources, set up airfields and projects, secret or otherwise, everywhere, and occupy half the nations of the earth (as if so fantastic, childish and gigantic a program as this were possible) in order to defend them and ourselves against the dubious power of a Soviet Russia which grows weaker and more ramshackle with each new conquest and expansion.

By such a program we antagonize the world and drive those who might be sympathetic into the arms of Communism (from which one day they will have to emerge the hard way). *Imposing* democracy upon peoples who have not earned it and do not understand it is never successful, for the structure degenerates almost immediately into a dictatorship or oligarchy of a vicious and corrupt nature. What goes on *inside* a nation should be none of our business so long as its aggression does not touch us directly. Backward nations must find their way and develop that system of government which is best for them, never forgetting the wise saying of Voltaire that "any people gets the government it deserves." Democracy in the sense of true representative government and in the sense of a republic is not something that can be given or bestowed, imposed or commanded. It is essentially a luxury which must be earned through literacy and prosperity, through wisdom and self-restraint, through knowledge and consideration and through fierce ideals of independence, liberty and the dignity of the individual man. It is true also that the good fortune of great natural wealth and resources, abundant food, good markets, internal or external, and all the factors involved in a sound, prosperous and permanent economic status, contribute much toward making any *real* government by the people a fact.

It is difficult for the elements and reality of such government to come into being in nations that are poor, illiterate, vastly overpopulated and that do not have enough of anything to go around. In such countries, either there must exist a kind of chaos in which the strong and unscrupulous come out on top or there must be a rigid autocracy or dictatorship in which everything, in theory but rarely in fact, is distributed equally among all the people. There has been in our time perhaps more loose talk about "democracy" than about any of the other vast abstractions that preoccupy so many of our Utopian thinkers—and among all vast abstractions, "democracy," with all its implications and perverted practice, is one of the vastest.

Throughout considerably more than half the world, the freedoms, the liberties, the living standards, the wages and a hundred other things existing in the U.S. are merely unbelievable and beyond conception. Bragging of them, in any of our many agencies of propaganda, without explaining them (even to our great good fortune in occupying one of the most important areas of concentrated natural wealth on earth) converts no one but merely creates envy, resentment and enmity.

When we criticize and resent the medieval, blustering abuse and treacherous tactics of Soviet Russia (which appears superficially to be a modern state), we should remember that in Russia or in any Asiatic country there was never an Age of Chivalry in which were formulated patterns of trust, honor, truth and the sacredness of an oath. We should not forget that the average Russian still thinks in terms of invasion by Sweden, by the Turks and Mongols, by Napoleon and last of all by the Nazis, and that the average Russian has *never* at any time known such things as free speech or the right of free assembly, and that he has *never* possessed more than a shabby suit of clothes, a pair of cheap shoes and with luck a roof over his head and a stove on which to sleep. If the men who negotiated the agreements of Yalta, Teheran and Potsdam had considered all these things during their negotiations, they would perhaps have been less optimistic and less trustful and the results would have been far less evil and disastrous for the whole world.

When truce negotiations fail in Korea, we forget that we are operating upon a plane quite different from that upon which the Chinese, the Russians, the Communists in general or even the Koreans themselves are operating. To Asiatic millions, and most of all to the politicians in power, another abstraction, "humanity," has very little meaning. Life itself is of small value, and the idea that to yield, to compromise for the common good is humane and civilized is frequently nonexistent. The smart and crafty deal, and above all the saving of face, are the important things, regardless of death, famine and suffering. We are dealing with another age, another civilization, indeed another world.

Much of the condemnation of Soviet Russian and Communist tactics and their success, should be leveled less at the Russians and Communists themselves than at those on our own side who conducted these negotiations and failed, either because they were intoxicated by their own "liberal" and Utopian ideas or because of their ignorance and lack of understanding of history and of the men with whom they were dealing. These were essentially the reasons why we have frequently appeared as a nation of tragic fools at Yalta, at Potsdam, at Teheran, in Korea and in the United Nations. They explain the reason for the inscrutable smiles of Stalin which appeared in the photographs of Yalta, Teheran and Potsdam, smiles which a good many of our people and worst of all, our negotiating representatives, mistook for smiles of benevolence.

The whole of the much vaunted "containment" policy is, in its eternal essence, a defensive and negative policy in which we undertake to engage financial and military support here, there and everywhere—in short, wherever, in the confusion of this revolutionary world, disorder or aggression breaks out. We are in the position of Canute commanding the waves to stand still, and we seem unable to distinguish between Communist conquest and the drive of small nations for independence and freedom from exploitation. At best it is a negative and defensive policy in which the initiative is always in the hands of our opponents: each time the enemy or the opposition acts, we merely *react*, sending troops, military supplies and even our conscripted soldiers into remote areas of the world where more often than not we have no right to be nor any justification for "occupation." It compels us to operate under the worst of military conditions, our forces dispersed here and there, at random, around an enormous perimeter encompassing virtually the whole of the world. It is obviously an operation that produces costs and tactics ruinous to any nation as well as a foreign policy of equal dispersal and feebleness which constantly involves us in contradictory actions and alliances—a policy which earns us in the end only the growing dislike and enmity of all peoples and nations. (It is clear that in the long run we cannot pursue such a policy without interfering in the internal affairs of peoples and nations everywhere, as indeed we are already doing.)

7

The United States is spending on national defense more than four times as much absolutely as ten of our European beneficiaries combined (some $53,200,000,000 as against a total of $11,800,000,000). It is also spending much more relatively—fifteen per cent of its gross national product (total value of goods and services produced) as against an average of seven per cent of the ten beneficiaries. Many Europeans argue that this is as it should be. They advocate a sort of international income tax. This rests on the theory that the man or country that produces more and earns more somehow owes the difference to the man or country that produces less and earns less.

HENRY HAZLITT in *Newsweek*

(The ten countries are Britain, France, Italy, Norway, Turkey, Greece, Portugal, the Netherlands, Belgium-Luxembourg and Denmark.)

At the same time, under our "containment" policy we are constantly engaged in aiding and propping up the rotting colonial empires and in establishing and afterward maintaining through military force (as in Korea) the independence of small scattered nations which *cannot* remain independent, unco-operative or intransigeant, either politically, economically or geographically, without huge support from the people of the U.S. in terms of money, real wealth and the lives of countless unwilling conscripts.

This senseless and intolerable burden can and inevitably must in the end destroy the United States itself, as Lenin predicted. It is a smug and arrogant policy, infected with the evils of power politics, and is rewarded largely and rightly by increasing resentment and even hatred everywhere.

Aside from the tragic drain on our youth, whether drafted for two of the best years of their lives or maimed or killed or imprisoned, the grandiose "containment" policy means an immense and constant drain in terms of money, a drain which, as pointed out by a Congressional committee, actually means that today the average citizen of the United States is paying the taxes of the British people who cannot be taxed further without economic extinction and the taxes of rich French and Italian citizens who refuse to pay their tax share of the expenses of government.

It means also an immense and perpetual drain upon the natural resources of this nation in the form of military supplies, farm machinery, oil and other vital minerals and of all the real wealth which has in the past been the very foundation and bulwark of our economy, our wealth, power, prestige and independence. When we have exhausted the iron ores, the copper, the zinc, the oil, the forests or what you will, by giving them away wholesale, we shall simply be left an impoverished and weakened nation. Like the weak and fading colonial empires of Europe, we will be forced to barter and beg for these things *outside* this country and in order to get them will be forced into constantly lowered wages, living standards and actual dietary deficiencies.

It is seemingly apparent that such drains cannot go on even much longer, especially under a policy that is merely negative and defensive and that sacrifices everything while gaining at best temporary and constantly shifting delays and checks which in the long run are meaningless and without lasting results of any kind.

The world revolution now in progress is not only the struggle for freedom and independence of formerly exploited nations. It is, simultaneously, a spontaneous and inevitable regrouping, geographically, politically and economically, upon a new and basic economic pattern, of the nations and peoples of the world. The various nuclei around which the groups are forming are the large, reasonably populated or underpopulated land masses with proper balances of real wealth and natural resources to support agriculture and industry, and with secondary balances between agriculture and industry themselves, which in turn provide the *interior* markets of a prosperous, self-contained and dynamic economy.

All this means that these fortunate land-mass nations can feed themselves, export food and produce industrial commodities out of their own natural wealth and resources. In the end these great and obvious advantages can serve to balance and equalize supplies of food and industrial commodities among the smaller and less fortunate nations and peoples grouped about them, provided a sound pattern of close economic co-operation is established. These smaller, less fortunate and what are frequently described as "backward" nations can have *no* wholly independent economic existence and consequently no *real* political independence, and as wholly independent nations can have nutritional, educational, living and human standards only of an inferior sort. In this shrunken world their only hope of anything better is economic co-operation and eventually political federation with the larger, richer, more fortunate nations existing within a workable geographic pattern and area.

The new pattern can be formed in two ways. It can come, as I have already indicated, from economic co-operation and union among groups of small, less-favored nations gathered about the nuclei of three or four great, rich and self-sufficient or *potentially* rich and self-sufficient land-mass nations; or it can be accomplished by the co-operation and eventual union of large groups of small nations, as in Europe, into units sufficiently large to attain the economic advantages of the great land-mass nations such as the U.S., Brazil and Russia.

Behind this immense revolution lies the paradox of alliances everywhere or the threat of alliances between Communism (or threatened Russian imperialism in the disguise of Communism) and intense nationalism—it does not matter whether in China, Bolivia, Brazil, Iran, Indo-China, Guatemala or elsewhere.

One of the great failures of our foreign policy throughout the world arises from the fact that we have permitted ourselves to be identified everywhere with the old, doomed and rotting colonial-imperialist small European nations which once imposed upon so much of the world the pattern of exploitation and economic and political domination. This fact lies at the core of our failure to win the support and trust of the once-exploited nations and peoples who are now in rebellion and revolution in all parts of the world but especially in Asia. We have not given these peoples a *real* choice between the practices of Russian Communist imperialism or Communism and those of a truly democratic world in which individualism, American capitalism and free enterprise are the very pillars of independence, solid economics, liberty and good living standards. We have appeared to these peoples themselves (and above all to their politicians, who have taken every advantage of the situation) in the role of colonial imperialists (which we certainly are not, largely because we are not forced to be so by grim necessity) and of supporters in almost every case of the rotting old European empires. We have never once said or even intimated that we are able to offer them a better choice than either Communism or decadent, outdated European imperialism and capitalism. We have, in brief, always appeared to them in the guise of Europeans rather than as Americans. Despite the fact that our own record in Cuba, the Philippines, Puerto Rico and elsewhere is a complete and utter refutation of the charge of imperialism and colonialism, we shall *appear* to the scattered nations in revolt to be ourselves guilty so long as in Indo-China, Hong Kong, Iran, the Near East and elsewhere we lend support diplomatically, militarily or economically to the waning empires based in Europe.

In the meanwhile we have sought by pouring out vast sums of money and real wealth and even American lives to *buy* the good will and co-operation of these peoples in revolution and have succeeded no more than we have succeeded in buying the good will of the dying European imperialist nations whom we have been supporting with even vaster amounts of money and real wealth.

None of these rebellious, awakening peoples will, in their hearts or even superficially, trust us or co-operate in any way so long as we remain identified with the economic colonial system of Europe, which represents, even in its capitalist pattern, the last remnants of feudalism and which in many respects is as remote from the realities of our time and of the future as many of the sixteenth-century concepts and practices of Soviet Russia. We cannot appear to these Asiatic peoples in the role of friend and benefactor while we are at the same time financing, attempting to restore to power and even providing arms to the very forces of the dying colonial empires, against which they are in rebellion.

This is exactly what we are doing in Indo-China and in Hong Kong and elsewhere in the world under a confused policy based upon the doomed past rather than upon the inevitable dynamic pattern of the future. We leave these awakening peoples with no choice but to turn to Russian and Communist comfort and promises of Utopia. We make it possible everywhere, even in South America, for the Communists to worm their way into the turmoil of countries in revolution striving for independence, and to create the impression that what in fact is merely an intense assertion of nationalism is really a Communist liberation, planned and carried out by Communist influence.

This pattern exists in Indo-China, in Guatemala, in Bolivia and imminently and potentially in Iran and Egypt and elsewhere. It has validity even in China, where we have backed the interests of the British in holding Hong Kong. At the same time Britain, by recognizing Red China and advocating her admission to the United Nations, is permitted to play the role of benefactor and friend while we are left to hold the bag in Korea. Neither morally nor in a practical sense have the French any right to be in Indo-China or the British to be in Hong Kong, and neither can maintain their positions there in the long run, as countless wise and realistic French and Britishers understand and even admit.

The rebellion in Indo-China, in Java and even to some extent in China are *not* Communist revolutions in any fundamental sense. They are mass surges of people moving everywhere toward independence and dignity in which the Communists through intrigue and in some cases with the financial backing and training of Moscow, have managed to gain dominant power. The aid we provide to the French in Indo-China only serves further to alienate from us *all* Asiatic peoples, including India, and to make the already doomed position of the French in Indo-China increasingly precarious and hopeless. Pouring money and materials into these countries through Point Four aid and foreign aid is meaningless so long as we join forces with those against whom they are struggling. This is the real meaning behind the utter failure of our policy in Java and the repudiation of all American aid in Burma. It lies at the very root of the difficulties we have with India, the actual leader of all Asia, and with Nehru, who has himself spent years in British prisons for fighting for the liberation of India from the British.

We are constantly espousing the dead past rather than the inevitable future in a battle which cannot be won and which in many cases makes the U.S. appear ridiculous. And in doing so we are providing ammunition for propaganda, aid and comfort to the Russians and the Communists everywhere. We have heard a great deal of talk during the Korean tragedy about the value of "face" in Asia, but all the "face" in the world is meaningless so long as we give aid and material support in arms to the ancient and traditional exploiters of these Asiatic peoples. By such a policy we help only to deliver these rebellious people into the hands of the Communist forces, wherever or whatever they may be, meanwhile pouring out hundreds of millions to "buy" the friendship of peoples who cannot afford to trust us even were they so inclined.

All this is the heritage of a policy beginning under Roosevelt and carrying through the Truman-Acheson period when the interests of Europe and those of Britain in particular were placed above those of Asia, South America and even our own national interests. The gravity of the situation is heightened by the fact that the awakening people everywhere are aware that the colonial empires are finished and that the old imperialist, colonial nations of Europe have not the force, either militarily or economically, now or ever again, to impose their will upon subject peoples. It is only through vast aid from the U.S. that they are able to maintain their present weak and static situation as exploiters of other weaker nations.

The only semblance of real force or power in the dying colonial empires is created out of the aid in money and arms with which we provide them, and Asiatic peoples and politicians are sharply aware of this fact. It is probable that these Asiatic peoples, illiterate, poverty-stricken, half-starved, discern the shape of the future far more clearly than does anyone in our State Department or even our government. The shape is one which calls for the economic and industrial development of these now struggling nations and for their co-operation economically on a basis of equality, dignity and mutual regard for sovereignty, within areas sufficiently large to provide markets and raw materials and make possible the free exchange of food supplies and commodities and the general raising of living standards, wages and purchasing power. It is a pattern in which we are constantly interfering, stupidly and aimlessly, in Korea, in Iran, in Java, in Hong Kong and elsewhere, but it is a pattern that will one day come inevitably into being, as it has already come partially into being in India.

We shall lose the battle abroad and what is more disastrous, at home, if we do not become aware of the realities of the revolution now going on in the world and act accordingly. In virtually every sense our present policies and actions are running exactly counter to the world revolution and to the vast irresistible surge toward new and inevitable world patterns of development.

We *can* become the leaders of the world, as many muddled Americans now claim we are, and we can accept our responsibilities, but only when we offer the nations and people now in rebellion something new and real which neither the nations of Europe nor Soviet Russia nor Communism can offer them.

8

These obstacles which exist in the underdeveloped countries themselves and can be corrected only by them, include in the Bank's opinion, the lack of traditions of political responsibility, the weakness of economic initiative; low standards of education and training; and insufficient understanding that economic progress requires patience, effort and self-denial.

WALL STREET JOURNAL in comment upon the World Bank Report on Investments in the Underdeveloped Nations

In summary, let me repeat, for it is the basis of this book and very likely the only basis for a peaceful world: the day of old-fashioned colonialism and imperialism is over. It no longer exists nor can exist save for a limited time within the borders of Soviet Russia's precarious, troubled and ramshackle imperialist state. The future of the world will be based upon *co-operation* on a fair and legitimate basis between the small, less fortunate nations and peoples and those nations which possess great land masses, reasonable populations, great natural resources and sound, largely self-sufficient economies. In this *co-operation* it is the smaller nations which derive in every case the greater benefits. It is with the destruction of these old empires and with the economic regrouping of the smaller nations that the world revolution is concerned. Even Soviet Russia, which possesses great land masses, wealth and is reasonably populated, cannot succeed in holding together a great, diverse self-contained empire by the methods of conquest and bitter exploitation she has followed thus far. She risks even the disintegration of interior Russia itself through racial, cultural, religious and lingual resentments, intrigue, low living standards, exploitation, political oppression and a hundred other things including, perhaps most of all, her contempt for man's inherent desire for freedom, independence and dignity which has never yet been wholly and completely suppressed for any long period.

It is co-operation among nations upon an economic basis that we must make understood and that we must practice—not the politically based weakness and ineffectiveness of the United Nations, but the real fact and force of *economic co-operation*. Giving away vast sums of money and material is not co-operation—neither is the propaganda of the Voice of America. Co-operation, particularly in the economic sense, is the acceptance of other nations and the peoples of other nations as equals and co-operators in a large economic plan in which the smaller nations receive by far the greater benefit. And in putting this into effect we should make it clear that we are not concerned with maintaining or re-establishing the old scattered empires, or in re-establishing the European capitalist system, which is so vastly different from our own as to be something wholly apart, or in hypocritically supporting corrupt and tyrannical individuals and regimes merely as pawns in our campaign against the expansion of the ramshackle empire of Russia.

It was the Truman-Acheson policy and before that the Roosevelt policy (if such things existed in crisis-to-crisis government) which have placed us before the world in revolution as Europeans rather than Americans and as the defenders and supporters of a system, almost a civilization, which has declined far more rapidly than any in the history of the world. From all of this the Communists and Russia have derived enormous aid, comfort and benefits.

We need, as I have said, to offer the nations of the world in revolution something different, an alternative, which is better than Communism or the dying imperialism of Europe. We have it to offer. It exists as a fact. It is the reason why today the United States is the richest and most powerful nation in the world, why her great corporations are owned *not* by a tiny minority of very rich individuals and families but by the people themselves, why the middle class, so hated by the Communist, is represented by ninety per cent upward of the people, why the American worker receives wages from thirty to ninety per cent higher than the wages of working-men of any other nation save Canada. . . .

Let us remain friends with Europe if we can, but let us not appear before the rest of the world as reactionaries seeking to re-establish what cannot be re-established. That is the role to which our State Department and two Presidents for the past fifteen years have committed us. It is a false role and a disastrous one. We have acted it badly and it may be costing us in the long run our very existence. Certainly it is costing us the friendship of peoples in every part of the world and constantly building up fresh suspicions, hatreds and fears which, especially in Russia and Asia, may explode into what well may be The Last War.

We are playing the politics of a vanished world, blindly and stupidly attempting to surround and contain what cannot be contained, blocking the free exchange of goods and keeping the world in a constant uproar by making alliances and setting up military installations everywhere. It is an antique pattern of power politics which in these times is not a policy at all but a confusion of embroilment.

It is common nowadays to hear talk of the menace of Asia and her millions and of the necessity of developing friendly relations and of keeping the vast resources of Asia from the control of Soviet Russia. Such talk is part of the sweeping pattern of wholesale generalizations that are put forward by those who advocate the absurd, dangerous and impossible conception of this country—of the U.S., aided *perhaps* by a few weakened allies in Europe, attempting to dominate and control the whole world. It is also a picture painted in meaningless words and loose phrases which falls apart at the very first analysis. Worse than that, it raises the suspicion and resentment of all the awakening nations of the East and fortifies the accusations that the United States does actually contemplate and even plan such a domination. It follows closely and encourages as well that worst of all handicaps to our friendly co-operation with other rising nations—the line that we are merely bolstering up in Asia what remains of the European colonial empires and consequently supporting a continuation or restoration of white domination and exploitation.

Regardless of the intentions of our policies toward awakening Asia (and they have been vague and muddled and without consistent direction since the very first episode in Indonesia), they appear only in a sinister light to the millions of Asiatics who know anything about them, and it is inevitable that they should appear so to the more enlightened and revolutionary leaders possessed of a long and bitter experience with the colonial exploitation of European nations.

The indifference, at times bordering on sympathy, with which Nehru regards Red Chinese aggression, is wholly explicable in these terms. Why should he, as a leader who has fought most of his life for the independence of India and suffered long periods of imprisonment for his activities at the hands of the British, trust the United States whose whole policy for more than twelve years has been to support and encourage and build up British power? For what reasons are we doing so? The answer that we are doing so in our own defense is not only cynical and wholly unsound, but actually alienates the whole of the Asiatic world.

Today Britain is India's debtor. Is it likely that Nehru or thousands of Asiatic leaders, small or large, will take a chance on ever returning to the old position of subservience and exploitation? India has never been grateful or fertile ground for Communist propaganda and growth because of countless factors, many of them religious. But if India and the Indian people today were confronted by the necessity of an absolute choice between the bitter fact of the British imperialism of the past and the bright promises, however false, of Communism in the future, who can doubt which way her millions of ignorant, half-starving and illiterate inhabitants would turn? Communism offers only bright promises, however fantastic and unsound, while Britain and Europe offer the reality of past humiliations and bitter experience. The dice are badly loaded. The United States has poured billions into Britain and is today supplying her with arms. By comparison, only a pittance, a token, has gone into India. What do Asiatics think of this? What would you as an Asiatic, limited in education, a victim of prejudices, experienced with regard to Europe only through exploitation, be thinking? We cannot have it both ways.

Let us say if we will that we have ties of culture, blood and tradition which bind us to the United Kingdom. In Asia this is a meaningless argument. It merely serves to increase suspicion and hostility. We cannot follow one policy based upon hard fact and at the same time another based upon sentimentality, certainly not and expect belief and faith from the suspicious and frequently cynical Oriental mind.

Asia, it should be remembered, is stirring and awakening from her long sleep for two reasons: (1) because of genuine yearnings for freedom and independence, arising largely from the ferment caused by increasing enlightenment through education, newspapers, radio and propaganda, and consciously expressed through a few articulate leaders rebellious against the old colonial powers; (2) because the European colonial empires no longer have the force nor the wealth to resist revolution or suppress rebellion as they had in the past, nor to exploit by force the raw materials, labor and vast markets of Asia.

We should never overlook the fact that our intentions, policies, plans and actions may well appear in one light to ourselves and in quite another light to the millions living outside the U.S., and especially to those millions in Asia.

The experience of those Asiatic millions with the nations of the West has not been a happy or desirable one in the past, and judging by that experience they have no reason to suppose, despite all the hundreds of millions poured out in aid and advice, that we in the United States have any but an eventually sinister purpose. This is especially true when we ourselves are not quite certain what our purposes are (save from a vague and muddled Utopian point of view or from the negative one of opposition to Soviet Russian influence), or why we seek to interfere, either by advice, aid or threat in an area so remote and complex as Asia.

I am not at all certain that even one American citizen in ten thousand could give any real explanation for all our multitudinous interferences, meddlings and activities, and I doubt that many of those in government who have helped to bring about our vast and disorganized program could give any very convincing explanation of a policy which, like Topsy, "just growed." We are extended everywhere in the world today with known and secret establishments and military installations. There is scarcely a nation in the world outside of Soviet Russia and her satellites where there are not all sorts of American agencies ranging from give-away programs to military installations and airfields and in some cases virtual occupation. Why? To what purpose? To say that it is to defend ourselves against Russia is an answer as meaningless to Asiatics as it is to many an informed and thoughtful European and American. Whatever else it may be, it is a policy of the utmost danger to our foreign relations and the good will of other nations everywhere, as time continues to demonstrate. It can bring about our own internal economic collapse. Above all it serves to maintain and perpetuate rather than to resolve the existing strains and confusions of the world and to prevent its return to work, trade and peace.

Millions in Asia and elsewhere cannot therefore resist asking "Why?" It must be remembered that in the Orient conditions of life, ancient traditions and differences in civilizations and philosophies make no allowance for the meddling, reforming "do-good" propensities of Anglo-Saxon nations. Altruism is not an outstanding quality in the miserably hard life and experience of Asiatic peoples and is usually viewed with suspicion and utter cynicism. On the other hand, in the Orient cynicism *is* a prevailing quality, born of a fierce struggle for mere existence, and among many Oriental peoples craft, duplicity and the ability to put over a "smart bargain" are considered credits and even virtues. Hypocrisy such as Anglo-Saxons know and demonstrate is virtually unknown in the Orient except as it has been introduced by the European colonial powers and by some of our own missionaries.

It is not astonishing then that our activities everywhere from Korea, where we have been carrying on a costly full-scale war upon Asiatic soil, to Ceylon, where we have exerted pressures to prevent the exportation of crude rubber to Red China in exchange for rice, are viewed with suspicion, and become rich grist to the mill of the Communist propagandist and politician.

Here again our leadership in the United Nations and our alliance with the defunct European empires have done us great damage. The enemy propagandist has only to say over the radio, in the press, in harangues on the street corner, "Look at the United Nations! All your old European oppressors and enemies are banded together with the U.S. against you. Only Russia has clean hands and can help you. Only Communism can back you up and seeks only your welfare."

It is well to remember that it was the European colonial empires and *not* Russia which for centuries oppressed and exploited the peoples of Asia. It was the European nations which set up a color line, race prejudice and, in the case of the British, refused to admit Indians living in their own country into British clubs in Bombay, in Calcutta and in other Indian cities and communities.

These things may seem variously profound or trivial but they are all of immense significance in Asia, as anyone with any *real* knowledge of Asia readily understands. The battle in Indo-China is not altogether a battle against Communists and Red China. In it are engaged countless Indo-Chinese, of all the small individual nationalities represented in the Indo-Chinese area, who hate French domination more than Chinese domination and many who are fighting not *for* the Red Chinese but *against* domination and exploitation by the French. Yet there are even those, principally in the armed forces of the U.S., who would, if they dared, advocate drafting American boys from Ohio, Iowa, Kansas and elsewhere and sending them into this struggle where they or the nation itself have no proper place and where our intervention can only serve to do us tragic harm in the long run.

It must be remembered again and again that Asiatic people have *had* experience with European colonial empires. They have had no experience with Communism. In propaganda today in Asia, Communism has all the advantages of bringing promises and golden ones, while anti-Communist propaganda coming from the West is desperately handicapped by the long black record of the past. When we in the United States associate ourselves with the nations responsible for that past and co-operate with them by interfering in their behalf in the Asiatic areas, we already have two strikes against us.

9

The threat hanging over the independence of Korea is greater than ever. A huge Chinese army is installed in the northern part of the country. There is a possibility of a letdown of national morale, if after all the sacrifices of the war, nothing is gained but the old unnatural and uneconomic line of partition.

THE FREEMAN, August 10, 1953

Every time we act as "police agents" for the United Nations (and we appear to be the *only* active "police agents" of this organization), we are automatically acting in behalf of those very forces which are suspect and hated in Asia. Remember that to the Asiatic, it is not only the Red Chinese and the native Viet-minh troops who are perhaps guilty of aggression. Long before, it was the French, the British, the Dutch, even the Portuguese, who set up the model. To many an Asiatic it is the merest hypocrisy to assert that we are helping the Indo-Chinese people to resist the aggression of Red China. What happens if we defeat the Red Chinese? The French are still there, unseated and unwanted, and Indo-China still does not have her independence. By simple logic and fact, it is the French we have protected from aggression and not the Indo-Chinese. No matter that we claim we are resisting Russian and Communist domination, no matter though we may honestly believe this; it does not appear thus in Asia, to the Asiatic, who is judging merely from his own cynical experience.

Whatever the eventual outcome in Korea, it will make very little difference to the general aspect of an Asia in ferment. Those who talk much of "saving face" in Korea are talking of a superficiality. Korea is devoted to us and our efforts simply because we offer her for the first time in centuries any real freedom or independence. Her particular hatreds are entirely Asiatic—for China, Japan and possibly Russia. Only by *our constant and perpetual support* and defense can she maintain that freedom and independence. She may well prove to be not the martyred heroic nation which the sentimental have made of her, but merely the albatross about our neck which can carry us deeper and deeper into tragic complications and future wars. Because we have no real reason to be in Korea, unless, as every Asiatic suspects, for reasons of power and exploitation. To say that a country so remote and so insignificant as Korea is our first line of defense is to say that every nation in every part of the world is also our "first line of defense"—a conception which is obviously fantastic and grotesque to the borders of megalomania. It is properly suspect not only by Asiatic nations but by many others. Yet this is a concept widely shared and widely exploited by considerable elements of our armed forces.

It is part of the world revolution that we must begin to think not of small, individual nations, separated everywhere by arbitrary trade restrictions, traditions, tribal and racial and religious enmities, but of great land masses united economically into free trading areas living in mutual co-operation. In other words we should think—if we are to have permanent peace and economic stability and prosperity—of Asia, of Russia, of a United Western Europe based upon the ideas of the geopoliticians, of North America, and even of the Western Hemisphere as such areas.

Our permanent occupation of Korea in order to maintain her economic and political independence artificially is an act against the whole trend of world revolution and the irresistible forces of our times. It permits her, at the expense of American money and lives, to maintain an archaic and quixotic condition of stubborn and bitter nonco-operation with her powerful surrounding neighbors and thus to become a perpetual running sore which cannot be cured until she chooses or is forced to enter into complete economic and eventually political co-operation with her powerful or potentially powerful neighbors, China, Japan and even Russia. By our action we involve ourselves in huge expenses and in future wars arising out of the inevitable enmity and economic pressures existing in China and Japan. And we actually prevent the Koreans from ever working out any really sound future upon a basis of compromise, and co-operation with the realities. Let me repeat again, the whole pressure of world forces is not toward greater and greater fragmentation into more small, helpless and troublesome nations, but toward larger and larger land-mass nations and combinations of nations upon a geographic basis.[6]

10

Americans are rightly famous, and beloved, for their generosity; but there was no genuine or Christian charity in Mr. Dulles' discriminatory promise of lavish material help for the rehabilitation of South Korea and not of North Korea. The American food parcel can be as true a symbol of Christian love as the cup of cold water; but the political, and even electoral, strings attached to such aid in Asia, in Italy, and in Berlin have robbed the gift of its virtue and induced either sycophancy or cynicism in those who receive it. The Good Samaritan did not ask to see the party card of the man he was taking to the inn.

Surely a Christian approach to modern world politics must include not only the Golden Rule itself ("do unto others . . .") but an attempt to see ourselves as others see us and to put ourselves imaginatively in the position of others.

TOM DRIBERG, British Labor M.P. in *Time* Magazine

The case of Korea is unique in all Asia, and whether we support or abandon her will make very little difference to our waning prestige in Asia. Millions of Asiatics will merely ask why we were there in the first place. Why should we cross the Pacific to take up the cause of a small nation and involve ourselves in a war with a great Asiatic nation like China which for more than a century, even after the Boxer troubles, had been our great friend? To the Asiatic mind, the answer that we did it to resist aggression, as a "police action," is merely foolish; and it is not impossible that history will show them to be right. For we have intervened in a situation which can never be solved permanently save on the basis of geography and economics. Unless it is solved in this way, we must stay in Korea indefinitely and eventually either retire and accept defeat or involve ourselves and the world in a war which may well be for us and will be certainly for all Europe the end of the road. With such a frightful prospect it is small wonder that many of our former allies and friends, who have neither any desire to be involved in another holocaust nor any reason to be dragged into it by the vagaries and irresponsibility of American "foreign policy," are cooling toward us and adopting a policy of neutralism.

Our proper course in Asia is confused for most Americans by the tendency of the lazy and uninformed mind to think of all other peoples as being more or less like ourselves and all other nations as having a considerable similarity—physically, materially and in development—to our own. It is this same laziness of thought, lack of imagination and of information which makes it possible for our own warmongers, our hysterical columnists, our military brass to build up the legend of the great Asian menace and preach the doctrine that if Russia controls Asia she will control the world.

Let's examine what it means to "control" Asia. It is, I think, a task which no nation in its right mind should desire to carry out or even attempt. It may well be that history will demonstrate how fortunate we were *not* to have inherited the burden of China, for with our talent for meddling and intervention and the absurd conviction of some that we can "buy" friendship, loyalty, "democracy" and peace, we could and probably would have poured more billions into China than we have poured into Europe with little effect save the bankruptcy of the American government and people. It is ironically possible that all the blunders of the Truman-Marshall-Acheson front in China have, despite everything, worked out for our own good and even to the eventual damage of Soviet Russia.

The conditions and problems of such vastly overpopulated nations as India and China, are virtually insoluble in terms of generations and even perhaps in terms of centuries. In each country there are from one to two hundred millions of people now living who were born and will die without ever having had enough to eat one day of their lives, and the people of both nations are subject to every sort of disease and handicap arising from malnutrition. Worst of all, they are steadily *increasing* their populations, while their resources from minerals to food remain stable or decline, and capital for investment in development under existing conditions is hard to come by or impossible to obtain. This is especially so in China where government financing and development of industry and even agriculture is under existing conditions the *only* solution.

Nowadays we hear much of "manpower." Usually the word is employed to mean fodder for cannon and only secondarily in relation to industry and agriculture, yet manpower for vast armies becomes increasingly unimportant in the world of modern warfare in which planes, radar and atomic bombs are all-important. Nearly always we hear "manpower" referred to as if it were an asset, yet the fact is that over great areas of the world such as Asia and even in parts of Europe, "manpower" exists as a virtual and deadly liability which handicaps or blocks altogether all efforts to solve profound economic, sociological, political and even nutritional problems.[7]

If, for example, the whole of Asia were isolated from Western influences, particularly the influences of Western knowledge, capital, technical, agricultural and industrial and engineering skills, it would within a short period of time fall into chaos and anarchy. Even Soviet Russia would not have the power either in resources, wealth, knowledge or technically skilled manpower to save the situation. Indeed, if all Asia were today handed over wholesale to Russian domination, the act could in the end only drag Russia into the maelstrom of general economic and political ruin. The fact is that the nations of Asia are themselves the only ones who can solve their problems of food, education, hygiene, population, literacy, politics or what you will. No amount of money or material or military intervention can in themselves accomplish this.

Most European nations are already in the first stages of a serious condition of overpopulation resembling that of India and China. The greatest problem of the British Isles is the problem of food, for which the financially embarrassed British government is forced to spend a third of its budget without affecting much the fact that until very recently most food was still on a rationed basis.

Most other European nations save France, Sweden and Norway,

face similar conditions. They *must* have sources of raw materials in order to produce the revenue through the processing and production of industrial commodities with which to buy food. Also they must have access to markets in which to sell their processed commodities. (Meanwhile our policy is to do everything possible throughout the world to block the establishment of free exchange of goods and raw materials.) France is an exception because France, including her North African colonies, has that remarkable economic balance between agriculture, food production and industry which for the most part permits her to maintain a balanced and very nearly self-sufficient economy despite every sort of *political* confusion and complication.

None of these throttling conditions of population, of food, scarcities, of oil, raw materials, etc. affects the major nations of the New World. The future lies *before* rather than *behind* them. Their greatest need lies in the development of industry and agriculture and the consequent utilization of their huge reservoir of resources. All nations in the Western Hemisphere, and in the final analysis even the United States, actually *need* population. The only exceptions are three or four small and isolated islands which are colonies or dependencies, such as Jamaica, Haiti and Puerto Rico. In the case of Brazil alone the doubling of her population overnight by sound immigration would be of the greatest possible benefit. With a uniformly sound agriculture and the utilization of millions of acres of unused and possible agricultural land, the U.S. could easily feed at existing dietary levels two to three times its existing population at a very conservative estimate.[8]

11

A tyranny in retreat is most vulnerable because on the one hand, it cannot give real freedom to its oppressed subjects and, on the other hand, it has lost the spell of absolute and consistent terror. Soviet policy in the satellite area since Stalin's death has been confused and vacillating, offering concessions here, intensifying repression there. This kind of wavering, unsure policy has been the prelude to serious disturbances, even to collapse.

THE FREEMAN, August 10, 1953

As in the case of Europe, so again the average American lazily or ignorantly maintains a vague physical picture of Russia which resembles his own U.S. and again he falls victim to the military and bureaucratic propaganda which constantly presents Russia as a vast, rich, united, powerful, productive world power which it is not.

If we take the vast land mass of Soviet Russia, we discover that the actual known real wealth and natural resources are small by comparison even with the united resources of Canada and the United States alone. By comparison Russia has very little reliable agricultural land which can be depended upon consistently to produce adequate amounts of food. By far the greater part of the vast land mass is desert, frozen tundras or dry blowing sand. A huge part of her territories lies within the barren Arctic Circle. And the greater part of her agricultural land, because of undependable rainfall and extremes of temperature, is fit only for raising occasional quick crops of wheat which are themselves subject to periodic failure through adverse weather conditions. Russia's balance of wheat for export is always small and is frequently found only by actually sacrificing the bread of her own people. Genuine famines and near famines have occurred frequently during Soviet Russian history.

Forest areas are perhaps Russia's greatest single asset, and these remain in regions where the soil, if cleared, cannot be converted to an agricultural and food potential. Means of transportation are primitive or nonexistent. Just as in China and India manpower becomes a liability, so in Russia the vast sterile distances and the huge expanses of barren territory become a handicap useful only as a military protection—and in the grim realities of an atomic world with long-distance planes they no longer serve even in that capacity.

Moreover, Russia is made up of countless races, tribes and subtribes of peoples speaking different languages and possessing utterly different religions, traditions and customs.

The fact is that since the beginning of greater Russia as a nation, its whole history, under the Czars or the Soviets, has been a history of gigantic expansion in which gains have never been consolidated or digested. The absorption of the smaller Middle European and Balkan nations can well become a liability rather than the dubious asset it now is, especially since the Soviet government continues unbroken the traditional Czarist policy of exploiting and pilfering newly taken territories rather than developing and absorbing them in an economic and co-operative sense.

Again the fact is that much of the "menace" of Russia is fictitious and has been created through propaganda out of Russia herself and by those forces in the Western World, particularly by generals and politicians in the United States, who want to expand their own power, influence and financial appropriations. All this has been of the greatest aid to Russia and the Comintern and in general has promoted on many occasions the effectiveness of her bluffing tactics in international affairs.

While the average American citizen has a lazy mental picture of Russia as a nation with schools, railroads, hard-surfaced roads, automobiles, modern telephones and a network of plane services, and is encouraged in this picture by the hysterical or warmongering elements which constantly emphasize the threat of Russian power and menace, the picture is grotesquely false. Schools, except in a few areas, are primitive. The distribution and mileage of railroads is far below that of the U.S. and by far the greater part of the railroads and equipment and rolling stock is antiquated and in wretched condition. Telephones, save in a few limited metropolitan areas, are primitive or unknown. Commercial plane service in the abundance and efficiency known in Europe, South America and the U.S. and Canada, does not exist. Living standards and diet are among the lowest in the world. Luxuries are unknown save to a small minority of Communist bureaucrats. Even what most Europeans or Americans regard as necessities, such things as dwelling places, shoes and clothing, are of shabby quality, scarce and ferociously expensive.

In all the strange and sinister maneuverings of the Korean War I have never seen one single mention out of the State Department or the armed forces that Russia's only means of transporting food and military supplies in quantity to carry on the Korean War is an antiquated single-track railroad, the old trans-Siberian railroad which takes nearly three weeks to make the journey from Moscow to Manchuria—a railroad which, in times of planes and bombs, could be kept permanently from operating. The concealment of this fact, or at least the failure to mention it, is consistent with the Acheson-State Department–United Nations policy of engaging in a full-scale war with no expectation of winning it.

Not only is Russia a ramshackle empire divided a hundred ways by the traditions, languages and religions of barbaric and semibarbaric peoples, but it has undertaken within the past decade to dominate and exploit within the borders of Europe proud people with a tradition of civilization and culture and living standards which the Russian people as a whole have not yet attained or even approached. These satellite nations are also divided by race, language and religion but they share a common hatred of Soviet Russia. This fact becomes increasingly apparent with the passing of each day and makes increasingly impossible the threat of invasion of Western Europe by large land forces, which are probably Russia's greatest military asset at the moment.

There has been much loose talk of how easy it would be for Russian armies to overrun Western Europe, but no modern army, even the Russian army with its capacity to live off the countryside and under conditions imposed on no other army save perhaps the Chinese, can maintain or carry out a war without adequate communication lines which cannot be cut. As circumstances have demonstrated within the past year, the communication lines of Russian armies invading Europe would be cut almost immediately at the first sign of a march West. Some millions of satellite peoples are only waiting to take to the forests and swamps as guerrilla troops, from where they would sally forth to sabotage railroads, raid ammunition dumps and in general disrupt all communications and sources of supplies. Even supposing that the huge Russian armies did invade Western Europe, there would be the colossal and insoluble problem of policing millions of proud and rebellious people, a task at which even the brilliantly trained and disciplined German armies failed during the occupation of so small an area as a part of France.

Moreover, during the past year there have been increasing signs of unrest and dissatisfaction within Russia's own borders, notably in the Ukraine and in Georgia. The Iron Curtain was devised for two purposes: (1) to prevent Russian citizens from discovering how much better off than they were the peoples of all Western Europe and indeed all the rest of the world save Asia and the Middle East; (2) to prevent outside nations and peoples from discovering how wretched and unstable were conditions inside Russia.

It has been fairly well established that but for the insane policy of Hitler and the S.S. the Ukraine and White Russia would have gone over at once to the German side, and they might again revolt against the Kremlin if the opportunity arose. It is also extremely unlikely that Russia could have held out during World War II against Nazi pressure and invasion and have saved Moscow except for the unceasing stream of military aid, supplies and matériel provided by the Allies, particularly the U.S. Aware of this fact, the Kremlin has steadily increased military appropriations for war material at the sacrifice of a sound economy, of decent living standards and indeed of every other factor in her existence. This situation cannot continue indefinitely, and with the advent of the atomic and hydrogen bombs it becomes increasingly meaningless, futile, and actually destructive to her own strength and power.

Even if these factors in Russia's sprawling and disunited weakness were not historical fact and fairly obvious from general sources of information, we should learn them through the one source which Soviet Russia cannot conceal within her own borders, the reports in her daily press, *Izvestia, Pravda* and the *Red Star*. There is irony in the fact that these newspapers are the principal media of internal Russian propaganda, and that in using them to tongue-lash the helpless and beaten citizenry for failure to produce or for the shabbiness and scarcity of Russian commodities in general, the Kremlin is forced to reveal the weaknesses of Russia's internal economy and the unrest which constantly makes itself felt here and there within her borders.

Yet the men of the Kremlin have been extremely shrewd in utilizing and building up the legend of her strength and invincibility, not only directly through Communist propaganda in other nations but through the warmongering and fellow-traveling elements in those nations which aid her greatly in constantly building up this same legend.

Actually Soviet Russia is in the same afflicted state as the ancient Czarist empire, and suffering from the same maladies—abysmal living standards for the great mass of the people, secret police, exile and concentration camps, forced labor, militarism and the vicious necessity of suppressing the rights of free speech or the right to assemble, of playing always upon the love of the homeland and the menace of invasion by European nations. In this shrunken world of course, the U.S. has been added to the enemies against whom the Russian people are protected by their government. There still exists the same passion to expand by establishing viciously exploited buffer states, with the same consequence that the more she expands the more rebellion and hatred she invites and the weaker and more unstable she becomes.

The truth is that the menace of Russia lies not in her own great strength and military power, which is overrated by our own armed forces, nor in the Comintern nor in the operations of Russian Communists in other countries. Where it lies is in the treason and co-operation of native citizens in these countries, mostly among the "intelligentsia," the mild Socialists and the "liberals in quotes" everywhere who have been consistently deceived into believing that they were serving Socialism and Communism when in reality they have been serving only the old Russian Czarist imperialism in a new disguise. It is never the Russian Communist agent who has worked evil and betrayed secrets in our own or in other countries. It has always been the native or naturalized scientist, bureaucrat or fellow traveler.

There is another menace and that is the possibility that Russia has been able to create not merely atomic and hydrogen explosions, but workable bombs which could be transported and used in the frightful wars of the future.

Against such a possibility, there is, as General Ridgway pointed out, no real defense. The victory, if there were a victory, would go to the nation, either the U.S. or Russia, which could first destroy the greatest number of key cities and industrial installations. We have by no means as yet explored all the terrible potentialities of atomic warfare, but, as has been pointed out so many times, it is possible that these potentialities may be so frightful that no nation would undertake their widespread use or even undertake war itself. Nevertheless, the warmongers in every country continue to utilize the horrors of atomic warfare to terrify the citizenry in general, to promote vast and perhaps useless land armies and navies and to carry on dangerous and aggressive tactics in the conduct of international affairs. It is this group in the U.S., including certain elements of the armed forces, which is responsible for the desperately dangerous course of maintaining troops and establishing military installations (many of them secret) in forty-nine different countries in the world, of destroying our friendship with almost as many nations and endangering our relations with foreign countries everywhere.

12

It is our business neither to save Soviet power from its follies nor to confuse the issue by attempting to assert ourselves into its difficulties. If our own beliefs are sound, it will continue to suffer, as it is suffering today, by the effects of its own unsoundness—its incompatibility with the deepest human needs—and it will eventually earn the retribution it so justly deserves. It is important that this process be permitted to reveal itself with such vividness and clarity that for generations to come, and let us hope forever, men will not again be tempted to seek their political fortunes through the degradation of fellow men, forgetting that it is they themselves who are thereby most deeply degraded.

GEORGE F. KENNAN in the *New Leader*

Our occupation forces and installations are merely so many triggers, any one of which touched at a sensitive moment could precipitate us into more and more wars on the sordid, futile and tragic basis of the war in Korea. Our warmongers and the military apparently believe that the borders of Soviet Russia and the U.S. are contiguous, that each might invade and conquer the other at any moment, and that all other nations are unimportant and can be trampled under foot the moment either Russia or the U.S. sees fit to precipitate a war. I doubt that ever in the history of the world has there been any "policy" so charged with constant and immediate danger or so calculated to make peace or even a return to normal conditions of trade impossible. To this faction (the warmongers and the military) it seems of small concern that the nations lying between us and Russia would be the most terrible sufferers in any such conflict. The growing "neutralism" of the European nations is merely a reasonable, sensible and civilized reaction, legitimate in every respect when all the factors from Russia's inherent weaknesses to our own meddling and aggressiveness are taken into consideration.

It seems clear and logical that if the reports on the effectiveness and horror of atomic warfare put forth by much of the armed forces brass and the warmongering columnists are true, then there is no need whatever for a conscripted army of a million and a half young Americans or huge and extravagant airplane carriers which could be vaporized by a single bomb. If we are to believe and follow these arguments (and in the case of atomic warfare they are sound enough) then both Army and Navy should be reduced to mere police force proportions and all effort and money should be expended upon the Air Forces.

Patently the only excuse we can have for an enormous land force is that we intend to impose indefinitely the presence of these forces upon other nations where they only serve to endanger and destroy friendship and good relations, or that they are to be used perpetually here and there all over the earth "repelling aggression" in remote and insignificant countries which are wholly outside our zone of influence and responsibility and where intervention, as in Korea, can only invite war.

One "police action" war such as the tragic blunder of Korea should have taught us that little or nothing is accomplished beyond involving ourselves more and more deeply in the web of perpetual police actions and wars in every part of the world. The Korean situation has not been settled and will not be settled until we withdraw entirely from an area in which we have no right to be and leave the peoples of that area to work out their own problems, which in the end they and they alone must do in any case.

It is quite obvious that there are only two possible justifications for the present size and vast expense of our land armies: (1) that we mean to continue forever or until we are thrown out the "occupation" of forty-nine foreign countries, compromising them and subjecting them to the risk of all the horrors of atomic warfare as a part of our "defense policy," and thus gradually losing their confidence and friendship; or (2) that we mean to continue into the distant future absurd and tragic "police actions" such as that in Korea where ninety-five per cent of the burden is carried by the U.S. In this third biggest war in our history thirty thousand unwillingly conscripted Americans were killed to little purpose and nearly 150,000 were maimed or suffered the miseries of imprisonment and torture by a cruel and barbaric enemy. If the American people continue indefinitely to support or to permit such a policy of meaningless extravagance and destruction then they will be getting, as Voltaire implied long ago, what they deserve. On the human side one is tempted to ask bluntly, What right has any politician or general to advocate the conscription of boys from Iowa, California or Ohio or where you will and send them all over the world to be killed, maimed, taken prisoner or at best to waste two of the best years of their lives in the quixotic and hypocritical assumption that: (1) it is part of a defense policy; (2) that it is worth sacrificing them to preserve the liberties of peoples who have never known liberty and frequently have no word in their languages to define such an abstraction?" I cannot resist observing that I do not believe that the whole of such a policy is worth the torture or the life of one unwilling conscript, even if it were not the most dangerous and destructive of policies to the peace and welfare of the world.

One cannot place all the blame for the confusion of the world upon the Russians. Let us suppose that Soviet Russia had armies on our Canadian border and a ring of airfields surrounding us, that they had armies in Mexico, as we have armies in Korea, airfields within striking distance over all Central America and the Caribbean, and virtually complete command of the seas, and were at the same time supplying arms and even soldiers to the nations bordering on our frontiers. Well?

No, it is indeed a muddled world and we cannot as a government deny that we have done much to muddle it still further and are continuing valiantly and persistently to do so.

III

A Brave New World

1

And we would do well to worry less about whether Europeans like us (the rich uncle is rarely the most sincerely loved member of the family circle) and to be more concerned with whether they respect us as a reliable, consistent partner in international affairs, clear in our purposes and realistic in the choice of means to realize these purposes.

EDITORIAL in the *Wall Street Journal*

MEANWHILE, the "good neighbor policy" in the Western Hemisphere has been virtually forgotten and the American people themselves have become slowly and inevitably aware through newspapers, radio and other mediums of what is being done with their money, of the muddled futility of our policies and of the fact that in the vast expenditure of money, material and lives, we have no consistent policy and are making little progress toward our asserted goal of peace and world prosperity. They are also sharply aware that anti-American feeling has been rising steadily from Burma to Britain and from Egypt to China. Indeed resentment against us in many parts of Europe could scarcely be greater if we put a sudden end to all economic aid. Indeed such action might greatly *decrease* the resentment among the great mass of people, since in many areas the billions poured into Europe have brought almost no direct benefit to them at all, but have only increased the wealth and domination of the small and rich minority long in control of banking and industry.

At the same time a new interest in the Latin-American nations and in Canada has come into being. With it has come the growing

76

conviction that our own future lies in this immensely rich Western Hemisphere rather than in a divided Europe hampered economically in countless ways or in a chaotic Asia where any immediate stability or prosperity and any likelihood of real co-operation seem remote indeed.

In other words to many an American today—and many of them men and women of great influence in the world—has come a doubt and a question. It is this: "Have we not been wasting far too great a share of our energies and our money and resources in attempting to revive the past instead of looking toward the future?"

Does not the sound basis of our future—and consequently to a large degree the future well-being of the world—lie in our own Western Hemisphere and not in Europe? Will not even Europe benefit more in the end if we concentrate on building the future upon a strong sound basis in this abundant underpopulated Western World rather than upon the shaky one of a European past which has to a large extent destroyed itself with all its once great wealth and power?

As in the past, there has arisen in response to these questions a cry of "isolationism," but this is nonsense. There is no possibility of isolation in the modern world unless a global catastrophe forces us to close our frontiers and concentrate wholly upon our own safety and defenses.

It is largely in this Western World that the pattern for the very antithesis of "isolationism" potentially exists and here that the clue to the future and *real co-operation* among nations actually lies. When the pattern is realized, we shall have laid the foundation upon which can be built a real and lasting structure of peace and abundance without the many cumbersome traditions, habits of mind and superstitions which continue to haunt the old world. *Here* is where we need to build and to establish the pattern of a sound future and real and enduring peace for the whole of the world. This Western Hemisphere is solid rock rather than shifting sand.

Conversely and cynically we might ask whether, for all the vast sums of money and material expended on Europe, in case of a world war between Russia and the United States we would be able to count upon most of the European nations as allies and whether even if we could count upon them, they would be of much help. Certainly almost the whole expense of such a war in money, material and even lives would be upon our shoulders and mean our inevitable and hopeless ruin. Western Europe today, which altogether occupies only a very small portion of the earth's surface, and a portion notably poor in resources compared even to those of Canada, is greatly overpopulated and cannot even feed itself. It is a poor foundation upon which to rely or to build a future—at least so long as Europe remains stubbornly disunited and unco-operative. As a Peruvian said to me, "Europe is like an aged woman who was once beautiful and admired and had a great success with men. She has a glorious past but not much future."

Certainly in the harsh terms of economic reality, Europe has little future in this revolutionary changing world with markets and sources of raw materials and food largely disappeared and disappearing, and most European states on the borders of bankruptcy. And lately there are signs that some European nations seek to pit the United States and Russia against each other, playing both ends against the middle and driving hard bargains with the two great powers of the world.

"Isolationism" is essentially a silly word and a meaningless one since it is not an absolute term but rather an epithet hurled in a quarrel between children on the level of "You are—I am not" kind of discussion. The fact is that in this Western Hemisphere lies a very nearly perfect laboratory in which to erect the pattern of economic co-operation which is the very antithesis of the idea which lies behind the vague word "isolationism" and the only basis upon which world peace and economic stability can ever be built.

The materials are all there—a huge land mass which, even in

the case of the United States, is still underpopulated, real wealth and natural resources which are virtually beyond computation, the greater part still wholly undeveloped and even unexplored, and a vast land mass which can if necessary, like Russia, be defended not only because of its huge size but because of the oceans which surround it.

Agriculturally this hemisphere could under reasonably efficient management supply the entire food deficit of the world wherever it falls below the level of sound nutrition. Also there exists on this Western Hemisphere the greatest reservoir (the U.S.) of scientific and technological knowledge in the world and on it exists by far the greatest reservoir of free capital held, not by small cliques and cartels as under European capitalism, but by the people themselves.

The new interest in Latin America, arising from the disillusionment of many an average American citizen with our past policies is immensely important to all of us in the Western Hemisphere. It means very likely a revival of the "good neighbor policy." This time it will be backed by the growing conviction of the rank and file of the American people themselves—a force far greater, more lasting and more fundamental than the forces behind the first attempt at such a policy.

The earlier program had the backing of Under Secretary Welles and a small group of informed and farsighted men in government. This new and slowly but steadily rising wave of support comes from the people themselves, and in this sense can be irresistible. It is clearly a part of the wave of repudiation which swept out of office by an overwhelming vote the Truman-Acheson influence, or at least its immediate influences, although the Pentagon and certain other elements in our government still prefer to ride looking backward rather than forward. That Mr. Acheson was aware of this reaction *before* the elections was proven by the brief visit he made to Brazil during the late summer of 1952. His visit was too hasty and too superficial and too obvious and too late to have much effect upon the elections in the United States, or any effect whatever upon the people of Latin America. This rising wave of interest will increase, provided the steady bombardment of propaganda from the military and those who would continue to concentrate the greater part or all of our support in Europe at the expense both of Latin America and Asia, can be diverted or at least modified.

Without much question, pressure from public opinion in the United States will in time force a policy of increasing co-operation with Western Hemisphere nations, regardless of whether the Eisenhower Administration chooses to support such a policy or not.

Ex-President Hoover in an address made some time ago, in the midst of the controversy over wholesale programs of aimless and indiscriminate world aid, stated that so far as this country and the world and even Western civilization were concerned, it was imperative that the United States should be maintained as a citadel of stability, economical and political, and as a fortress of free government. I would extend the limits of this statement by saying that the *whole* of the *Western* Hemisphere can and should be made into a citadel. It seems quite obvious that a citadel—a rock which would give stability to a shaken world, a nucleus about which to build a new and better world—cannot be created within generations or even centuries in Asia, or upon the shifting chaotic economic and cultural sands of half-medieval, half-Asiatic Russia. In short, if we are to have any semblance of order, peace and economic stability in the world within foreseeable time, it will have to come from a strong union of nations possessed of huge natural resources, great interior strength, self-contained and still *underpopulated*, rather than from vastly overpopulated, isolated, highly nationalist countries working as small economic units. The only area, large or small, in which all conditions necessary for economic stability exist is the Western Hemisphere.

2

The United Nations, in its present form, has not met all our expecta-
tions . . . It does not provide adequate security. The . . . Charter reflects
serious inadequacies. One inadequacy sprang from ignorance. When we
were in San Francisco in the spring of 1945, none of us knew of the
atomic bomb which was to fall on Hiroshima. The Charter is thus a
pre-Atomic Age charter. . . . A second inadequacy sprang from the fact
that the three leaders who planned the United Nations . . . inevitably . . .
looked upon the United Nations as a kind of peacetime prolongation of
the wartime triumvirate. . . . We now see the inadequacy of an organ-
ization whose effective functioning depends upon cooperation with a
nation which is dominated by an international party seeking world
domination.

JOHN FOSTER DULLES, in a speech before the
American Bar Association, August 26, 1953

Considering the record of the United Nations organization and in
particular the increasing confusion and bitternesses which surround
it and the use to which it has been put as a spy center and propaganda platform by Soviet Russia, the outlook it offers for world
government or peace is dim indeed. Even Walter Lippmann, the
most conservative and lofty of our North American commentators
and long a supporter of the United Nations, recently stated that
many of the closest friends of the organization doubted that it could
long continue to exist.

Its mistakes and failure to function effectively are based very
largely upon virtually the identical errors that brought about the
lingering death of the League of Nations. In the first place, it persistently seeks political and even military rather than economic solutions for the troubles of the world, though they arise directly from
maladjustments of supplies of food and raw materials, access to
markets and overpopulation. Secondly, like the League, the U.N.
still operates under the kind of political philosophy of which Talley-
rand and Palmerston were the prime exponents more than a century

ago—a politic of power bargaining, balances of power and political deals. It is a politic which, in a highly industrialized, shrunken and overpopulated world, has not only become obsolete but actually perilous and explosive. In the third place, the U.N. gives equal representation to all nations regardless of standards of literacy or responsibility, natural wealth, power, skill or of any standard you may choose. Under such a system, the smaller nations are inevitably forced to become parts of power blocs entirely dominated by two or three great and strong nations. This was exactly what happened to the League of Nations when it became merely an instrument of world political maneuverings for Great Britain and France, and other nations began to withdraw one by one.

Much the same process has taken place in the U.N. where the United States and Soviet Russia have become all-dominant and have broken the representation into two blocs—one supporting the U.S., the other Soviet Russia.

Soviet Russia from time to time has given reason to suspect that she might withdraw altogether from the organization. With the American people, the prestige of the U.N. has fallen to a record low from which, in the face of persistent economic pressures and world revolutionary forces, it is unlikely to recover.

To date no nation, and least of all the U.S., with its huge toll of lives, material and money, has derived any great benefit from the U.N. organization. More and more, the great nations tend to settle their differences unilaterally and independently or on the basis of power blocs while ignoring the United Nations organization completely.

The hazy and benevolent idea of a United Nations organization, implying but never *arriving* at the fact of world government or order, may be a comfort to some people and, as Senator Taft suggested, the institution may be of some benefit as a debating society, but the assertion that it functions as a means of world government and the enforcement of order is merely ridiculous. The only real

powerful enough to *impose* order and peace upon the whole world, as Rome did upon the whole of the known world for nearly eight hundred years. One thing is certain—that the future peace and well-being of mankind will be determined from now on through conceivable time by economics, food, markets, raw materials and populations.

The opportunity is ripe. Slowly but solidly a great many Americans are beginning to understand where the future lies. The realization of a plan to integrate the Western Hemisphere is of immense importance not only to the nations within it (and the smaller they are the more important will be the final results and benefits) but to the world. Here can be created a pattern which excludes the old colonial imperialism of Europe and the satellite-exploitation of Soviet Russia, a pattern of growing, economic and finally political co-operation and development, with a dynamic economy based upon the constantly wealth-creating system of American capitalism, in which ultimately the rest of the world might well participate.

3

We Americans have a strange—and to me disturbing—attitude toward the subject of power. We don't like the word. We don't like the concept. We are suspicious of people who talk about it. We like to feel that the adjustment of conflicting interests is something that can be taken care of by juridical norms and institutional devices, voluntarily accepted and not involving violence to the feelings or interests of anyone. We like to feel that this is the way our own life is arranged. We like to feel that if this principle were to be understood and observed by others as it is by us, it would put an end to many of the misunderstandings and conflicts that have marked our time.

But we ignore the fact that power underlies our own society as it underlies every other order of human affairs distinguishable from chaos. Order and civilization are not self-engendering. They do not flow from themselves or even from any universal and enlightened understanding of political institutions in the abstract.

GEORGE F. KENNAN

In the Western Hemisphere today there are three nations possessing great land masses, huge reserves of natural resources and having an actual need for more population. These are Brazil, Canada and the United States. In the United States and Canada reserves of coal, of oil and oil-bearing shales appear to be virtually inexhaustible. The size of the new reserves of oil discovered in Canada has not even been estimated but it is clear that it is immense. Discoveries of vast deposits of iron ore and other valuable minerals continue to be made almost daily. In Brazil exploration to discover these vital assets of a modern world has in reality not even begun.

Both Brazil and Canada are larger than the United States but neither has yet attained the point of industrial and economic development for which the United States stands today as a symbol throughout the world. Nor has either nation as yet developed that fundamental and powerful balance between agriculture and industry which makes any modern nation or economic coalition of nations very nearly impregnable and undefeatable in an economic sense, both within its borders and in relation to the world outside. (It should never be forgotten that victory in two great world conflicts was largely determined by the vast industrial productivity of the United States, its capacity to feed itself and its allies, and by the immense and constantly renewable financial reserves arising from the first two factors. Productivity in agriculture or industry, either actual or potential, elsewhere in the world outside the Western Hemisphere is small by comparison.)

To illustrate more clearly what is meant by the agricultural-industrial balance, I might point out that the total investment in land, buildings, machinery and livestock in the United States is greater than the whole investment in industry, although the United States is by far the greatest industrial producer in the world. More than fifty per cent of the nation's economy is supported by an agricultural base which not only feeds the nation and exports food but constantly creates wealth and provides the wages, profits and *purchasing power* that absorb the products of industry, rendering the need for export of second or third importance.

It is essentially a very nearly self-sufficient economy that gives this nation an immense advantage over those countries which must live by processing in order to eat and consequently must have immense external sources of raw materials and large and available external markets. As our population increases at the rate of two and a half millions a year, this interior market and purchasing power continues to grow and expand upon the still abundant base of natural resources and real wealth. (I am not talking here of mere money, which in reality is not wealth at all but simply a kind of measure of the actual value of food and commodities—a fact becoming abundantly clear in a world universally afflicted by inflation.)

For the United States, the point at which manpower ceases to be an asset and becomes a liability as in Asia and parts of Europe is still remote in relation to the food potential or to general purchasing power, productivity and living standards. In the case of such a nation as Brazil it is centuries away.

It is just such a powerful and self-sufficient economy that lies immediately in prospect before Brazil. This colossus of the South has vast unexploited resources and an agricultural potential countless times greater than the existing production. Within a comparatively short time, under progressive and sound conditions, Brazil could become the *greatest* exporting nation in the world—certainly in terms of food and especially meat and the raw materials desperately needed elsewhere in the world and possibly in industrial commodities—a point which I wish to discuss in detail a little later.

Today in the northern continent of the Western Hemisphere, understanding and co-operation among the three large nations, Mexico, Canada and the United States, have never been more friendly. Although there exists between the United States and Canada the longest single frontier in the world, there are no fortifications and no armies guarding it on either side. The same is true of the border between the United States and Mexico. There is an increasingly lively exchange in trade and even in manpower and capital among these nations. Indeed, the American-Canadian border is today criss-crossed by a network of pipelines transferring oil and natural gas from one country to the other. With the inevitable joint develop-ment of the great St. Lawrence River seaway, which will bring oceangoing vessels into the very heart of the United States to lake ports such as Cleveland, Detroit and Chicago, the two nations will share the largest common waterway in the world and enjoy huge supplies of electrical power derived from a single source, as they do already in a small way. The same kind of co-operation occurs between Mexico and the United States, who now share the waters of the bordering Rio Grande River for irrigation purposes and eventually perhaps will share them for power.

Here in this vast rich area of the northern continent there already exists a nucleus for hemispheric co-operation and development, despite many contradictory factors such as language, tradition and historical association. Although Canada still remains in name a part of the loose association of commonwealths within the British sphere of influence, her economy and her people and indeed their habits of mind are far closer to ours in the United States than to those of the British Isles. Psychologically and in material development they belong to the New World and its pattern of economic and capitalist development. In many respects Mexico is closer to the United States than to the mother country Spain. Certainly this is true in the economic sense.

During the past two years more than four billions of dollars of American capital have gone into Canada for the development of its resources, its industry and its agriculture. Yet the value of the Canadian dollar rose at the same time to a value higher than that of the American dollar. Moreover this huge investment of North American capital has tended largely to cure previously existing dollar shortages. Let me point out here—and this is immensely

important in the parallel case of Brazil—that for every dollar of
the four billions invested by Americans in Canada, the Canadians
will realize within a short time through the development and exploitation of her resources at least three or four dollars in terms of
developed wealth, production and export in world markets.

Let us put the whole question quite simply. If a healthy, intelligent young man arriving from Mars looked about in this world
for the area offering the greatest opportunities for a future career,
in any field, whether business, science, agriculture or industry,
where would he turn? Certainly not to Asia nor even to Europe.
Certainly not to Soviet Russia nor to Africa, with its immense
climatic and physical and racial difficulties. He would, beyond any
doubt, turn to the Western Hemisphere where almost every opportunity awaits him—as indeed it awaits the whole suffering world.

Let us suppose for a start that we should extend (as it must be
extended if there is to be either real peace or real progress in the
world) the pattern of the largely self-sufficient economy of the
United States to include wholly Canada, Mexico and Brazil. Let us
suppose we develop it gradually, as it is being developed today,
through increasing economic co-operation accompanied by the investment of capital, thus generating constantly more wealth and
capital and food and the means of utilizing *more* population at high
standards of diet and living.[1]

Then let us suppose that through co-operation, under the pattern
already developed in Canada, and to some degree in Mexico and in
Peru through the new "opening up" policy of that potentially rich
South American country, the pattern were extended to other Western Hemisphere nations which have huge resources and real wealth
but need capital, skills and experience in order to convert this static
wealth into the dynamic, constantly self-recreative wealth of useful
and commercial commodities needed not only within the borders
of the given nations but elsewhere throughout the world. Such a
development within this hemisphere would provide a constantly

expanding and constantly richer area and volume of production and prosperity and purchasing power for all the inhabitants of North and South America.

Let us go one step further and suppose that between the United States, Canada and a vast and rich country such as Brazil, there could be established an agreement under which there would be no custom barriers, no passports, a free exchange of citizens and goods among the three nations. Let Brazilians come freely to settle in the United States and Canada and North Americans and Canadians go freely to settle in Brazil. Let us suppose that the United States assumed the Brazilian debt (which in terms of our own national debt would be insignificant and in terms of our foreign aid program merely unimportant) and that a common currency among the three nations were established.

The economic development of Brazil would very quickly be vaster and more rapid than that of any great nation in the history of the world. All three nations would benefit enormously, Brazil and Canada far more even than the United States, which is already enormously developed and provides a reservoir of capital and skills and organization indispensable to the rapid development of new countries. This pattern could in turn be expanded in time to include the remaining nations of the Western Hemisphere as they chose to join it. In every case such an economic union, even the political aspects of it, could only bring the greatest benefits in terms of living standards, diet, education, well-being, political freedom and prosperity to the mass of the people in the smaller and less developed nations.

Upon such a pattern, which is in effect only an economic extension of the traditional Monroe Doctrine, can be built the strongest, richest and most benevolent power the world has ever known, capable of stabilizing world prosperity and food supplies and in the end of extending its own pattern into other parts of the world. We should then have a real, workable and gradually growing but

solid basis for world government. For such a government would recognize the realities of the modern world. It would be founded upon
economics and a real sharing and distribution of raw materials, food
markets and means of production, rather than upon a ramshackle,
determined and visionary political system such as the United Nations.
The antiquated complex Metternich pattern of shifting political
intrigue and bargains and artificial military alliances with which the
U.N. concerns itself rarely comprehends the dignity and permanent
realities of the fundamental economics that today determine the
fate of individual peoples and in the end of the whole world.

This is perhaps a prodigious conception. It is neither a premature
nor a visionary one, for the pattern already exists in part within
the Western Hemisphere. And it is not impossible that it will come
about eventually through necessity and the pressures of a confused
world in revolution. It is a pattern in which in the beginning there
is no immediate role for any nation either in Europe or in Asia. The
leadership must be undertaken in the New World because all the
cards are in her hands and all the potentialities, so enormous, are
rooted in this fabulously rich Western Hemisphere. The world
will never find salvation by continuing and greater fragmentation
into smaller and smaller nationalistic units with no economic excuse or possibility for existence, but only by increasing union about
a nucleus and increasing economic co-operation within those constantly expanding areas to the point where it becomes permament
and complete.[2]

This is not imperialism. It is not colonialism. It certainly bears
no resemblance whatever to the pattern of pilfering and exploitation
set up by the Soviet Union in the satellite nations. It is merely co-
operation for the good of all, and most of all for the less developed
and smaller nations, to whom the pattern must bring by far the
greater benefits in every possible way.

Imperialism, colonialism and all forms of overseas or foreign exploitation, including especially the half-feudal system of conquest,

hostages, purges and economic rape set up by Russia and her satellites, belong to the barbaric past, regardless of the fact that they still exist in more or less vestigial form in the twentieth century. They are dead, slain by the declining economic and military status and generally increasing impotence of the key European colonial nations, by the confusion spread by Communism and Communist propaganda throughout the world and by the rising nationalism of peoples everywhere. The antiquated Russian pattern of conquest contains within itself the seeds of its own destruction, and the more the pattern expands the more this will be true.

The *new* pattern is merely one of co-operation in a completely modern sense, the kind of co-operation that is represented already by the relationship between this country and Canada with their general sharing and investment of capital, savings and profits within the borders of a vast area, and by the operations of many American corporations already having investments in foreign nations. It is essentially a constructive and dynamic pattern rather than a retrograde and negative philosophy such as that represented by the Keynesian theories and by much or all of the Socialist programs, or the muddled tragi-comic Utopia of the United Nations organization. The old cries of "imperialism," "colonial exploitation" and that absurd phrase "the Colossus of the North" are all obsolete and have little if any validity.

That is what this book is about.

4

. . . there are few important issues of national policy that can be understood today except in relation to our international position. And even the quality of the statesmanship of our national leaders often becomes manifest primarily in their reaction to problems that are at least partly problems of international life. The conscientious citizen therefore obviously requires as broad and enlightened an understanding of this subject as he can get.

GEORGE F. KENNAN in an address before the Alumni
of Princeton University, February 18, 1953

In considering the construction of an economic and political citadel within the borders of the Western Hemisphere, it is necessary to take into account the conditions and the difficulties with which we would have to deal. Certain factors favor such a co-operative alliance and others create what appear, on the surface at least, to be powerful obstacles to such a union.

North and South America together extend almost from one pole to the other, bisected by the equator. No other great land mass in the world contains such a wide variety of climates, of soils, of mineral resources, of lakes and mountains and potential water power all in combination and well distributed. No other single area of comparable size, indeed perhaps not the rest of the world taken together, contains such immense reservoirs of natural wealth or so much actual and potential agricultural land capable of high production.

In North America, the United States occupies the very heartland of wealth, with favorable climatic conditions and huge areas containing much of the richest and most productive soil on earth. Brazil, an even larger nation, geographically speaking, occupies a similar area south of the equator extending across nearly the whole of South America. Just as the United States provided a natural nucleus for the development of the northern continent, so Brazil occupies a similar natural, geographic and strategic position in the vast land mass of South America. It is essentially the heartland of South America, geographically, as well as in terms of population and immense natural and potential wealth, both industrial and agricultural.

The future of Brazil as the *great* nation of South America is inevitable. The most interesting factor is the rate of speed at which this development will occur. Without such a nucleus as Brazil, the co-operation of other South American nations in an economic and eventually a political union within the Western Hemisphere would be dubious indeed. Brazil is certainly on her way toward such a dominating position in terms of growing population, increasing development of agriculture and exploration and exploitation of natural wealth and the building of a huge industrial potential.

Most important of all is the rapid development of a middle class— that is to say a class fitting the Marxian definition of the *bourgeoisie*: a group of citizens possessing security, savings, a sizeable income, purchasing power, the capacity to produce wealth, a share in profits and capital development, and existing in sufficient numbers to stabilize the whole of a nation's economy.

Probably the greatest handicap to the development and above all to the political stability of the Latin-American nations throughout history has been the lack of this middle class. The development of the Latin-American nations has been along Latin rather than composite Anglo-Saxon lines. One way is as good as the other, culturally. But owing to their political and economic traditions and their historical background, the nations of South America have lagged behind the United States and Canada in their economic and social development.

The blight of the Spanish and the Portuguese empires still hangs over the Latin-American nations, and even beclouds their judgment of the vast difference between exploitation on the one hand and development and co-operation on the other. It is a bitter tradition, imposed centuries ago by nations that looked upon the colonies of the New World not as a part or potential adjunct or even asset of the nations themselves but merely as territories to be exploited ruthlessly to the advantage of the governing and wealthy class at home, from king or emperor downward. From the time of Pizarro, the policy was never one of development but of exploitation. Even today the mere mention of foreign capital investment raises immediately in the mind of most Latin-Americans the old specters of the Spanish and Portuguese empires and their bitter exploitation.

As one by one the Latin-American nations obtained their independence and the great empires of Spain and Portugal declined to the status of third-rate powers, the pattern of exploitation was not annihilated; it was merely taken over in almost every case by a small feudal minority which owned most of the land and resources and meant to hang on to them just as desperately as did the exploiters of the old empires or the cartelist class of European capitalism today. The general policy continued to be one largely of exploitation rather than development, and the feudal absentee landlord pattern of lordly ownership of vast estates became the universal rule.

Those of us who have lived much in Europe know those Latin-American families, once possessed of vast wealth and many of them still rich, who lived most of the year in Paris, in Biarritz, Deauville and the Côte d'Azur. They were essentially the families who in wealth and influence inherited the rule of the Spanish and Portuguese viceroys. And for every one of these, there were four or five other families that lived nearly all the year in the great houses of Rio de Janeiro, Buenos Aires, Lima and other capitals. They owned immense farms, *estancias*, *fazendas*, *fincas*, cattle and mines which, often enough, they left to the management of what were in reality little more than tax farmers. These men managed the operations, drew down the huge profits and turned them over to the property-holders. This small minority owned everything, but expended as little as possible upon fertility, maintenance, wages, housing and welfare.

In their economic pattern they were not unlike many of the great landholders in the British Isles, especially those who had huge holdings in coal, who operated throughout the nineteenth century—and a few of them up until nationalization of the coal industry—in a similar fashion. In Latin America there was always on these vast holdings a "great house," occupied by the owners for at most a few weeks a year. Otherwise there were frequently only hovels lived in by the workers who were under the direction and dictation not of a well-educated, intelligent agricultural operator or engineer but of men who sought the biggest profits at the lowest costs. In many

Latin-American nations, there has really never been any middle class and in some, such as Bolivia, there is no middle class today.

There exists also another notable and important difference between the composite Anglo-Saxon-American culture and social organization and that of Latin America. It is founded perhaps upon the inherent individualism of the people of most Latin nations, but many other influences have contributed toward it. In the Latin-American nations there has rarely existed that feeling of common citizenship, co-operation and civic duty that is represented in the U.S. by such organizations as the Red Cross, the Parent Teachers' Associations, the Y.M. and Y.W.C.A.'s, the service clubs, the settlement houses and by scores of other bodies. Such organizations as the Chambers of Commerce, St. Lawrence Waterways Association or the American Forestry Association or the Audubon Society or the Izaak Walton League or The Friends of the Land are virtually unknown.

In the Latin-American nations, and indeed in nearly all Latin nations, the aspect of American civilization known as "common good" and "common effort" and "co-operation" is nearly non-existent. In addition to the individualism of nearly all Latin people, at least three other factors have functioned for centuries to shape their present culture. One was the domination of government, both in the colonial-imperial period and today, by small groups, originally an aristocracy through inheritance and later on a clique of wealthy families or political adventurers or military men. A second influence is the sharp division in many Latin-American nations between a wealthy aristocracy and a mass of Indian, Negro or mixed blood citizens existing at very low standards of material comfort, income and education. The idea that the citizens of a community might meet together, regardless of social status, wealth or education, to solve their common problems, all the way from installing a sewage system to setting up recreation facilities, is almost completely unknown.

The third factor is both traditional and cultural. Not only in Latin-American nations but even in European nations of Latin background or influence, the functions represented by charity, education, welfare, civic co-operation and many other things have been regarded since the Middle Ages as the province of the Roman Catholic Church and in most cases are left to the church with little or no participation by the citizenry.

In all the studies and books which have been written concerning sociological, economic and political development in the U.S., reference is rarely made to the civic-co-operation aspect of American life or to its vast influence in consolidating the social life of the nation and bringing about a general sense of unity and common effort. While such an impulse exists in the British Isles, the practice has never approached in scope or intensity the degree which it has attained in the U.S.

In short the average American citizenry has voluntarily and spontaneously taken upon itself many of the functions which elsewhere are regarded as those of a Socialist government or of the Roman Catholic Church. It is almost impossible to overestimate this factor of American life, either in terms of economics and sociology or of civilization, which it represents to a very high degree. The mockery directed against this common effort by the late Sinclair Lewis and by H. L. Mencken was, as we have come to understand these things, shallow and superficial and without understanding of its profounder significance and effect upon American life and civilization. All of it is encompassed in the faith of that very great man, Thomas Jefferson, in the soundness of the reason and heart of the great mass of plain people and particularly of the middle class. Indeed, this civic impulse and its manifestations, born of the middle class and carried out by it, has been one of the stoutest bulwarks against the absurdities and evils of Marxian Socialism in all of its manifestations. The average American trusts far more the decisions of a local "town hall" committee than he does any decree by government politicians, even to the President of the U.S., and rightly so. In the past twenty years, under New Deal, Fair Deal, and the propaganda of Socialist doctrines of every kind, the nation came perilously close to losing this great sense of responsible citizenship expressed through the spontaneous and conscientious action of the citizenry itself. It would have been perhaps the greatest loss that our nation could have experienced.

Such an impulse and influence, put into direct action, could work miracles in the development, economic, political and sociological, of all Latin-American nations. Fortunately here and there it has begun to manifest itself, notably perhaps in Brazil. One of the most important factors in the development of stability in government as well as in economy throughout Latin America would be the growth of a sense of common citizenship and its values as an antidote to the general and overdeveloped individualism. In its most extreme manifestation, this characteristic resolves itself into the isolation of individual families concerned selfishly only with their own safety, prosperity and common actions, to the exclusion of any thought of co-operation in the fields of civic development, political reform and the development of natural resources.[3]

In the United States, the pattern of development, save in a few Southern states, was wholly different from that of the Latin-American nations. When the thirteen colonies, weary of exploitation by the Georges and the great landowning and banking families of the British Isles, secured their independence, there existed within the nation—save in limited portions of the South—no great land-holding or banking class to take over and continue the old line of exploitation. Generally speaking, everyone started from scratch in a new country that was immensely rich and undeveloped.

When Hamilton and his followers and some of the Bostonian merchants attempted to set up special privileges for the propertied class in the British tradition, their efforts were defeated by Jefferson, Franklin, Monroe, Madison and in general the followers of French Revolutionary ideas. Save in the South, where slavery provided cheap labor and a certain pattern was already set, there never existed in the United States the general tradition of the great absentee land-owners any more than there existed among the whole people the European tradition of special privilege in the way of cartels, monop-oly, closed family capital and land. Whenever, in the history of the nation, there appeared tendencies in these directions, they were sup-pressed or annihilated sooner or later by popular feeling and legisla-tion.

The best evidence of the economic and social evils that may arise when such a feudal system extends into modern times, lies in our own Southern states where the exploitation of agricultural land under slavery and a privileged and frequently an "overseer" absentee system led to such a rapid loss of fertility that at last even slave labor became unprofitable and uneconomic.

The Southern states were well on their way to economic dis-integration under such a system long before the War Between the States and would eventually have touched economic bottom if the war had never occurred. The war possibly speeded the decline by a generation but the old South, with its feudal land system and unbalanced agricultural economy, was already doomed by its own greed and ignorance and futility. It is likewise significant that the rapid rise of the South from poverty to wealth within the last generation or two came about through the rapid breakdown of the last remnants of the absentee landholding system and through the dispersal of industry throughout the area. The establishment of new industries and better-managed and frequently smaller farms and plantations operated on the spot by the owner himself has con-tinued with a steadily increasing effect to bring about that balance between industry and agriculture which is the very foundation of the stability, income, purchasing power and living standards not only of nations but of given areas within nations.[4]

During all the period up to and for a generation or more after the War Between the States, the South never had a real middle class except for professional people and a few shopkeepers representing *in toto* only a very tiny minority of the population. There was never any bourgeoisie, which the Communists hate so passionately because it is the biggest barrier to their progress.

The new and rising industrial economy of the North and the rapid growth of a middle class with actual investment in capital, land and industrial operations, made the break between the South and the rest of the nation inevitable. It was the first really decisive struggle in the world between the last remnants of old feudal family, closed, cartel systems of capitalism based upon land, and that modern pattern of capitalism, industry and development, shared wealth and investment, which is almost wholly American and different from that of almost every other nation in the world. The old traces of feudal and landholding cartel capitalism have not even today wholly disappeared from Britain despite the violent swing from closed and privileged capitalism to Socialism and government ownership, a change that in time may be modified by the fundamental British talent for compromise and adjustment and even readjustment.

With the loss of the American colonies (perhaps the most tragic event in the history of Britain and of the world) the policies of the British privileged classes and of the government toward colonies, especially those settled by her own people, underwent a change. Development and co-operation replaced exploitation. Under this new policy the economic development of Canada followed lines very different from those of the British Isles or the older colonies and closely similar to the pattern of development in the United States. As a result, in Canada today capital wealth is not confined to a privileged few, but is largely shared, as in the U.S., through property ownership, savings and invested capital.

In the Latin-American nations no such developments as these ever occurred until very recently, and then in only a few countries. Of these, Brazil has the best record for developing a genuine middle class. In terms of land development and ownership, however, she has still a long way to go, for the prosperous small farmer and the actual *resident* owner remain the exception in comparison to those who hold the vast acreages of agricultural and cattle land.

A number of young Americans come to me from time to time with plans of going to Brazil. They have heard that this is a country of vast opportunity (which it is). But like so many other Americans, they lazily or ignorantly think of the country as being exactly like the United States, with middle-sized and large cities scattered everywhere, with remarkable facilities for transportation of all kinds, with a great dominant and prosperous middle class, with miles upon miles of prosperous small farms having farm machinery in quantity, one or two automobiles, refrigerators, deep freezes, television sets, radios—all built near hard-surfaced roads capable of transporting anything anywhere at any time of the year.

Of course such conditions are still rare in Brazil (and in many areas nonexistent) or in any other Latin-American nation. What is vastly important, the huge dispersed purchasing power represented by the machinery, the automobiles, the radios, the electric current or any of the other industrial commodities and manifestations to be found on the average American farm even in some of the backward areas, is practically nonexistent or is only now beginning to be developed. All the things listed above and the dynamic, self-generating economy and wealth which they represent are essentially the manifestations of a vast middle class which, economically speaking, includes most industrial workers and farmers.

Generally speaking, in Brazil the pattern of *resident* land ownership of reasonably sized farms, operated scientifically to produce wealth and fertility, has, wherever it exists, been largely the creation not of old native Brazilians, many of them still living dreamily in the blighted economy of the old empires, but of her immigrant population, the Italians, the Germans, the Dutch, the Japanese and others. The tendency of these immigrants has been to settle in colonies where as a rule they continue to speak their own languages, to maintain their own cultures and traditions and to live among themselves in a semico-operative fashion. It is really only thus that they can establish themselves in the face of the old "estate" tradition which offers them few opportunities for work save on the feudal basis of field laborers on the vast *fazendas*, with little or no opportunity to rise in the world.

Becoming alarmed during World War II over the insistent national cohesion and the loyalty to their mother countries and traditions of some of these small colonies (which in a few cases have not even learned to speak Portuguese, the language of Brazil) the Brazilian government attempted to prevent their future formation and rise by a policy of dispersing immigrants. Immediately the newcomers discovered that they were, singly, up against the wall of the old absentee landlord tradition, became disillusioned and, despite the vast apparent opportunities of the new country, chose to return to Europe in considerable numbers. Indeed, one group of Italians literally fought their way aboard an Italian ship at Rio, fearful that the Brazilian police meant to prevent them from returning home.

I suspect that many a young American going to Brazil in the rosy hopes of making a prosperous future on the last great world frontier would suffer a similar disillusionment and quick and violent reaction to the lingering traditions of the Portuguese empire.

Moreover, the task of opening new frontiers (which the Brazilian government attempts to make attractive by tax concession and otherwise) is made difficult and rigorous by lack of communications and above all of proper roads and transportation.

The old Portuguese tradition of great holdings of agricultural land as a source of wealth, operated under the "steward tax-farming" absentee system, is going much the way of the similar social economy of our Southern states, save in the case of a few modern, scientifically run operations. On many of the typical estates, modern or scientific agricultural practices have largely been ignored in the past and the production of the land in terms of food and fibre or of real wealth has gone steadily downhill, making some of these properties no longer profitable. Side by side with the old social pattern there have existed the evil agricultural practices with which we in the United States were also familiar and of which we ourselves were guilty during a similar pioneer stage of our development.

Principal among these evils, and one shared throughout history by all nations opening up new country with vast possibilities, is the tendency to treat agricultural land not as a constantly renewable asset and source of wealth capable steadily of providing food, profits, prosperity and new incomes and purchasing power, but as a kind of mine to be exploited and abandoned when its riches are exhausted.[5]

In most cases, there has been little attempt in Brazil to increase and even to maintain the fertility of a piece of land. The tendency has been to exploit quickly the initial residue of virgin fertility and then move on to the new, rich and virgin lands which exist in such vast quantity. We in the United States have no right to criticize, since our own pattern of agricultural development was virtually the same until we came to the Pacific Ocean and there was no more free virgin land. Then we began to acquire the attitude to agricultural land prevalent in Europe, where there is so little of it in relation to the total population that it becomes immensely valuable and in many cases is not for sale at any price.

Brazil is still a very long way from being in any such condition but her rapid and sometimes careless development of agricultural land has created another serious problem—that of transportation.

Throughout Brazil, the agricultural and in some cases the industrial development, has far outstripped such factors as transportation, schools, communication, sewage disposal, electric power and many others, and great and productive areas of the country are without adequate, quick, efficient and reasonably priced means of transporting their products and general abundance. In the case of cattle transport (on which many costly pounds of meat are lost per head through the shrinkage of animals on a long, hard, slow trip to market) or in the transport of perishable foodstuffs, the cost to the Brazilian economy is very great in terms of higher prices to the consumer and in added expenses and loss to the producer. Many a Brazilian asks, "What is the use of opening up all this new country when there is no means, or only very faulty and expensive means, of bringing the products of the new country cheaply and in abundance to the great city markets and the seaports for export?" The losses in meat from bad means of transportation undoubtedly run into millions of pounds of good meat each year, and the losses in profits to the cattle breeder and feeder and the nation are tremendous.

The railroads are largely government-owned and most of them, like all government-owned railroads everywhere in the world, are inefficient and badly run; they lose money constantly for the tax-payers every year. In some areas of Brazil there has been a tendency to by-pass railroads altogether and to jump directly from the jungle frontier trail to trucks. For people and even for some commodities, there has been a tendency to transportation by air. Obviously the transportation of cattle or heavy bulk food of any kind by air is still impractical at this stage of development, and the roads used by the trucks are hopelessly inadequate. Frequently, they are merely trails suffocating with dust in the dry season and waist deep in mud after a day or two of rain.

Lack of transportation facilities has not only handicapped Brazilian agricultural and meat production and export, it has also hampered mining and industrial development. Many of Brazil's richest natural resources lie in areas wholly without transportation facilities or means of communication.

This widespread lack of transportation has done more than to handicap the development of the country upon a *sound* agricultural base and to discourage small resident ownership; it is partly responsible also for the development of an even greater evil. That is the tendency and even the desire of countless Brazilians and even immigrants and the descendants of immigrants to crowd into great cities such as Rio, São Paulo and Pernambuco. The immense and rapid increase in the city populations in Brazil has not occurred entirely through the growth of industry and of city opportunities. Much of it has come about through the desire of Brazilians and in particular of the native-born population to live under better conditions, where there is amusement, diversion and easier living than is to be found in the remote areas handicapped by poor transportation and communication.

The native Brazilian frequently has a strong taste for the sidewalks, the cafés and for just wandering happily about the streets at night until two in the morning. He is not by nature an instinctive farmer as is so much of the more recent immigrant population, and he is not too happy in the village. It is largely for this reason that Brazil is a nation of great and large cities with vast areas in between where there are only tiny villages or no settlements of any kind.

The size and rapid growth of these great Brazilian metropolitan centers has created and is daily creating more and more grave problems of water and electricity supplies, housing, sewage disposal and many other things. A really modern transportation system could do more to remove many of Brazil's most serious handicaps and to solve her problems than perhaps any other factor. It could promote the rapid development of the vast natural wealth of the nation and in doing so check both the old habits of exploitation and the paralyzing disruptive forces arising from the disreputable marriage of Communism and extreme nationalism.

The average Brazilian and indeed the average Latin American thinks of the United States largely in terms of New York City and Chicago and perhaps of Miami, Florida. He seldom, if ever, realizes that the few vast cities of a nation are not its greatest assets but frequently serious liabilities, creating many economic and social problems, including transportation and traffic, and constantly hovering on the verge of bankruptcy despite steadily increasing taxes. The average Brazilian is immensely proud of Rio and its large population and especially of São Paulo which has grown from a small town to a great city of two and a half million population in less than two generations. It rarely occurs to him that these great and rapidly growing cities are creating constantly increasing problems of housing, of sewage disposal, of electricity, of taxation and finance, of social and political unrest, and that Brazil and her economy would be far better off if her population were dispersed among smaller cities of substantial size scattered more or less evenly through the vast area already opened up or in the process of being developed.

It is difficult to make many Brazilians understand that the foundation of our United States economy, and especially of our high living standards and the general distribution of wealth among a truly huge middle class, is a sound and widespread agriculture, a dispersed rather than a concentrated industry, and perhaps above all the existence in every part of the nation of smaller cities and large towns such as St. Louis, Omaha, Des Moines, Minneapolis, Tulsa, et al. (Here I have named only a few out of the hundreds where millions of people lead contented, secure, solid and prosperous lives, many of them without ever once seeing New York or Chicago.)

The dispersal of industry and agriculture, the existence of the countless smaller cities and large towns, have been made possible in the United States almost entirely by the creation of modern and efficient means of communication and transportation. Transportation facilities also make possible the constant movement of the American population, which in turn has its bearing upon the truly immense and constant investment in automobiles, gasoline, rubber tires, restaurants, tourist camps, roadside stands, motels and a thousand other things, and, of course, upon the whole vast system of service in the form of garages, filling stations, truck transportation, etc. All of these serve to create a turnover of money, employment and purchasing power within a dynamic economy and actually and constantly create new wealth. This is a pattern that is barely developed or nonexistent in most of the nations of the world outside the U.S.

Brazil, like nearly all Latin-American nations, needs four principal elements to make her development of wealth, a stable economy and government and a prosperous middle class possible. These are capital, immigration, transportation and a middle class itself.

In many countries throughout the world, the lack of capital and in some cases the lack of skills, knowledge and experience are so great as to create almost insuperable difficulties or at least to slow down progress to a snail's pace.

All of these can be supplied by the United States in abundance and if supplied upon a basis of economic *co-operation*, and better still under actual *economic union*, they could bring about a rapid rise in the literacy, the economic and even the cultural status of the *whole people* of Latin America at a rate hitherto unknown in history.

This pattern of co-operation in a modern world, based almost wholly upon the workings of economics and redounding to the advantage of the undeveloped nations—a pattern that we have already begun to develop and that must in the end replace the old structure of imperialism, colonialism and the barbaric Russian-style exploitation of satellite nations—furnishes us with a point of the utmost value in combatting the growth of communist ideas in Latin America. Yet it is a point that is rarely employed and never explicitly stated.

Peru, through a recently established policy of co-operation with American capital and enterprise, made upon a sound, sharing, and clearly understood basis, has within a surprisingly short space of time already begun to feel tremendous results. A new prosperity has raised living standards and caused a perceptible increase in a middle class, based upon trade and services, the latter one of the important elements in the balanced prosperity of the middle class of the United States. Moreover, it has brought about in Peru the only hard, established currency value in Latin America, with the exception of Venezuela, another nation with a program of co-operation, and of Panama where currency has a wholly artificial basis in the Canal Zone economy.

Conversely nonco-operative nations such as Bolivia, in its present status, face only disaster. Guatemala under a Communist-influenced government is at the moment in the process of rapid economic decay.

Brazil has suffered from time to time from all the political troubles of most Latin-American nations. Most of these—the inequality in the distribution of wealth, the backwardness of much of the lower economic strata of society, the military dictatorships, an over-whelming burden of bureaucracy, and the intrigues and struggles for power as well as many other conditions and situations—have largely arisen from the blight and traditions of the old Spanish and Portuguese empires. But even beyond this factor they have been brought about through failure to develop natural wealth and to distribute it more or less evenly through profit and savings, invest-ment and opportunity. Although some of these Latin-American nations, like Brazil and Peru, are actually older than the United States in terms of settlement by a hundred years or more, they are with regard to the opening up and development of their natural resources and real wealth about where the United States was a century or two ago.

One other factor has handicapped the rapid development of Brazil as it has consistently handicapped the development of nearly all Latin-American nations and at times the development and stability of such Latin nations as France and Italy. That is the unwillingness of the governments, the people's representatives and even the people themselves to impose or accept adequate taxation for the develop-ment of resources, transportation, school and other elements having greatly to do with prosperity, high wages, purchasing power and a generally dynamic economy. There has always been a Latin tradi-tion against paying taxes which arose perhaps out of the abuses of past royal practices of the Bourbons and of the old empires. It is a tradition which since the time of Runnymede has never really been dominant in Anglo-Saxon countries. Citizens of the U.S. are among the highest taxpayers in the world and on the whole their attitude toward paying taxes is that taxes are a good thing *when* the revenues are wisely used in a practical fashion. The recent and rising resentment among American taxpayers at the high rates, particularly in the field of income taxes, has grown from the conviction that much of the revenue raised has been wasted by overlavish and misdirected foreign aid, by extravagance, bureaucratic inefficiency and occasionally corruption in the operations of the armed forces and, under the Truman Administration, by corruption and the wholesale expansion of bureaucracy.

Despite this recent resentment against the extravagances of half-formed and unrealized and unrealizable policies, the average intelligent citizen in the U.S. is quite aware that on the whole fairly heavy and *sound* taxation is a good thing. It provides him with good roads over a vast area. It supplies him with good schools for his children, with police protection, with agencies which secure his investments and protect him from the swindler and the avaricious banker or loan shark. It provides him with great national parks and the finest recreation areas in the world. He recognizes the fact that the taxes come back to him many times over in the actual creation of increasing wealth, health, research, experiment, transportation and in a hundred other ways, unknown in large parts of the world and rarely developed to the same degree in most other nations.

This is an attitude toward taxation which seldom exists in Latin or Latin-American nations and never in the Orient. In both places taxes are looked upon largely as exploitation and as a burden from which small benefits are derived, a burden which, in the past and in living tradition, was placed upon the shoulders of the major part of the citizenry for the private benefit of a king, a privileged class or a clique of corrupt politicians temporarily in power. Even today in France and Italy the privileged classes, the cartelized and family industrial groups, do not bear their fair share of taxes for the development and the maintenance of public services of all kinds. The tax laws are inadequate and the common tradition in the privileged classes is to evade as much as possible the paying of all taxes. It is the slowly dawning realization of this fact that has created the growing resentment of American citizens over the tremendously high income taxes he is paying. He has come to understand, as congressional committees eventually pointed out, that actually he is paying, in terms of foreign and military aid, the taxes which the citizens of other nations refuse to pay.

The tax rates of most Latin-American nations and in particular of so rich and potentially rich a country as Brazil are hopelessly inadequate to meet the great needs for schools, for roads, for hospitals and in general for the opening up and development of the nation. For every extra dollar paid in taxes, if spent wisely and honestly, the average Brazilian would in time profit by at least ten dollars.[6]

The fact is that Brazil needs honesty in government and adequate revenues from taxes for the development of the nation as much as she needs transportation, immigration, education and capital and skills and experience. Largely speaking these same needs are even more evident in most other Latin-American nations.

One of the obvious factors in American economy and the American pattern of capitalism is that wealth, when properly managed, generates wealth and more wealth—better transportation and communication, better education, greater ingenuity and genius, better living standards. The endless demand for industrial commodities in the United States came into existence because there was sufficient purchasing power to create not only the demand for such things but the ability to pay for them. In this very process more employment and more purchasing power were generated for whole new segments of the population. Essentially these factors mark the differences between the dynamic industrial and agricultural development under the capitalist system in the United States and the static and limited conditions of European cartel capitalism or the paralyzing effect of the rigid Marxian-Socialist system. Such a dynamic development under capitalism has never yet existed in Latin America although there are signs of it in Brazil and in Peru. The basis for it is there in the incredibly vast and virtually untouched wealth of the Latin-American nations, but this dynamic economy cannot be achieved either under the ground rules of Socialism nor under those of European capitalism with its closed and restrictive rules of monopoly and cartelism.

Many of Brazil's difficulties, those that are directly financial and also those concerning the development and opening up of the country, the efficiency of her government and even her business operations, have their roots in the impulse during the past fifteen years or less toward Socialist measures and the Welfare State. The inefficiency and inadequacy of her railroads and general transportation, the grave faults in her postal and telegraph system, the numerous and tiresome complications which even a casual tourist must go through in order to visit Brazil, and much of the government corruption, are all rooted in an immense, inefficient and mediocre bureaucracy that works only a few hours a day and serves largely to paralyze development of the enormous Brazilian economic potential. If the vast burden of this bureaucracy and the resulting red tape could be curtailed and the saving spent upon more and better schools, better transportation, a sound immigration policy and other lesser factors, the results within a short space of time would be astonishing not only to Brazil but to the world and most of all to the lower levels of Brazil's own human society which the socialist bureaucracy, *in theory*, was set up to benefit.

The intense nationalists, and their fair-weather friends the Communists, insist that the potential oil of the Brazilian nation remain in the possession of the government and in control of a burdensome, clumsy bureaucracy devoid of all initiative. The principal result of this situation is that today Brazil imports very nearly all of her fuel derived from a base of petroleum at a huge cost, which handicaps the development of the nation enormously both in the industrial and agricultural fields.

Brazil undoubtedly has vast reserves of oil. She has whole known mountains of seventy per cent pure iron ore, more potential cheap water power than any nation in the world, perhaps more manganese than all the rest of the world put together. But the development of all these riches and many more for the good of the whole nation has steadily been blocked, directly or indirectly, by nationalist policies and by the vast and clumsy bureaucracy existing within Brazil's partially socialized government.

If the United States or indeed Great Britain or any of the great oil-producing and processing nations had left the discovery and development of oil resources to government bureaucracies, probably ninety per cent of the world's oil reserves would still be undiscovered and undeveloped, a condition which would have cast a blight upon all industry and transportation, and in a thousand other ways affected the economic welfare of people everywhere in the world.

Initiative is the very last of the characteristics of the professional bureaucrat. In most cases, and particularly at the lower levels, the bureaucrat has chosen to be a bureaucrat because he is without ambition, curiosity, creative energy or even vitality and is looking first of all for the security of a government job, from which it is difficult to expel him no matter what his stupidities, his incompetence, his dishonesty or his laziness. After the security of his routine job, he will have a pension, which again will give him security paid for by other citizens. He lives a drone's life, mechanical, uninspired and colorless, on a treadmill with guards in the form of civil service which prevent him from falling off it. In the end he dies without having contributed much to the world in any sense and without even having found much enjoyment in living. He is immensely expensive and depressing to the economy of any nation, and can, like Brazil's own pirana fish, if allowed to increase indefinitely, succeed in changing quickly enough a living nation into a meat-bare economic skeleton.

It is small wonder that to the French, one of the most bureaucracy-ridden peoples of the world, the word *"fonctionnaire"* or bureaucrat has become an expression of abuse and a dirty word.

5

In the Atlantic Charter freedom of worship and freedom of speech were equated with freedom from want and freedom from fear. These freedoms are in entirely different categories. Freedom of worship and freedom of speech are natural rights springing from the nature of man. Freedom from want and freedom from fear pertain to the accidental conditions of our economic order and psychological milieu.

Our frontier fathers never looked for freedom from want and freedom from fear. They endured want and they overcame fear for the more basic freedoms to use their God-given talents to subdue hostile forces and establish peaceful living conditions.

THE VERY REVEREND EDWARD B. BUNN, S.J., President of Georgetown University, Washington, D.C., in an address at Loyola College, February 17, 1953

Under its guise of a Socialist Welfare State, Brazil has enacted a considerable number of laws which serve only to handicap the economic and social welfare not only of the nation but of the individual. One is a law which makes it impossible to discharge any worker who has had the same employer for ten years, except by way of red tape and processes so tiresome and long-drawn-out that many an employer will pay blackmail money in order to induce the resignation of a worker who has become lazy, insolent, inefficient or dishonest. Another absurd law is that which permits any government worker to retire after twenty-five years on full pension. A worker might begin by sweeping a bureaucrat's office at the age of fifteen and be able to retire at forty, to be kept the rest of his life, if he chooses (and what bureaucrat does not), by the taxpayers and the nonbureaucratic elements of Brazilian society who are actually working for economic and consequently *social* progress and the development of the *whole* nation.

Not only is such a law a vast burden in terms of taxes and money but it can and in many cases does mean that at least twenty years upward of work by countless bureaucrats is lost in a country which actually needs for its development more and more population and more work from its people. Indeed, in its final workings, it may be that such a Socialist law will so embarrass and handicap a government that in time there will be insufficient funds to pay the pensions of the prematurely retired workers, a situation that will automatically put an end to a law which even a beginning student in mathematics could foresee would be unworkable. The two laws which I have cited, as well as some others, are all a part of the Socialist folly which universally only lowers the welfare of nations and peoples rather than improves it.

No nation in the world so needs a policy of co-operation in capital, skills, knowledge and good will as Brazil. This is not only because she is perhaps the potentially richest nation in the world today, but because she has a vast reservoir of intelligence, skill, ability, initiative and vitality which is being obscured and handicapped in developing the nation by government bureaucracy, government ownership, and the whole stultifying rigmarole of Socialist laws, and by the connivance of the blind nationalists with the unscrupulous and demagogic radicals and Communists.

Because of these conditions, much of Brazil's population, especially on the lower economic levels, is not permitted to participate in the vast potential wealth which, if developed, could and would raise it to the status of solid middle class, far beyond the need of relief and elaborate Socialistic security measures. Nor are they permitted to work toward the realization of that generative process whereby wealth creates more wealth, which is the mark of a free economy and the pattern of capitalism within the United States. Again, as in all Socialist or even partly Socialist regimes, mediocrity is enthroned, initiative stifled, vitality dimmed—and all at the final expense of the people themselves. Pensions and handouts have never been able to supplant the great advantages, either to governments or to individuals, of a free, dynamic and growing and wealth-creating economy.

Many of Brazil's financial and economic difficulties during the past few years have arisen also from activities and manipulations of that class of citizen who finds speculation more stimulating than the real and sound development of wealth. The vast undeveloped wealth of Brazil and the rapid growth of her cities has led to the kind of speculation which the Socialists and Communists very properly condemn as one of the worst evils of "capitalism." Indeed, this speculation, and its accompaniment, the "quick buck" fortune, has given rise to a whole library of Brazilian jokes on the subject, particularly in the areas surrounding Rio de Janeiro and São Paulo where one can witness its worst manifestations.

There is a saying that the Paulista who does not make forty per cent on an investment does not think it worth while to put out the money. This general intoxication with speculation has a certain self-generating quality. The Brazilian tells himself and all his friends that Brazil is the richest nation in the world and that everything there—land, mines, houses, office buildings and even general commodities—are really worth much more than people realize. But on the whole he has little inclination to develop and translate this potential into real wealth, exports, living standards and prosperity for the whole of the people.

This intoxication with the "future" of Brazil produces the psychology which has marked every speculative boom in history, from the time of the Mississippi Bubble to the Florida land boom. Number One sells a piece of land to Number Two at a profit, Number Two sells it to Number Three at a profit, Three sells it to Number Four at a profit and it is resold to the original owner at a profit, and the process begins all over again. All this works very well, creating fictitious profits in terms of money but none at all in terms of fundamental real wealth or any of the benefits which accompany a dynamic and really productive economy. And presently there arrives a time when the buyer begins to become nervous and stops buying at constantly increasing prices. Then there is no market and prices begin to fall rapidly, panic follows and there is a general scramble to get out from under. This has been going on for some time now in Brazil, particularly in the São Paulo area which is the economic heart of the nation.

The Paulista is justly proud of the rapid development of his great and beautiful city; but he is inclined to overlook the fact that much of its size and much of its prosperity is built upon the quicksand of this intoxicating speculation and has no real and solid economic foundation, and therefore can collapse under stress into sudden disaster. This speculation on the *future* of Brazil with little effort to doing much about the *present* in some ways is symbolized by many a São Paulo skyscraper office building, hotel or apartment. They have countless rooms and offices, but the elevators are so small or insufficient in number that people stand in queues to go up or down.

As the speculative prices keep rising the currency buys less and less and all the evils of inflation become evident, fundamentally because the commodities exchanged in the boom process have no such real value as the high prices would indicate. Agricultural land and real estate generally have been priced far beyond any possible real value in terms of return on the investment. Meanwhile the development of industry and agriculture, the building of transportation facilities, the translation of the country's great inert and now useless mineral wealth into industrial products for export to establish foreign exchange, make little progress.

Many Brazilians are today aware of the spuriousness and danger of this sort of speculation in a new and potentially rich nation which by developing and expanding its vast natural resources could easily and quickly attain the wealth and productive power of the great economic nucleus now existing in North America. Indeed, at the time of writing many sound and sober Brazilians suspect that the crash and the evil time of reckoning is at hand.

This speculation is familiar to every new and developing nation with great natural resources and potential real wealth. It can only be checked and a sound basis of genuine prosperity established by road-building, a better agriculture, the increasing development of industry and the establishment of a real wealth-creating economy that will make the country really as rich as the Brazilian speculator tries to persuade himself it is. A fancy for speculation and quick profits through manipulation of money has always been one of the less solid and less attractive characteristics of the Brazilian. It is more dangerous than ever today, not only because of the inevitable risks to the individual which accompany all boom speculative maneuvers, but in the political sense, for it is creating an increasing cost of living for the great mass of the people while the value of the currency constantly declines. In this respect the speculators are as great aids to the Communist cause as are the intense nationalists with their hidebound and shortsighted restrictions upon the real development and welfare of the nation.

It is the intense nationalist throughout Latin America who is continually mouthing the shopworn Communist phrases concerning "the American invasion," "the Colossus of the North," "exploitation by foreign capital," etc., etc., etc. These nationalist politicians, and those who follow them, might well study history and especially the history of the United States for the answer to their accusations. The opening up of the country, its development, the original transportation facilities and much of American industrial development, were *not* financed by American capital, for there was not much of it and what there was could provide only a small fraction of the amount that was needed. Much, and in the beginning, most of the opening up and development of the vast rich area of the United States was financed by capital from Britain, France, Germany, Switzerland and elsewhere.

The important fact is that for every dollar in interest or profit that passed out of the United States into the hands of the capitalists of other nations there was at least one thousand dollars profit for the people of the United States, simply through the rapid development of the country and the rapid generation of wealth made possible through the use of foreign capital. Somewhat the same process is going on today in Canada; and the co-operation of Brazil with the vast sources of American capital available could bring about there the same rapid development on terms even better than those on which the foundations of the United States were built.

The future wealth and power to be derived from the co-operation of three such great nations as Canada, Brazil and the United States with all Latin America is almost beyond human comprehension. Let me point out that an economic union of Canada, Brazil and the United States alone could and would provide an economic bloc of a size and invulnerability that exists or could exist nowhere else in the world, and one which would inevitably attract into its orbit the rest of Latin America, for the good of all concerned.

It is important to consider at some length the case of Brazil because it represents on a grand scale many of the problems which confront smaller and less fortunate nations now in the process of achieving political independence and struggling at the same time toward economic freedom from exploitation under the old colonial and European capitalist patterns. None of them, even so vast a country as India, has potential wealth and power comparable to those of Brazil, but in many of them are represented the same forces that are at work in Brazil today—the blight of the absentee landowner, the semi-socialized bureaucracy, the small wealthy or military classes which seek to maintain absolute domination, the fanatical class of extreme nationalists playing into the hands of the Communists, who are unceasing in their efforts to penetrate government and create dissension, the destructive tendency toward speculation and inflation and, on the whole, the lack of any general, sound and comprehensive plan for the economic development of the nation's resources, living standards and general potentialities.

Some of the nations are certain in time to exert an influence upon world affairs, if only by reason of their natural wealth and resources and capacity to produce food. Nearly all of these nations are today in a state of economic confusion and stress and many of them are suffering from disturbed political conditions which arise from the economic disorders. Indeed, in some of them there is a vicious circle in operation. In other words, economic stresses, poverty, inflation and low living standards produce political unrest, unstable government and capricious and temporary laws, which in turn block co-operation with the capital skills and knowledge coming from the outside. And this in turn prevents the sound economic development which would produce a middle class, stable government and cure the political unrest. Fundamentally and in virtually every case the progress of these rising nations is checked or blocked altogether by trade restrictions, by lack of free exchange in commodities and currencies and even ideas and in general by the restrictions which have grown up frequently in time of war and have been kept over long past the period of any reason for their existence. This applies of course to such annoyances as passports and visas, which within the memory of many citizens now alive simply did not exist save in the cases of medieval nations such as Czarist Russia. Aside from the fact that it was a much happier world than the one harassed by the petty bureaucratic restrictions which infect free passage from one nation to another today, it was a much more civilized world and one that was infinitely more prosperous than the one in which we live at the moment.

Ostensibly passports and visas were set up as a safeguard in wartime to prevent the free circulation of foreign agents and spies, but even under war conditions they are wholly ineffective if any clever spy chooses to circumvent them. How much more so are they in more peaceable times. The U.S. is one of the worst practitioners of all this archaic bureaucratic nonsense. The system never entraps any *important* enemy agent but catches only small fry and sometimes wholly innocent individuals, of no importance, occasionally with heartbreaking and tragic results. Any spy wishing to enter the U.S. can find a hundred means of doing so with no trouble at all. Indeed during the past ten or fifteen years it has been unnecessary for spies to operate here at all, since so much secret information has been made freely available to other countries through our own government officials and employees and even scientists employed by us and our allies.

The persistence of these idiotic restrictions in the case of the U.S. has arisen from the ignorance and bigotry of Congressmen and the pettiness of the average bureaucratic mind. Those who have encountered the operations of the existing laws under the administration of many of our consular offices abroad are left with the impression that they are really living in darkest Czarist Russia or playing a part in the cheapest sort of Hollywood spy melodrama. I shall not go into the red tape, delay and inefficiency.

One hears in Brazil continually the plaint of dollar shortages, yet Brazil is one of the most exacting nations with regard to passports and visas, and each year loses hundreds of millions of dollars in American tourist money by making entry and exit from the country so difficult and so tiresome. Yet Brazil is potentially one of the great tourist countries of the world, with wonderful scenery and beaches, any climate you desire, and provides summer while the U.S. is in the full rigor of winter. Again, through bureaucratic paralysis, Brazil has failed to release the veritable flood of dollars to be had merely by opening up the country and making some provision for the comfort and entertainment of visitors. It is the easiest money that any country can earn, since little but service is given in exchange.

The endless and tiresome restrictions on tourism, trade, the free exchange of commodities and raw materials, and in general the bars to improvement of conditions everywhere have arisen in part at least from those elements in every country and, most of all in our own, which perpetually conduct war, "crisis and menace" propaganda tinctured frequently by the technique of The Big Lie. They manage to keep the world in an uproar when what the entire world seeks most is a chance merely to settle down, work, prosper and spend money . . . which in the end is the only route to world peace.

Let us jump far—very far—into a hypothetical future and suppose that Brazil and the United States came to an economic agreement under which American capital could be freely invested in Brazil, and Brazilian capital, if it chose, in the U.S., under which Brazilians might come to live in the U.S. and Americans could take their capital to Brazil, invest it and live there—an agreement under which the two nations shared a common economy with eventually a common currency and possibly in the end political federation. Under such a basis of co-operation the development of Brazil into one of the richest nations in the world and one of the great would be the inevitable result.

The benefits to the great mass of the Brazilian people would be almost inconceivably rapid and the only sufferers would be the Communists, the speculators, the extreme nationalists and those military and political elements which in many Latin America nations look upon government as a kind of private racket which they fight to monopolize. The mere introduction and establishment of the wealth-generating system of American capitalism, coupled with American technological skills, knowledge and science, would within a short time truly create a revolution, but a revolution of the utmost benefit to the Brazilian people as a whole. Who can doubt that the benefits to the average Brazilian citizen and certainly to the lower economic brackets would be countless times as great as any benefits which might accrue to the average American citizen.

Such a pattern is not impossible of achievement. The worst obstacles would be ancient prejudices and traditions and the opposition of the small wealthy privileged class of Brazil, although this group too could not but benefit in the end.

6

Economic control is not merely control of a sector of human life which can be separated from the rest; it is the control of the means for all our ends.

FREDERICK MAYER

While Brazil has been slowly creating wealth and building a sound middle class, the Republic of Argentina has been moving exactly in the opposite direction. She has been destroying whatever middle class she already possessed and moving directly into the ranks of a totalitarian-Socialist economy which has still to prove its benefits in any degree whatever in any country where it has ever been put into operation.

Argentina, like all Latin America, suffered from the blight of a very nearly feudal land economy, and, being economically a country based almost wholly upon agriculture and cattle with little or no industry and few natural resources in terms of raw materials, it was inevitable that the explosion when it came would in this modern world be a violent one.

Argentina was already going the way of the cotton aristocracy of the American South. The bad agricultural and grazing methods generally in practice were greatly reducing the productivity of her chief source of real wealth. As her productivity declined, her economy, based almost wholly on the export of food commodities, was affected in countless ways, notably by the rise of the cost of living and the lowering of living standards, which created a widespread unrest among the people on the lower economic levels.

With her agricultural and cattle production declining, it was impossible for her to increase her population without serious social troubles. This was especially true when the opportunities for rising into the status of middle class living by the establishment of savings and consequently dispersed capital ownership were limited by the fact that most of the population worked at low wages in one form of agricultural employment or another (including of course the whole huge meat-packing and wheat export business whose basis was wholly agricultural).

Misgovernment and political corruption deriving from the old Spanish imperialist tradition undoubtedly contributed to the forces that brought about the Peronist *coup d'état* and a military revolution of the sort which has long plagued the Latin-American nations, but the fundamental causes were economic. Progressive legislation and evolutionary development might have brought about changes for the better, but in the *coup d'état*, the state fell temporarily into the hands of a military clique unprepared either by experience or education or wisdom to bring about the necessary reforms or even to conceive of them. Then after a time, it fell into the hands of an extraordinary pair of adventurers and demagogues whose tenure of power depended not on any planned or sensible amelioration of conditions or knowledge and experience. Rather, it was maintained only by buying votes with extraordinary promises which could not be fulfilled and finally by the whole typical totalitarian progression from demagoguery to force and tyranny and a police state—the earmarks of the totalitarian regime in any country whether it exists under the name of Nazism, Fascism or Communism (all being one form or another of Socialism).

Not only were Peron and Evita adventurers in the purest sense, they were extraordinarily ill-equipped either by education or experience or natural genius or character and ability to lead the nation into reform and growth. And they were guilty of the colossal fundamental mistake, made by the leaders of certain other basically agricultural nations, of looking north to the U.S. and even toward Europe and of believing that industrialization alone would prove to be the total solution of all problems and bring about the genuine prosperity and contentment which was necessary for such a regime to continue under any circumstances save those of violence and oppression. In other words they looked at the U.S. and said to themselves, "Industry has made this incredibly rich and powerful nation so we must become an industrial nation in order to be the United States of South America." Of course they overlooked other basic factors in the astonishing growth of the U.S.: (1) the great base of natural and varied raw materials available within the borders of the nation for industrial use; (2) the immense agricultural wealth and purchasing power to support industry; (3) the kind of dynamic self-generating economy which Socialism is incapable of producing.

Peron and those about him also overlooked the dilemma which before their eyes, was bringing about the rapid decline of the larger once-powerful European colonial nations—that *without* vast free markets, cheap and abundant supplies of raw materials, plus abundant and cheap sources and supplies of food and, most of all, a balance between industry and agriculture, heavily populated nations in this modern world inevitably decline in wealth and power to a position of inferiority.

Argentina had no colonial empire and no great internal sources of the cheap raw materials vital to industrial development and to any great enduring modern nation. She did have food. She could at the moment at least feed her population at a reasonable level and cost although future possibilities, with an increasing population and a declining soil fertility and production, were not too bright. And she could and did export food which provided virtually the whole of her international exchange and her purchasing power as a nation. But essentially, without a balance between agriculture and industry, she had not the means of becoming a great nation. And by the time the outlines of the program for bringing about the industrial revolution became evident, there was virtually no private capital available in adequate amounts within the borders of the Argentine "Republic." Most liquid capital had fled abroad in vast quantity. The behavior of the Peron regime had frightened off any possible investment of foreign capital and the national government credit had fallen so low that other nations were unwilling to lend her capital or even to give her credit on the importation of commodities of all sorts.[7]

It was at this point that the Peronists embarked upon the final step of chaos—that of attempting to make agriculture and the cattle industry pay for their quixotic dream of becoming a rich industrial nation alone. The method, like that of all Socialist-Communist states, was to take over agriculture and cattle by fixing the prices paid to the producer, selling the products abroad at as high a price as possible, and keeping the difference for the government—a pattern which inevitably serves to throttle production and the spontaneous creation of both food and wealth, which in the case of Argentina were virtually identical.

The result was that Argentina found itself saddled not only by political tyranny but by economic imbecility as well. In 1952 the second greatest producer of wheat and the greatest exporter of meat in the world found itself actually *importing* wheat and setting up two "meatless" days a week in order to feed her own people inadequately and have meat to export in order to provide at least some foreign exchange.

The result was something close to economic and political anarchy which has steadily increased rather than diminished. Inflation, which has devalued the currency to a point where all the demagogic wage raises of the Peronist regime have long since failed to keep pace with the price of things, creates increasing havoc. There are great shortages of ordinary conveniences and even necessities and people stand in queues to buy food. What was once one of the richest and most luxurious and beautiful cities in the world has become a sad and shabby spectacle of decay, with the great houses closed and boarded up and the city haunted by ancient jalopies and littered with Socialist housing and recreation projects which were in need of repair before they were ever finished.

And Argentina, which once proudly considered herself the United States of South America, and the most dominant of the Latin-American nations, has become a disorganized economic ruin and a third-rate nation. By now it has become increasingly evident that she cannot ever regain her former position of importance without abandoning her Socialist principles and adopting a really extensive pattern of co-operation within the orbit and influence of much larger and economically more favored nations. No amount of intense and passionate nationalism or patriotism can compensate for economic disadvantages in this modern world. That some such idea has crystallized in the brain of Peron is attested by his abortive visit to Chile in an effort to unify the economy of the two nations and by his constant propaganda against the "imperialism" (ridiculous phrase) of "the Colossus of the North." The Chileans gave Peron a rather cold reception and little came of his proposals, perhaps because the Chileans understood too well that Argentina was already an economic ruin and that such co-operation as Peron proposed would turn out to be a liability rather than an asset.

The visit to Chile was at least some evidence that the nation *could* be saved and perhaps restored by economic co-operation with other nations on an expanding basis—nations that have the natural resources and raw materials that Argentina does *not* have and which could be exchanged for the food that under a reasonable government she produced in great quantities. This is but one more sign of the dynamic move throughout the world toward the creation of larger and larger economic areas and away from fragmentation into smaller and smaller economically handicapped independent nations.

Granted that misgovernment, Socialist ideas and ignorance have confused and made Argentina's problems at least temporarily insoluble, the whole story serves to demonstrate at least two facts: (1) that it is today impossible for nations, even as important as Argentina once was, without colonies or great diversified internal wealth, to realize the ambition of great wealth and power as wholly independent nations; and (2) that no amount of Socialism, government restrictions, regulations and benefits can alter this circumstance. The future of Argentina, in terms of prosperity and even decent living standards for the great bulk of her people, is dim or indeed invisible without close economic co-operation with larger and richer nations. In jumping from the blight of the Spanish empire into the blight of planned Socialism, the nation merely jumped from the frying pan into the fire.

Internationally, of course, Argentina, or rather Peron, has, in desperation, followed the usual course—that of making gestures of friendship and co-operation toward the head of all Communism, Soviet Russia. These gestures have, of course, been welcomed largely for two reasons: (1) to alarm the non-Communist, non-Socialist powers; (2) to create the impression that by moving in on a government and nation wrecked by a vicious combination of intense nationalism and Socialism, Russia and the Comintern are making progress in taking over the world.

The process also works in a backhanded fashion by encouraging the warmongers in the world and particularly in the U.S., who at once begin to shout again about the "Russian menace," and how we must protect ourselves against it. The fact is, however, that Communism and the Comintern, regardless of their resemblance to *all* dictatorial, bureaucratic, totalitarian governments, whether they are called Fascist or Communist, had nothing whatever to do with the disastrous revolution in the Argentine "Republic." Actually the gestures of friendship on both the Russian and the Argentine side arise out of weakness and the fact that neither nation has at the present time anywhere else to go but into each other's arms.

7

Those who would give up essential liberty to purchase a little temporary safety deserve neither liberty nor safety.

BENJAMIN FRANKLIN

In all this discussion, the emphasis among Latin-American nations has been placed upon Brazil for a variety of sound reasons. In the first place, Brazil is potentially and actually by far the richest of all the Latin-American countries. She is also the most populous, with more people than all the rest of the Latin-American nations put together. The prospects of economic and political stability on an enduring basis are brighter in Brazil than anywhere else in Latin America save in Peru. All the elements necessary to it are present, provided they are wisely developed in a fashion which places emphasis upon the immense value of a balance between agriculture and industry and that these two elements are developed equally and soundly and at a correlated rate of speed. (Brazil has already been burned by the attempt to develop her cities and industry more rapidly than her agriculture and transportation, with a resulting rapid rise in the cost of food and other commodities and the political unrest which inevitably accompanies such a condition.)

Moreover, in establishing a solid middle class sharing the whole wealth of the nation and its development, Brazil is considerably in advance of most Latin-American nations. The old blight of the Portuguese empire was never quite so virulent as the Spanish blight and it is disappearing with fair rapidity. Also Brazil has consistently maintained a close friendship with the United States, even at times when our own behavior, particularly in the realm of State Department tactlessness and general neglect, has hurt Brazilian pride. Temperamentally and psychologically the Brazilian is much closer to the United States and to the general American temperament than is any other Latin-American nation. Like this country, Brazil is made up of a blend of many peoples, cultures and even races, and in facing the problems arising from such a mixture, she has been in some respects more advanced and more liberal in the past than the United States. The Brazilian by disposition is extremely friendly and open and hospitable, characteristics which are not so evident among the peoples of the more austere Spanish-American nations.

But more important than all this is the basic fact that Brazil is a great land mass, possessed of huge natural resources and real wealth, with potentially vast internal markets for both agricultural and industrial commodities which in size and balance could render her economy almost self-sufficient. The more her population increases, the better it will be for the development of a truly dynamic and largely self-sufficient economy.

It is inevitable that under these conditions she must dominate economically and in the end politically the whole of the fabulously rich South American continent. It is inconceivable that circumstances should arise to prevent this. The rapidity with which this power, wealth and domination can be achieved is a matter which Brazilians alone control through their right of choice and co-operation with the United States and Canada in a countless number of fields, and by their own willingness to abandon the policy of "quick buck" speculation in favor of one based upon sound and progressive development. Fundamentally, and as is proper and inevitable, the development of Brazil into the completely dominant nation of Latin America and one of the world's two or three great powers lies entirely in the hands of the Brazilians themselves. Even a united and co-operating Europe has not the immense natural basis for wealth and power of Brazil.

Again the picture of development that emerges in Latin America is of a powerful economic nucleus, represented by Brazil, around which the economy of smaller, less fortunate Latin-American or at least South American nations will eventually be integrated for the good of all, and most of all for the smaller, less fortunate nations. The inevitability of such a pattern under future world conditions seems assured, especially in any world in which there is permanent peace and economic stability and prosperity. The rapidity with which the pattern may emerge is dependent, as it is in Central Europe and in Russia, upon the internal development and realization of economic advantages which *cannot* be developed under a Communist-Marxian Socialist system or even under the old privileged cartel-capitalist system of European nations.

Under present conditions, political and even military alliances and treaties are meaningless, temporary and constantly shifting. They will continue to be so until some sound and permanent economic basis for their existence is established through free exchange of goods, raw materials, food and manufactured commodities and eventually through a common currency and economy over large areas.[8]

IV

Dynamic Capitalism vs. Capitalism by Inertia

1

The American struggles against the natural obstacles which oppose him; the adversaries of the Russian are men. The former combats the wilderness; the latter civilization with all its weapons and arts. The conquests of the one are gained by the ploughshare; those of the other by the sword. The American relies upon personal interest to accomplish his ends, and gives free scope to the unguided actions and common sense of the citizens. Their starting point is different, their ends are not the same; yet each of them seems destined by Heaven to sway half the globe.

DE TOCQUEVILLE, *Democracy in America* (1833)

ONE of the greatest weaknesses of American public opinion and decision and even foreign policy is the common tendency of the man in the street to think, consciously or unconsciously, of all other countries in the physical terms of his own United States. This is a weakness and an error which certainly is not confined to the less prosperous, less educated and less prominent members of society, although it does reflect one of the many defects of our generally loose system of education. The error extends even to individuals on a high level of government in Congress and in the Administration. When many an individual talks or thinks of Russia, as he thinks of Brazil, he sees in his mind's eye, half-unconsciously, a nation of great factories, of roads and railroads which lead anywhere and everywhere, making even the most remote parts of the wilderness accessible. He envisages, unconsciously, a nation where modern hospitals and schools, refrigerators, housing developments exist in every province, every city, every town. Unconsciously, he thinks of the workers as having automobiles, radios and television, as living on mechanized farms in a country where one can drive for miles in the best and most remarkable of automobiles, over excellent roads, past farm after farm on which there are one or two cars, several tractors, television, radio, refrigerators and deep freeze machinery. Lazily and carelessly, he frequently conceives of whole networks of roads and railroads capable of transporting quickly and efficiently commodities, people, troops and ammunition. The general vague picture in his mind is preposterously wrong, but it is useful both to the military, who harp constantly upon "the Russian menace," and, under certain circumstances, to the ardent Communist. The real Russia bears little or no resemblance to such a picture.

The word "unconsciously" I use advisedly, for these people, even up to a man like Truman, who have had little experience either with geography or world economics, or experience in other countries, or the experience of *living* with other peoples or nations, and frequently not even of a moderately good general education, see the rest of the world in terms of the world which immediately surrounds them. Many of them make no effort to see or understand the rest of the world in terms of reality or fact, and many lack the imagination or the powers of abstract thought to conceive of any foreign nation in terms of anything with which they are not themselves familiar in an immediate sense.

If it were possible for *every* American citizen to understand and know the other nations of the world as well as a few Americans are able to, the American people would be infinitely more cynical and isolationist. They would say to themselves, "At least some of these other nations possess the wealth, the power to create as rich, as prosperous and as free a world as our own. All that they lack is the will to establish an ordered, productive, co-operative, prosperous life in which the wealth is well distributed without any resort to Socialist methods. If the other nations do not choose to create such a world, then there is no reason why we in the United States should go on aiding and supporting them and attempting to keep them going economically, and trying to raise them, by intervening in their affairs, even at times by force, to the level of our own freedom and living standards and material welfare, which seem to the rest of the world little short of fabulous."

This would be a wholly inaccurate, hasty and unfair judgment, yet it would be the inevitable one. Some such thought occurs at times even to people with a great deal of information and understanding. But the judgment would overlook, for example, the fact that in the States there has never been, even in our most vulgar periods of great individual wealth, the sense of privilege and class which is still deeply rooted in the British Isles. It would overlook the fact that almost the first characteristic of the French is their intense individualism, with a consequent lack of will and ability to co-operate in any political or economic sense even in time of crisis; and that Latin America still suffers from the blight of the Spanish and Portuguese empires and the patterns of politics and privilege and general corruption deriving from them, although the empires themselves have long ceased to exist. Nor would it take into consideration the fact that the U.S. has never known the deep-rooted and persistent traditions of class privilege and occasionally tyranny and corruption which derive from feudalism and the divine right of kings, and are still apparent in Europe, either directly or in the evidence of the pendular Socialist reaction against them. The handicaps of most Asiatic nations—decadence, tradition, caste, overpopulation and other factors—are indeed infinite and cannot quickly be altered and are so remote from the history, tradition and experience of the average American citizen as to be inconceivable to him.

The handicaps listed above—and one might cite examples and details almost without end—have never really existed in the United States. As a young nation and the very first of the great democracies, we fell upon one of the richest areas of the world, filled with natural resources and vast real wealth of every sort, to be had merely for the taking. Added to this was a considerable amount of genuine ingenuity flowing from almost every possible cultural, racial and intellectual source introduced by the tremendous wave of immigration of the nineteenth century. Every type of person was included, from intellectuals driven out of their own countries for intellectual or political reasons down to the common laborer who played so vital a part in the building of our industrial economy.

We in the United States did not enter the industrial era (which has now progressed into the chemical and electronic eras) burdened by the huge populations and limited natural resources of the Asiatic nations. And unlike the European nations, we were not forced by lack of internal resources to abandon a sound and self-sufficient agriculture and to create vast colonial empires as a source of raw materials and natural resources and as markets for the processed raw materials manufactured in the homeland.

We in the United States never made the mistake or *were forced* to commit the mistake of putting *all* our eggs into one industrial basket. In Europe this process created rapidly swelling populations that could not be fed adequately save by importing vast quantities of food from overseas. This situation in turn depressed wages and living standards and raised taxes as populations increased rapidly and agriculture came to be neglected or almost wholly abandoned. The evils of this system of almost total industrialization in which whole nations came to live by processing raw materials into marketable commodities for exportation and through which many nations, notably the United Kingdom, grew immensely rich and powerful in the short space of little more than a century, became crucial and desperate the moment war on a grand world scale exposed the weaknesses, dangers and evils of a national economy far out of balance on the sides of industry and population.

2

Whatever may be said for or against him, Keynes was, essentially, the prophet of economic patchwork.

Time Magazine, September 7, 1953

Two wars within a generation have virtually brought about the liquidation of the British Empire as a colonial empire and reduced the United Kingdom to a comparative insignificance from which she is unlikely to emerge unless she becomes part of a common economy with the United States and the commonwealths, dominions and even the colonies. I do not mean by a common economy such an economy as existed during the heyday of the British Empire when the wealth of colonial possessions was funneled off into the hands of a small class within the United Kingdom, which thus completely dominated the banking, industrial and carrying trade. I am talking about a mutually beneficial economy in which the principles of free trade and eventually a common currency would be accepted and put into use within a given but extensive economic orbit. Economic privilege would be extended through high wages (and consequent purchasing power) to *all* economic classes. With this would go the ability of *all* economic classes to own shares in *all* great corporation and industrial undertakings.

Such a process would of course maintain living standards and prosperity in the United Kingdom and even undoubtedly *improve* them far above present levels for the great bulk of the British people. However, the United Kingdom in itself would be forced inevitably to accept a realistic position as a nation of minor importance in a vast economic pattern which included all the English-speaking nations and possibly India. Great Britain, although her experience and leadership would have some value, could no longer be the head and heart of such an impressive economic union but only one of the small component parts.

This is a position which neither Labor nor Tory forces are as yet willing to accept or even to mention, although actually in many respects it already exists. With the colonial empire no longer in existence, the poverty in natural resources and real wealth plus the overpopulation of the British Isles and a sharp decline in *controlled* overseas market makes the position inevitable.

There has been great resistance to such an idea from British politicians of all parties for reasons which can be well understood by any informed and sympathetic observer.

The Socialist-Labor groups will not acknowledge that it is inevitable because their whole campaign for domination is based upon their assertion and perhaps their genuine conviction in some cases that the United Kingdom can and will regain its old position of wealth and domination through their efforts, thus demonstrating to the world that Socialism in practice can actually be endured by or may even benefit a great nation.

The Conservatives avert their heads from the reality because such a spectacle is deeply painful to the wounded pride of lost prestige, and because they hope that somehow, by some miracle, the inevitable will be averted. The Communists and extreme radicals use the actual strains and difficulties of the United Kingdom to make hay by urging Britain to abandon not only her whole concept of imperial grandeur but even that of co-operation with the United States and the commonwealths and dominions, to join up with the unhappy Soviet Republics—a course that would be economically and socially disastrous by every standard of political, ideological, traditional or historical judgment.

Thus there is really no leader or party in the United Kingdom able or willing to take the long, sound and realistic view and to start building, *not* upon shaky and/or discredited ideas of Colonel Blimp imperialism or of neo-Communist Russian imperialism, but upon a basis of reality and inevitability—not even though it would mean the welfare eventually not only of the home islands themselves but of the Indian, Canadian, South African, Australian and American world as well, and in the end even of the whole world.

Winston Churchill, a great man and a man of vision, cannot be expected at his age or with his traditional background and pride, to step forward and say, "We must face the facts and begin to work upon a basis of new ideas in the terms of inevitability and reality.

We can never restore the old colonial empire. It was indispensable as a source of raw materials and markets to all that Great Britain once was. Nor can we slip deeper into the slough of Socialism until we become merely an inferior ally of the 'Communist' imperialism of Russia. Nor can we count indefinitely upon vast dollar support from the United States to shore up our shaken economy. We must hitch up our trousers and go to work to save and preserve the living standards, the great traditions, the cultural importance, all the things which Britain has contributed to the world. We can only do so by accepting a position of wealth, importance and power considerably below that of our glorious past and by co-operating at the same time with the more favored members of the English-speaking world. We must abandon our old position of domination for one of co-operation."

We cannot expect such action from the great warrior and statesman who has literally *lived* the very life of the British Empire for nearly sixty years as a kind of symbol. It is too much to expect from the man who observed, "I did not become Prime Minister to assist in the liquidation of the British Empire."

On the other side, leadership and such a declaration *might* be made by a man like Aneurin Bevan. But Bevan, moved by an inordinate dose of personal ambition, has apparently chosen the role of demagogue and tightrope walker to that of leader and statesman, and so to sacrifice the good of the home islands to his own desires.

3

Competition quickly and severely punishes managements that are stupid or lazy or get out of touch with conditions. In the tough struggle between Communism and private enterprise, business needs the spur and the discipline of stiff competition to keep it dynamic and well managed.
SUMNER SLICHTER in the *Atlantic Monthly*

The whole business of the so-called "sterling bloc" with its restrictions, limitations and artificialities is not the answer to Britain's problem. That is a makeshift, temporary affair born of the economic desperation of the home islands, deprived by war and the gradual falling apart of the empire of the basic elements of their economy— raw materials, controlled markets, shipping, capital, banking and insurance. It is a kind of international "cartelism" which sacrifices the interests and welfare of the great majority to the small minority. Worse, the "sterling bloc" pattern has created and is still creating dissatisfaction and something close to open rebellion among the peoples in the colonies, dominions and commonwealths still under the control or influence of the home islands or still co-operating or arbitrarily contained within the "sterling bloc."

The situation will grow increasingly difficult and become a constantly greater threat to the attempts to hold together economically what remains of the colonial empire and even the dominions and commonwealths for the benefit of the United Kingdom. For this is being done at the expense of the prosperity of great, rich or potentially rich parts of the old Empire. The operations of the "sterling bloc" benefit nobody but the subjects of the United Kingdom, primarily those engaged in industry and banking and only secondarily and indirectly the great mass of the people. For them there is little genuinely *shared* and distributed wealth except as it is shared through heavy taxes and the operations financed by these heavy taxes, of an expensive, clumsy and awkward Socialist bureaucracy. This is at best a self-devouring economy which fails in every way to *create* more wealth as does the free-ranging dynamic American capitalist economy. On the contrary it actually operates to devour wealth and to throttle production, expansion and all the manifestations of a truly dynamic economy.

The "sterling bloc" economy solves nothing, even within the United Kingdom. It is in effect a complete denial of the free trade policy which built the industrial wealth and power of the Empire, at the sacrifice of her agriculture and food supply. More than that, it goes back to a factor, perhaps the fundamental one, which brought the Labor government into power and created the present "adjustable" revolution by compromise, so typical of British history.

This is a factor almost unknown in the United States and poorly understood by the average American, but one which converted to the Socialist-Labor doctrines not only vast numbers of workers, but equally great numbers of professional and middle-income Britishers. It is the circumstance that wealth in the British Isles has always been badly and unjustly and unwisely distributed and that the Empire was created, operated and existed to benefit financially and economically in a direct fashion a comparatively small segment of the British nation. The shares or stock in the great corporations, even the land and the natural wealth and resources, or the working capital behind Britain's once vast banking system, were never shared or even well distributed among the majority of Britishers and certainly not among the workingmen, who frequently lived in slums and considered themselves lucky if they owned a bicycle.

This great wealth was held and controlled and manipulated by a comparatively few families and a few financial combinations of men with great fortunes. Until one war and then another brought about higher and higher income and especially inheritance taxes, most of the national wealth continued to gravitate perpetually into the possession or control of these families or small groups. In many cases the families themselves were never concerned with the building or even the management or control of these immense and steadily accumulating fortunes. There existed a kind of "ring" into which few outsiders ever managed to penetrate, unless they made big fortunes outside the realms of industry, inherited land or coal properties, as did the Beaverbrooks, the Northcliffes, the Camroses and other wealthy newspaper barons, all of whom amassed wealth out of journalism and newspapers.

In extreme cases vast fortunes were founded simply upon the existence of coal beneath the big land holdings which this family or that one had happened to acquire perhaps centuries earlier and which still belonged to them intact through the system of primogeniture, entail, and the gradual and inevitable accumulation resulting from economic inertia coupled with the rise of British general economy during the Industrial Age. In countless instances individual enterprise, ingenuity and creative initiative had little to do with the case. Competition rarely entered the picture until too late when static British industry found itself unable to compete with Indian, Japanese or even in some fields German and American industry.

In many cases, if indeed not in most cases, the operations of the mines were not even conducted by the owners or members of their families but by stewards and clerks hired for the job. The owner had little contact with the workers and little or no understanding of the operations or of his economic obligations. Frequently he had little or no interest in the housing, the welfare, the living standards or even the wages paid to the coal miner. He simply sat in the Elizabethan or Georgian Great House of the estate, or in Paris or the Riviera or in the huge London house, while the money piled up and he or his agents reinvested it within the limited ring of the privileged to build still greater wealth. And so the coal industry became in the end to be the very core and hotbed of every kind of labor trouble and radicalism and the first of the industries to be nationalized. The pattern was one which has rarely if ever occurred under American capitalism, not through any special virtue of the American people but because the conditions and circumstances out of which the British pattern grew, did not exist in the U.S.[1]

The same story is largely true of the cotton industry which in the nineteenth century was one of the great sources of British wealth. Capital was originally invested by the already land-rich families and small "rings" of plutocrat capitalists. Managers were hired and, for a couple of generations, with cheap raw cotton available and overseas markets which could consume all the Manchester mills produced, families and banks grew wealthier and wealthier. But little of this wealth ever seeped down to the workers or the lower middle class. In this fashion, also, fortunes were built in the shipping and shipbuilding trades, while the Tyneside worker, the clerk, the deckhand and even the company manager benefited scarcely at all. The workers lived in what were and to some extent still are the very worst slums existing on earth.

In this process the rich grew richer and, as living costs and taxes rose, the poor grew poorer, until as mismanagement and extreme conservatism brought about the loss of the cotton and coal trades and created disastrous unemployment, the degrading dole came into existence and finally the inevitable Socialist explosion with its program of nationalization of industry.

This system, which might be described as "wealth through inertia," was virtually universal in Britain and made for great concentration of wealth on the highest level. On the lowest level, in times of stress, it made for an abominable system of doles which helped to ruin morally a whole generation of British workers and to bring into power the Labor Party. Not even the lower middle and professional classes benefited, for they had little if any capital and in most cases no opportunity whatever to invest "on the inside" in the vast industrial enterprises and banking rings. They were forced to live upon small salaries with little margin for creating capital out of savings, while the capital of the wealthy families and rings steadily increased, and unrest and unemployment and labor troubles and radicals multiplied.

Worst of all, the system did *not* produce a dynamic, growing, changing, improving industry or economy, constantly *creating* wealth by distributing it and so creating more and more new purchasing power. Instead, it produced a static economy which operated well enough so long as other nations (actually much richer potentially in real wealth and natural resources) were too undeveloped industrially to offer competition. Or so long as the general prosperity of the Western World was so great that there was no need to worry about markets, *interior* purchasing power, competition, the growing industrial production of smaller nations, currency balances to provide food or the countless other problems that arrived to plague Britain along with a world-wide economic revolution.[2]

India and Japan, armed economically with industrially cheap labor—far cheaper even than the low-paid British cotton workers —and equipped as well with machinery far more modern than that in use in Britain, ran the cotton industry of the United Kingdom virtually out of existence in the Indian market. Even the American cotton industry, paying wages three to four times as great as those of the Manchester worker, was able to compete because its looms were more modern and efficient and turned out much more cotton goods per man hour, per pound or dollar. India largely supplies her own vast interior market for cotton goods. At one time she was even forced to establish a protective tariff because the Japanese were manufacturing and selling cotton at prices lower even than those of Indian cotton. How then could an antiquated, hierarchical, static cotton industry, dependent upon world markets (since, un-like India, she had an insufficient market at home) prosper or even survive in the British Isles? Of course, it did not survive and quite possibly can never be re-established in a world deep in revolution and vastly changed from that of the nineteenth century.

The same archaic mechanical conditions existed in the coal industry, which in the nineteenth century was, together with cotton, the industrial foundation of the economy and wealth of the British Empire. Methods, machinery, and even wages went unchanged so long as the money poured in from the dirty tramp steamers that carried coal to all parts of the world. Then, between the two world wars, world conditions began to change rapidly, but the coal industry in Britain did not change with it. Markets for coal declined. The coal industry in Britain continued to exist largely in an aura of strikes and doles. It was not surprising—indeed it was inevitable —that workers of the coal industry should vote solidly for a Labor government, thus eventually bringing about the nationalization of the industry. Meanwhile the owners of the land were heavily compensated by the government, frequently at appraisal figures far too generous, considering the true economic state of Great Britain and the possibilities of her future.

Under nationalization coal production increased, wages were greatly increased, but the general economic situation was not greatly improved. In 1951 and 1952, coal was actually imported into Britain from the United States where from a vast supply generally regarded as inexhaustible, coal production per day per man was almost seven times as great as in Britain. Meanwhile much of the actual capital paid in compensation to the families which once owned the land by inheritance has been or is being taken by inheritance taxes and the revenues from that capital by income taxes.[3] Actually this wealth and the vast tax revenues to be derived from it are being or have been destroyed.

It is not just to say that the Labor Party and Socialist ideas were wholly responsible for the rapid decline of prestige and economic conditions in the United Kingdom immediately following the war and from which the United Kingdom has by no means as yet emerged. The fundamental causes of the decline were the enormous changes in world conditions, the almost total liquidation of British overseas capital, the huge burden of two wars within a generation, the decline in the shipping trade, the moving of the world banking center across the Atlantic, the incapacity of the British Isles to feed their people, the general disintegration of the British colonial empire and many other factors operating upon each other in a generally disastrous fashion.

But, to repeat, it is probable that the worst thing, short of utter anarchy, that could have happened to Britain in her weakened and distressed economic condition was the coming into power of the Socialist-Labor government and the putting into operation of many of its ideological principles. While the immediate welfare of the working classes has been without question somewhat improved (at least in terms of material living standards and wages based upon currency which is meaningless under inflationary conditions), a perpetuation of the conditions which brought about this artificial and bureaucratic improvement, or even their long-time continuation, could be disastrous in tax burdens, restrictions and in the general self-devouring aspects of all Socialist economies.

4

You can call the roll of countries and see Communism, Socialism and Fascism or some other kind of ism rolling toward totalitarian government. Amidst all these nations, the American flag and free enterprise exemplify joint relationship, collective bargaining and a high standard of living unequalled elsewhere. Our task is to keep what we've got and retain what we have achieved.

JOHN L. LEWIS

The destructive forces of the Socialist-Labor-Fabian-Socialist pattern are all indirect and not so clearly apparent as the obvious abuses which existed under the old capitalist system—a capitalism peculiar to Europe rather than to the United States. You cannot see so easily the mediocrity and incompetence of vast bureaucracies because bureaucracy conceals itself like the squid in a constant cloud of red tape, shifted responsibilities, dishonest bookkeeping and general "passing the buck," and tends to attract the people without skill, color or ambition, or initiative, individuality and character, or even frequently without adequate brains or education. You cannot see (until the results fly back and hit you in the face) that when capital and dynamic, growing taxable wealth and profits are destroyed and not permitted to function, someone has to pay the bills. In the end, under any Marxian Socialist pattern, the low-income worker ends up holding the bag—not only in increased taxes and economic sacrifice but in countless other intangible ways such as loss of freedom of residence and occupation, regulations of farms and small businesses and so on. In the satellite countries even the pitiful savings of the industrial workers have been wiped out from time to time by currency devaluations (which is simply *increased* vicious confiscatory taxation in another form, benefiting the Socialist bureaucratic government through trickery).

If, as in the process of nationalization, vast taxable capital and the revenues derived from it are destroyed or driven out, while the inefficiency of production under government bureaucracy is increased and the huge costs of an inefficient and unproductive bureaucracy continue to mount, someone must pay the bill. And the ones who pay are *all* the people and most of all the *productive* worker. For as great lump sums of capital and income subject to taxation are destroyed by nationalization or confiscatory taxes or capital levies, the burden is spread out and is borne more and more by the people of small or modest incomes.

Meanwhile, under the Socialist-Labor system, wealth, of whatever kind, is not being built up. At best it is merely maintained at a static level. And as time advances, it becomes increasingly clear *in practice* that government ownership of public utilities, resources and industry in general, or even the collectivization of agricultural lands and farms under the Russian or any other extreme system, do *not* result in better living standards, greater production, cheaper and better food and housing, fewer and lower taxes, or even higher manifestations of culture and civilization.

Analyzing and balancing all the factors involved under the Socialist system and under the dispersed, co-operative American capitalist system, one sees that they become in essence mathematical. When added together, they produce a material picture of both systems which is almost mathematically exact and provides a virtually exact means of assessing the virtues, the failures and results of both systems. This mathematical reduction is devastating in opposition to the highfalutin promises of Socialism in any of its forms or of the amorphous and sloppy Welfare State.

The Socialist ideas, which are in the main not new at all but merely a restatement on a larger scale of the systems of the primitive communal societies of early man or of still-existing primitive tribes, have always been the product of minds that were either highly impractical and unrealistic or, as in the case of Marx, were stimulated by some psychological grudge against society, mankind and even nature itself.[4]

In the Socialist principle, there is really very little if anything that is constructive in terms of individual human endeavor, thought and action. Consequently it contains very little if anything that contributes to the general advance of the arts and civilization any more than to an advance in general welfare. On the contrary, the Socialist doctrine, in theory and in reality and in practice, tends to produce governments and "leaders" of a mud-colored mediocrity and lack of distinction. In extreme cases it leads to a dictatorship of a ruthless nature as under Hitler, Mussolini and Stalin—each a highly individualized, ruthless individual of psychopathic tendencies. Marxian Socialism tends, as in Russia, to produce a doctrinaire "culture" in which genius, creative ability and original thought are all suppressed or deformed to comply with the current color of bureaucratic thought and ideology. Under Stalin, of course, this tendency arrived at the point of *reductio ad absurdum*, especially in the fields of science and music.

It is significant that more and more people, especially in the ranks of the lower-income groups, are beginning to understand that Socialism, with its vast government expenses, its denial of the rewards of competition and individual achievement, its stultifying mediocrity, its vast and expensive bureaucracies, does *not* provide the material or spiritual blessings, the rewards—either in terms of material well-being or cultural and scientific advance—that its partisans have always proclaimed and have never been able to demonstrate or materialize at any time in any nation.

It does not matter whether the general principle is labeled Communism, Socialism or by one of the names used to designate the splinter groups adhering fundamentally to both doctrines. In theory and dialectics all of these groups have succeeded to a great degree in creating confusion of thought, principle, foresight and action. They are responsible for the debasement and deformation of meaning of such words as "democracy" and "liberalism." "Socialism" itself has frequently managed, partly through confusions of thoughts, to disguise itself under such names as the "Welfare State" and in some manifestations, now mostly canceled out, the "New Deal."

5

The Germans, those craftsmen Bornstedt, Marx, and Engels—especially Marx—are plotting their usual mischief here. Vanity, malice, squabbles, theoretical intolerance and practical cowardice, endless theorizing about life, activity, and simplicity, and in practice a total absence of life, activity, simplicity. The single word bourgeois *has become an epithet which they repeat* ad nauseam, *though they themselves are ingrained* bourgeois *from head to foot. In a word, lies and stupidity, stupidity and lies. In such company you cannot breathe freely.*

MICHAEL BAKUNIN, quoted by E. H. Carr in *Michael Bakunin*, p. 146

One of the greatest confusions has been created by the assumption and even the assertion that the co-operative movements, which have been successful here and there in the world, and particularly in the field of agriculture, are at base Socialism. Nothing could be less true, for the formation of any genuine and spontaneous co-operative *not* government planned, financed and managed, represents the attempt of the individual to solve his problems by organizing a number of individuals like himself, either for buying and selling or other purposes. This is quite *outside* of government and frequently in defiance of government regulations and controls, rather than a matter of working *within* government.

The moment a co-operative becomes a "government" and therefore "captive" co-operative, it ceases to be a true co-operative in any sense of the word and becomes merely another bureaucracy. It thereby loses its primary purpose, which is to give efficient outlet to the capacity of individuals to work together in solving their own problems without appeal to government for aid or intervention. The total failure of the agricultural and housing co-operatives set up under the New Deal is pure evidence of what happens when a "co-operative" is established as a government bureaucracy. The sad record and striking failure of the Soviet "collective" farms, also mis-named "co-operatives" is another notable example of what happens to the "co-operative" which is merely a government bureaucracy.

The record of the highly successful Farm Bureau in the United States is on the other hand evidence of what happens when a co-operative is the manifestation of the free will of individual citizens to work together *outside* government. Not only has the organiza-tion become rich and solved many of the farmer's problems, it also exerts great power upon government itself as the servant rather than as the master of the people. The National Grange, first of the farmers' great genuine co-operatives, came into being as an active and concrete means of battling the shameless and predatory railroad shipping rates of a half-century ago. It is possibly the least Socialist organization in the world and its members detest every principle of Socialism, even in its mildest forms.

One might as well say that labor unions are Socialism. Even in this field the issue has been confused by those labor leaders, either Communist or Socialist in conviction, who constantly attempt to involve government in their activities and to place responsibility for decisions, actions and labor peace on the shoulders of govern-ment. It was this tactic which led to the scandalous "deal" between Philip Murray and a weak, stubborn and confused President during the steel strike of 1951. Such tactics in the end merely weaken the power of organized labor until eventually unions are completely dominated and controlled by government as in Soviet Russia. Or they find themselves in the weakened and embarrassing situation of becoming government *itself*, as the British unions did when the

Labor government came into power, and so were unable to strike against themselves or against government. Actually the more labor unions seek to force decisions and impose their own proper responsibilities or those of management upon government, the more they weaken themselves, lose their individuality and independence and approach the status of mere bureaucracy with their power and freedom to act completely nullified.[5]

One of the worst points of confusion—that of Socialism versus Communism—has been constantly created and supported and even exploited by both Socialists and Communists. On the one hand the Communists assert that they are Socialists and on the other hand the Socialists constantly assert that Socialism and Communism are not the same and do not spring from the same roots. Actually the Communists are much nearer to the truth but their assertions that they are in reality Socialists is constantly and hotly denied by what is left in the United States of the Socialist theorists. The difference in reality is one of degree. The progress from Socialism, government ownership of public utilities, resources and industry to Communism and tyrannical bureaucracy is only a short step easily and imperceptibly made.

Indeed, as the pattern of practice and experience is becoming clear to the world, it is more and more evident that Socialism, in the manifestations listed just above, must either be repudiated, which Great Britain is now attempting to do, or must progress deeper and deeper into the kind of state in which a tyrannical bureaucracy or oligarchy and finally a dictatorship (as in the case of Stalin and Tito) is the end result. It is this progression which is made clear in George Orwell's brilliant book *1984.*

In the history of Europe during the past generation or two from Kerensky onward, it has always been the Socialists, with the aid of the "intellectuals," who have betrayed one country after another into the hands of absolute Marxian Communism or the final mockery of dominating and ruthless Russian Imperialist Communism. The progression has always begun with a "Socialist" government growing steadily less liberal and more radical until it is finally kidnaped by the Communists, acting often enough in reality as agents for a sixteenth-century imperialist Russia. One cannot resist quoting the old saw that "one can no more be a little Marxist than one can be a little pregnant."

Once started on the road, the very principles and the necessities of Socialism inevitably generate more and more rapidly growing bureaucracies, government regulations and restrictions of currency, labor and even occupation, and place of residence. More and more, liberties and dignity are exchanged for "security" and "benefits," until the whole squalid picture ends in a debasement of material living standards and, worse, what amounts to the virtual degradation of the human spirit. This progression was evident in the worst aspects of the New Deal and in virtually all the aspects of the political and demagogic Welfare State.

But the one fact which emerges in our time and becomes clearer each day is the failure of the Communist-Socialist principles to produce either a better civilization or permanently better income, abundance and constantly rising living conditions. The experiments have been conducted in public in our times by Hitler and Mussolini, Stalin and Tito, Peron and the Labor Party in Great Britain. None of these individuals and governments, who based their operations and practices upon a dialectic base of Marxian theory, have produced anything they promised upon a *permanent, dynamic* and *growing* basis. They have on the other hand, produced enormous bureaucracies and taxes, war, inflation, currency devaluations used as a weapon of desperation, and economic and financial anarchy.

In every case, save perhaps that of Great Britain, they have left the people, and especially the small people, worse off in practical and material standards of living than they were before. In the ultimate and lowest and most complete stage of Marxian development, in which there emerges a tyrannical oligarchy or dictator such as Stalin, Hitler, Mussolini and Peron, the inevitable drive is toward the ultimate diversion of war as a hedge against internal failure and disaster. It may take the form of war by actual arms or war by the underground methods of the Cominform and the bitter and ludicrous pattern of spies and secret agents adapted from Czarist Russia by the Soviet Marxian tyranny.

6

The formation of the Western world took place through the struggle of the feudal lords against the kings, of the kings among themselves, the feudal lords among themselves, the young cities against the feudal lords—a plurality of social groups born from a soil in full vigor, where power produced wealth, and wealth power. Today we get the same impression of force and vitality not from Europe but from the United States, with its vigorous pluralism: churches, economic forces, great trade unions, all kinds of associations.

JULES MONNEROT in *The Freeman*

The Socialist experiment in Great Britain, temporarily checked by a political reversal of economic and social principles, has already gone far enough for the people to discover that with the active establishment of Socialist principles there come restriction of freedom, taxes which wipe out any reward for working longer and harder or more skillfully to get ahead, and absurd health and medical programs which could in time bankrupt the nation and which already constitute such an unbearable economic burden that they have had to be curtailed sharply.

It has also become evident that industry, under the incompetent management of an expensive bureaucracy, not only operates less efficiently and less profitably in terms of the general economy, production and welfare, but no longer supplies vast sources of taxes, which now must be transferred to the shoulders of the whole citizenry who in turn must support the added and steadily increasing huge expense of bureaucratic expansion.

It could be said with justification that the experiment has already failed in the United Kingdom, less violently but just as surely, as it has failed under Hitler, Tito, Stalin, Peron or any of the Marxian Socialist "Welfare State" governments.

The process of *de*-Socializing which is being attempted in Great Britain at the moment is an extremely difficult one. Very possibly this nation, pregnant with Socialist doctrine, can only be *de*-Socialized with the violence and pain which accompanies an abortion. Certainly the transition from Socialism to the American form of co-operative capitalism becomes almost impossible, since much of the mass capital which *could* take over and finance the return of the industry to private management has already been destroyed or driven into the colonies, and the possibility of investment out of savings by countless small income people, as in the United States, has been wiped out by the heavy taxes necessitated by the expense of a huge bureaucracy and an ever-increasing program of "social benefits." Such a progression can and does reach the point where these "benefits" become in terms of increasing taxes, more expensive than if they were purchased outright under a system of free enterprise. The only other alternative is bankruptcy of government or through one more step downward the Orwellian state in which the individual becomes a combination of pensioner and slave.

In this sense, the rule of the Labor-Socialist government in Britain over a period of years has been one of the greatest obstacles to the solution of British problems, which were in any case very nearly insoluble, and to her economic recovery in any notably rapid and solid way. In other words, two violently opposed and conflicting forces have operated to the gradual but steady deterioration of Britain's chances for recovery: (1) the closed, cartelist system of capitalism by inertia, the limitations and evils of which eventually brought about the Socialist-Labor revolution; (2) the Socialist-Labor government that partially destroyed the old system which, however unsound, could still have produced the concrete wealth with profits and heavy tax revenues, that are so badly needed in Britain. And all

this in time of world crisis. It might be said that the principle of
the vicious circle is in full operation today in every phase of British
economic operations, from nationalized industry to the artificialities
of the "sterling bloc" economy.[6] It is also abundantly evident that
only the vast sums provided by the dynamic American anti-Socialist
economy in the forms of direct and military aid, have prevented
total collapse and bankruptcy of the British Isles.

7

*It is not by the intermeddling of the omniscient and omnipotent State,
but by the prudence and energy of the people, that England has hitherto
been carried forward in civilization; and it is to the same prudence and
the same energy that we now look with comfort and good hope. Our
rulers will best promote the improvement of the nation by strictly con-
fining themselves to their own legitimate duties, by leaving capital to
find its most lucrative course, commodities their fair price, industry and
intelligence their natural reward, idleness and folly their natural punish-
ment, by maintaining peace, by defending property, by diminishing the
price of law, and by observing economy in every department of the
State. Let the government do this; the people will assuredly do the rest.*
THOMAS MACAULAY, Essay on Southey's *Colloquies*

At this point it might be well to clarify the difference between
dynamic American co-operative capitalism and the monopolist capitalism of inertia which in the past was, and in some countries even
today, is dominant in Europe. The Socialists, Communists and Welfare Staters constantly harp upon the evils of "capitalism" and have
defiled the true meaning of the word as thoroughly as they defiled
the true sense of the words "democracy" and "liberal."

In essence capitalism means simply money which works for you.
In the best sense it means money which is the result of savings working in a dynamic fashion to create more wealth. It does not necessarily mean that all capitalists are millionaires or that all capitalists
are necessarily the product of closed rings, monopolies and cartels
or are capitalists by virtue of great inherited wealth, increasing

through the force of inertia. In the U.S. a capitalist may well be a schoolteacher who has saved a little money out of her meager salary and invested it in General Motors stock, or an industrial worker who owns shares of stock in the company for which he works, or a great labor union which has invested its vast funds in stocks, bonds and real estate, or a college or endowed institute of research which has invested its funds in good common stocks or in a business corporation. Any farmer, by virtue of land ownership, is a capitalist.

Capitalism or at least American capitalism means merely that people have put their money and savings to work to increase and develop industry, agriculture or what you will and in doing so are promoting not only profits for themselves but employment and profits and better living standards for others and general economic prosperity for the nation. That indeed is a pretty fair picture of dispersed capitalism in the United States although it does not bear much resemblance to the pattern of cartel capitalism in Europe.

Unfortunately capitalism in Europe in the past and even in the present has seldom if ever represented all the small shareholders or the great organizations and institutions listed above. It has been represented almost wholly by "rings" or bankers and millionaires working in tight and frequently monopolistic operations, or by whole industries belonging to a single family. Its worst manifestation, as we have seen, was the coal industry in Britain, where families representing great inherited wealth or acreage simply dominated a large operation, lived off the huge incomes and showed little concern and very little direct interest in the operations or in the welfare of employees. Shares and stocks in "good things" were and still are seldom available in Europe to the small investor, whose wages or salaries were and are rarely high enough to permit many savings which *could* be invested. Or else the "good things" were kept for the closed groups. The idea of capital as "shared wealth," paying high wages which in turn create new and constantly increasing purchasing power, and participated in by great numbers of the people, has never had either much support, understanding or practice in Europe.

This was especially true in England, France, Italy and Germany and to a large extent it is still true in most European nations (including England where these comments on a closed capitalistic system operating under cartels apply to the area of private enterprise still remaining under the nationalization program).

This sort of monopolistic capital, increasing constantly within a privileged "ring," has been steadily reinforced and encouraged by the cartel system in European industry and capitalism. Under this system prices and profits were in many cases manipulated and even determined arbitrarily by monopolistic enterprises or by agreements among combinations of monopolistic enterprises within one country and even within a single industry, such as the steel and chemical industries, throughout all Europe. All of these factors were directly and largely responsible for the rise of Marxian Communism and Socialism in the beginning, and they have continued to be responsible over more than a century for the steady growth and spread of these doctrines.

In a sense *European* capitalism today is simply the furthest extension of medievalism and feudalism or the right to keep the rich rich and the poor poor. In the minds of probably most capitalists in Europe, this doctrine is not far removed from the divine right of kings and in many cases is as ardently supported, especially among the cartelists, as the doctrine of the divine right is supported among frowsy, obscure, poverty-stricken royalists. Indeed many a cartelist, monopolist European capitalist is, in his mental processes and acuteness, not far removed from the romantic royalist, and in our torn, distressed revolutionary world, is becoming very nearly as obsolete.

It is this European type of capitalism which has overlaid the term "capitalism" in general with a shadow of discredit and in the minds of many Europeans even with infamy. Because of this, it is essential once and for all to distinguish American *dispersed co-operative* capitalism as something quite different in its operations as well as in its results from the closed, cartelist "ring" capitalism of Europe.[7]

It should be remembered that the Marxian accusations against "capitalism" and "colonialism" are still largely valid when applied to European capitalism but not at all valid when applied to the dynamic dispersed American variety. By the same measure, a "pro- letariat" in the Communist sense exists in some degree in every European nation and is virtually nonexistent in the U.S. Also in the U.S. much of the more extreme "New Deal" and "Welfare State" legislation was not the product of a profound necessity but intro- duced and promoted by the egghead element, resembling the Fabian Socialists in England, or by unscrupulous and demagogic politicians. Virtually all of these extreme measures have since been nullified and abandoned because of their obvious unsoundness.

American co-operative dispersed capitalism has grown out of American life and history which, in their economic and sociological aspects and roots, are quite different from European life, history and tradition. To understand the very great difference it is necessary to go deep into American history, the reasons for the founding of the nation and for the special pattern of its economic, sociological and political development.

In the first place, the United States, as a nation and as a capitalist nation, was not founded by the remnants of privileged or feudal landholding families, but by people of small wealth and privilege or none at all, seeking an opportunity not only for economic freedom but for intellectual and spiritual liberty. From the very beginning, these people were forced to "hang together or to hang separately." There were the menaces and hardships of frontier life, of Indian attack, of involvement in the imperialist and colonial wars between England and France. Here those wars were in reality manifestations of a struggle to dominate this vast rich continent *not* by the *people* of England and France, but for the benefit of the rich "monopolistic" capitalists of Britain and France—the royal families, the bankers, and that small minority which had inherited great wealth or lands and titles that gave them enormous privilege and prestige even among the wretched, downtrodden, small people whom they oppressed. These elements and their operations comprised the "cartel" system of the eighteenth century.

The motives and factors behind these wars eventually led in France to the world-shattering effects of the French Revolution. In more conservative Britain they led to the steady creation of immense capital wealth during the nineteenth century, to the rise of the British Empire and the creation of vast "closed" fortunes and industries, and to the breaking down of the agricultural wealth formerly tied in with the inherited land fortunes. In Britain agriculture went very nearly out of existence and agricultural land was converted rapidly and in a wholesale fashion into deer parks and ideal coursing for hunting foxes. What farmland still continued to be cultivated during the industrial nineteenth century (after the repeal of the Corn Laws which sacrificed agriculture to the free trade interests of industry and the great industrial fortunes) was largely held by individual farmers on lease from the great estate owners.[8]

Added to the already existing system of primogeniture was the system of entailed estates, which by law could not be broken up by inheritors, and even entailed leases. These became the basic principles of the land economy of Great Britain, which operated constantly to concentrate and maintain wealth in the hands of a minority, which grew increasingly smaller as the population rapidly increased. At the same time the free capital of the owners, the profits from estates and the capital raised with estates as security were turned into industrial development and presently fortified the fortunes of the great landholders with steadily growing accumulations of industrial wealth and profits throughout the nineteenth century. Occasional great fortunes, amassed out of such commodities as beer and cotton and newspapers, remained to a great extent fixed and closed fortunes, fortified frequently by marriage within the already established rings. All this still further concentrated the wealth in the hands of a small number of people—indeed in the hands of a smaller and smaller minority as population doubled and tripled.

8

Anything that represents a real force has a chance to assert itself. This vitality manifests itself by powerful transformations of social energy. Faith changes into power, and power or confidence into wealth. Wealth, in turn, supports power or science. All of these forces influence the political world which influences them in turn by suppressing what encounters the strongest resistance from the voting masses. It is a cycle of continuous energy conversion.

In the United States, "capitalism" does not hide. It tells the public its version of the link between business profits and national prosperity. It does not believe that its interest and profit represent Evil and Satan. In France, the bankers and business leaders appear to the eyes of the naïve as something akin to the acolytes of a secret cult, a mixture of alchemist and high priest of Baal. The capitalists have allowed themselves to be saddled by Marxists with an inferiority complex.

JULES MONNEROT in *The Freeman*

The tradition of inherited, concentrated, entailed and accumulating wealth never existed in the United States. Even the great plantations and estates in the South were never subject to this closed and concentrated pattern. What is supremely significant in tracing the divergent courses of European and American capitalism, is that in the United States nearly everybody started from scratch. Neither the great inherited fortunes rooted in feudal land estates, nor the privilege, or prestige or class differences of Europe existed on the new continent, a factor of truly vast importance, in terms of economics, sociology and even culture.[9]

The individuals and families who immigrated and settled the United States during its early history had before them a vast continent thousands of times richer than the British Isles in potential natural wealth of all kinds, but these were riches which had to be developed; they were not already sources of great wealth and income increasing steadily through the principle of "capitalistic inertia," simply to be had through the death of the head of the family. To develop this very nearly incalculable natural wealth existing on the American continent required ingenuity, strength, some capital and frequently a great capacity to deal with actual hardships and the perils of the frontier. Above all the principle and dynamic force of competition, unhampered by tradition or cartelist, monopolistic "rings" came into existence and general practice as a basic force in the operations of American capitalism.

Under American custom and habit, which ignored primogeniture, the tendency was always, as later on in France, to spread the ownership of land wider and wider rather than to concentrate it into single vast fortunes protected by law and by skilled management from waste and dispersal through the follies and extravagances of the inheritors. Great inherited American fortunes were rarely protected by entailment or its counterpart, the trust fund, until the very end of the nineteenth century and the beginning of the twentieth. Foolish or extravagant heirs were permitted to waste and lose their fortunes if they chose. Thus arose, out of a kind of folk tradition, the expression "from shirt sleeves to shirt sleeves in three generations," a progression which was almost impossible under the British sytem. Thus American fortunes were constantly in a state of flux and dispersal, or were being invested in new projects which in turn created new wealth, a process very nearly impossible under English custom and law.

Moreover, the enormous wealth encompassed by the huge American wilderness provided opportunity for everyone. A bold, adventurous and enterprising young man might possess fortunes in minerals, or forests, or coal mines, or large areas of rich agricultural land merely by staking a claim to them. As a rule, the area was pretty much determined by what the claimant felt he could manage with the capital, the hired men and the beasts he had at his disposal.

During the whole long period of the opening of the vast frontier any young American of reasonable health, intelligence and enterprise was potentially a rich man, a landholder and a capitalist, and thousands of them in time became so.[10]

The vast amount of wealth to be developed out of the new continent produced a certain element of adventure and even carelessness with regard to capital and money. It was expended and sometimes wasted carelessly in gambling and speculative adventures and throughout the nineteenth century it was common to hear of men who "had made and lost five or six fortunes." This was, of course, to some degree a wasteful process, especially in the field of agriculture. Farming became frequently enough a process of exhausting as rapidly as possible the fertility of one piece of land and then moving westward and claiming for nothing another piece sometimes more fertile than the original wasted holding. However, this abundance and the gambling speculative instinct and tradition served again to disperse wealth and to make it highly fluid and keep it constantly invested in new ventures which developed the country and later on developed industry far beyond the point of efficiency attained by European and especially British industry.

In this pattern of a constantly expanding and dynamic economy, more and more purchasing power in terms of employment was created. Indeed there were periods when there were great shortages of labor to develop and process the enormous natural riches of the nation—a condition unheard of in Europe for centuries—and millions of Europeans were welcomed as immigrants. This is a condition which vast, rich Brazil will face once a real and dynamic program of developing her natural resources is undertaken.

Even today in the United States, long after virtually all *free* wealth is possessed, there are more jobs than people. This, in itself, is a result of the very circumstances which made American capitalism so different from that of Europe. It is the perfect evidence of the universal advantages of a dynamic, dispersed capitalism over a closed and static one.

This entire process was exactly the opposite of that taking place in Europe and the British Isles where there was no free land or real wealth and natural resources to be had for the taking, and where opportunity to make a fortune and to rise in the world was extremely rare and discernible only to the very shrewdest, ablest and most ambitious of men. Generally speaking, the processes of capitalist and industrial development in Europe and England consisted very largely in hanging on to what you had and investing with extreme caution only in "good things."[11]

Such a process blocked opportunity for the young and for a really dynamic industrial development in which methods and efficiency were constantly increased and sharpened by competition and personal ambition. In England, as elsewhere in Europe, the principle that high or even adequate wages for the worker increased purchasing power and created constantly expanding markets was never understood and is not generally understood today. Certainly it has in such countries as France few advocates and much violent opposition.[12]

9

Perhaps his [Veblen's] greatest merit, as Author Heilbroner makes clear was that he saw the one great truth Marx never saw; the "working class" had no real desire to rebel against the bourgeoise but wanted to become more like it.

TIME Magazine in a review of *The Worldly Philosophers* by Robert L. Heilbroner

Coupled with the immensely rigid and static condition of wealth in Britain and its concentration in the hands of a small minority of people, went another sociological manifestation which was really never known in the United States—a manifestation which might be described as "knowing one's station." It was part of a rigid hierarchical system which at times, within the memory of the writer, approached the rigidity of the Hindu caste system. Under it the son of a baker was supposed to remain the son of a baker, the son of a gardener, a gardener, the son of a lawyer, a lawyer. In the extreme material snobbery and vulgarity of the British nincteenth century, the farmhand, the tenant, the small employee was often enough quite literally expected to salute or pull the forelock at the approach of his employer and virtually to abase himself at the approach of a marquess or a duke. Marriage between members of different social and economic levels was regarded with distaste and frequently met with violent opposition and even public condemnation in smaller communities. Not only was the opportunity lacking for the "lower classes" to advance themselves but they were not supposed even to entertain the idea of such opportunity. There was a general condemnation of "rising above one's station." And, of course, there existed a genuine awe in the middle class snobbery which arose from the spectacle of a coronet. In most cases the title represented not the accomplishment or brilliance or distinction of the individual but an inheritance from some ancestor, frequently remote, who had made some distinguished contribution to the safety or welfare of the nation, or who, more recently, had acquired a vast industrial fortune and purchased a title. Behind this title or near it lay the concentrated static wealth of great land holdings or the invested industrial wealth originally based upon it.[13] Or perhaps the impoverished Marquess had married a millionaire brewer's daughter. A minor process which persistently operated toward concentration of wealth in the titled entailed classes.

During the nineteenth century and especially in the early twentieth century, the bestowal of great titles became increasingly frequent and the process of "buying a title" became at times, as under Lloyd George, a scandal. No longer was a title bestowed because the recipient, as under the Restoration, was a mistress or a by-blow, or because he had made a great contribution to the general welfare of the nation, but because an individual, possessing a great fortune, made a rich contribution to the political party in power.

Throughout British society of the last two centuries, the respect for large, entailed fortunes increased steadily and alliances were made constantly between members of old titled landholding families with a noble history and the daughters of rich brewers, bankers and "persons in trade." This process tended steadily toward further concentration of the great "closed" fortunes in the hands of a minority.[14] It also served to maintain British nobility and aristocracy upon a secure, bourgeois basis, while in France great names and titles grew, on the whole, poorer and poorer, as they made "suitable" marriages within their own impoverished ranks.

As this wealthy entrenched minority in Britain exerted a power in government out of all proportion to its numbers, and exerted this power in many ways not always related to mere expenditure of wealth, the government itself came at times virtually under the control of the very rich. This element frequently dominated the tactics of the party in power and so determined policies often enough directed consciously or unconsciously toward its own benefit and advantage. Moreover, it was from among the offspring and notably the second sons of this element that most of the clergy of the Church of England were drawn, as well as great numbers of experienced and trained politicians. Very frequently they were men of genius and skill but they had known from the time they were infants every possible advantage of prestige, education, fortune and political patronage. What chance against them had the sons of the baker or the gardener who dared be ambitious enough to make an attempt to rise above his station?

It is true that during the nineteenth century now and then, a single man here and there rose to political power from the lower ranks of the hierarchy. However, it was not until after the First World War, which brought the first tremor of the collapse of the British Empire, that men of humble birth began, through the swelling tide of political and economic indignation represented by the Labor Party, to rise to positions high in government and to threaten the stronghold of entrenched "closed" fortunes. By then, of course, it was too late. Chamberlain, Baldwin, and the then Sir John Simon and Sir Samuel Hoare, all representatives of conservative capitalism, had created the conditions for Hitler's inevitable rise to power which led to the Second World War and with it the final stages in the decline of the wealth and power that were represented by the British Empire.

It is especially significant that these men were in themselves representative of the "gold console," entailed, closed, guarded and protected concentrated wealth, especially industrial wealth, represented by the small minority of British citizens. Either they were themselves men of great wealth or they were closely tied in with the vast closed industrial fortunes in their roles as bankers and lawyers. These men represented the special rather musty point of view of the small minority, and through appeasement and consistently bad judgment in every international crisis they accepted defeat after defeat and decline after decline in international affairs merely in order "to keep the shop open" and maintain the British capitalist pattern of economic inertia.

Policies and points of view which had proven sound in the building of the British Empire in the nineteenth-century world of conquered colonies and conquered markets proved only disastrous in a world which was changing rapidly without notice by the British economic oligarchy—a world no longer subject to the balance of power politics, a world in which half the earth was not held by weak half-savage peoples, easily conquered, dominated and exploited, and a world in which the ferment of radicalism and even revolution had begun to bubble and stir. The great fortunes began to collapse and dribble away before the rising indignation and resentment of the people, the Socialist Utopian promises of the Labor Party, adverse legislation, steadily increasing taxes and under the vast destructive and revolutionary pressures of two world wars.

These great fortunes and this pool of concentrated wealth were no longer a tower of strength but a menace, sociologically, politically, humanly and even economically. Even the remote but vast adventure of the East India Company had played out. By the time the income tax, a crude and arbitrary way of distributing wealth, had come into existence, it was too late. Crisis after crisis had made the tax no longer a means of distributing wealth more evenly, but a confiscatory disaster which virtually destroyed the British capitalist system with its many undeniable virtues as well as its antediluvian evils.

It could be said with justification that the capitalist system of Great Britain eventually destroyed itself in the final maneuvers of Chamberlain, Baldwin, Hoare, Simon and their special class. Almost alone among all those in or out of government, whose background and tradition represented the long pattern of "closed" wealth and inherited privilege, Winston Churchill saw the dark shadow of disaster on the horizon. A man actually of limited wealth but sharing all the prestige and advantages of the small privileged minority, he was saved by his own experience, his brilliance and genius from the class and minority into which he was born. He was saved by his own experience and intuition, brilliance and genius from the pompous materialistic dullness and blindness which afflicted the whole world of his conservative party down to its very roots. And he never belonged in reality to the specious category of the "liberal" with inherited wealth and a bad conscience, which is fairly common both in Britain and in this country.

Had this already menaced and rotting oligarchy heeded his warnings and followed his leadership, the final catastrophe which virtually wiped out wealth and privilege in Britain might have been averted or at least modified. But the leaders of the archaic Tory group repudiated him and threw him out of office and out of the counsels of the party in favor of advocates of old worn-out nineteenth-century beliefs and policies. They seemed not to realize that these policies were already shabby, tattered and useless in the savagely changing world and that the men with whom they were dealing were not Metternichs and Talleyrands who appeased and traded and bargained the human rights and dignities of whole peoples, but madmen like Hitler and Mussolini and Stalin to whom appeasement was a silly and meaningless gesture at which to thumb the nose.

In essence, a long chain of events, in which the pattern of British capitalism played a large role, brought about the end of the old scattered Empire "on which the sun never sets." Although the British capitalist never saw it, and only a few see it today, it was the beginning of an era in which the shift of power is toward those nations which have great concentrated, natural resources and real wealth within their own borders, or toward groups of smaller contiguous nations which have neither wealth nor the population to stand alone but are irresistibly drawn into the orbits of the nations which possess great and rich land masses and are reasonably or actually underpopulated—those nations which can feed themselves and create and maintain high living standards, and produce great quantities both of food and industrial commodities. The great colonial empires, whether French or Belgian, Dutch or British, were beginning to fall apart, and the exploitation of remote colonies and peoples for the benefit of a small concentrated minority in the imperial homelands had begun to become virtually a thing of the past.

The reasons for this revolution are almost endless but the reasons that can be raised for any optimistic appraisal of the future of scattered empires are virtually nonexistent. The Roman Empire spent eight hundred years in the process of decay and fall. These so-called modern colonial empires have had an existence of little more than a century and a half.

As has been argued above, the operations of American and European capitalism have been different from the very beginning. These differences arose largely from contrasting economic and sociological patterns. In the United States capitalist development was never overlaid by the traditions, the customs, the ways of thinking characteristic of the system of vast inherited wealth and privilege that came out of the remote past of the Dark Ages down through the years of feudalism, the era of the great land barons, to the time of the great industrial barons of the nineteenth century.

But the base of perhaps the greatest difference in the dynamic capitalism of the U.S. as compared to that of Europe and in particular of England lay in the vital principles of competition and dispersed investment and possession of capital and the high wages and purchasing power largely derived from these two factors. Added together with certain other elements such as the great natural wealth of the nation, these served to create a capitalism that was once possessed of dynamic qualities rather than inertia.

Across the channel from Britain, France, through the blood and violence of the French Revolution, managed to shatter in her own special fashion much of the medieval pattern and tradition with which her progress was afflicted for centuries. The great landholdings of the church and the nobility and the royal family were broken up and distributed. This meant that long inherited landholdings kept permanently intact rarely provided the base of capital for the industrial revolution which followed so closely upon the heels of the Revolution and the Napoleonic conquests. In other words the development of the industrial revolution in France came later and advanced more slowly than elsewhere partly because land-based capital scarcely existed and because political agitation and revolution continued intermittently until after the overthrow of Napoleon III.

The origins of great accumulations of capital and industrial ownership in France were quite different from those in the British Isles. The old nobility, the old distinguished landowner had been largely ruined and did not begin to regain his economic prestige until much later and then very frequently only through marriage with great bourgeois industrial and Jewish banking fortunes.

The industrial development in France was chiefly a bourgeois development in which the Jewish and Huguenot bankers, rather than the ancient Catholic families of nobility, played a great role. The history of the average industrial baron in France was quite different from that of his counterpart in England. In France, more frequently than not, he worked his way upward to success and wealth from a humble situation in life; in the course of his progress he never had to contend with the generally accepted idea that a man was presumptuous and rising above his station when he attempted to make his way in the world and enjoy the advantages which went frequently with great wealth. The French Revolution had swept the way clear for him and it was a matter of small consequence if he was not accepted in the rigid, ruined, seedy society of the old Catholic nobility. He was not facing the opposition of an ancient aristocratic society which at the same time was fortified politically and economically by a great and slowly accumulated mass of entailed wealth, acquired through caution, inertia and privilege and by frequent advantageous marriages with brewers' daughters.

The French capitalist and his bourgeois fellow industrialists had all the wealth and made their weight felt in politics. The old ruined aristocracy was powerless save in clerical and sometimes in intellectual circles. In the French capitalist family, marriage was planned and was carried out virtually on two bases alone. There was the occasional marriage of a daughter into the old aristocracy for the sake of the title and a somewhat withered prestige. And there was the usual marriage within a "ring" of fellow industrialists and bankers or even to cousins in order to keep the fortune in the family. This latter process was so constant as to be regarded as conventional and has become the theme of many a novel and play since the time of Balzac who lived in the very heyday of this development.[15]

Although the pattern of the industrial revolution and of the concentration and maintenance of great wealth within the limits of a small minority was in France quite different from that in England, there was likeness in the intensity and care expended on keeping the mass of capital intact and in the possession of the small group. It was out of this condition that monopoly and cartelism grew in France—a cartelism that also worked primarily for the good of the small, compact and rich minority which constantly admitted to the "ring" new millionaires who had made their way up from the farm or the humbler quarters of Paris, Marseilles or Bordeaux. It was only in a secondary fashion that this wealth benefited the whole of the people by producing a certain amount of employment and of foreign exchange.

Cartelism in France as in other industrial European nations extended at times beyond the borders of the nation, even taking the form of unpatriotic or disloyal alliances with similar capitalists and industrialists in other nations. The outcry of the Popular Front in the thirties against the Comité des Forges, which controlled the great French steel industry, and against the *"deux cents familles,"* whom it accused of controlling French banking and industry, was a valid and real protest, although frequently enough it came from the mouths of Communist hypocrites and frauds. It still remains so. No more than British capitalism does French capitalism represent the co-operative capitalism closely participated in by great numbers of the people, as in the American system. The pattern of closed capitalism in France from the very beginning has differed from the American system in methods, opportunities and results.

Very little of the billions of American dollars sent into France under foreign aid plans has found its way to the more humble levels of French society. The money has been retained to enlarge and modernize industrial establishments not for the benefit of great numbers of small stockholders or for an increase in the wages and living standards of the workers, but to increase factory production and other profit-making investments which will perhaps contribute indirectly to the general national economy but essentially will benefit only an extremely small group of cartel monopolists, many of them not too scrupulous in the matter of tax payments.

Even in the case where American foreign aid money has been expended on French government projects, very little of the vast subsidy found its direct way to the working man in terms of increased wages; for the outcry went up from the large employers that if wages were raised on government projects it would disrupt the whole scale of wages throughout the nation and create a burden upon nongovernment industry and enterprise. The same outcry went up in the case of wages offered in the beginning to French workmen hired for the construction of American military installations within the borders of France and her colonies. Low wages, inflated prices and the vicious, almost universal indirect system of taxation in France place a tax burden upon lower income groups that is out of all proportion to the size of incomes and profits in the upper bracket group.

This situation lies at the very foundation of the strength of the Communist vote in France and has given rise to an evil and destructive economic situation in which an enormous and elaborate bureaucracy has become necessary to administer the complex system of pensions, subsidies for large families and a hundred other manifestations of the Socialist state. Obviously a high standard of wages for the workmen would make unnecessary many of these expensive governmental bureaus and subsidizing tricks which not only add to the general tax burden but actually place the burden of fair wages and decent income not upon the industrialist, landowner and in the long run banker, but upon the government itself and so upon the people.

Low wages and inflated living costs, as has been pointed out elsewhere, not only create unrest, radicalism and sympathy with the Communist party, they also throttle the general purchasing power which could do much to create prosperity and stabilize the economy of the nation. The French worker or even the *petit bourgeois* has no margin left from his income to invest as savings or to purchase the simplest commodities. The purchase of such things as automobiles, refrigerators, good radios or a hundred items which to the average American worker are necessities is simply out of the question for the French worker or even the members of what might be called "the lower middle class."

At the moment, the economy of France represents a remarkable spectacle of the combination of the evils of two systems—those of Socialist bureaucracy and of cartelism—and the repercussions are, of course, felt in the confusion of French politics. As always in our times, the political unrest and confusion are not the primary part of a disastrous picture, nor the fundamental causes of the difficulties but merely a reflection and a result of economic confusion, maladjustments and hardships.

There is little question that of all the nations of Europe, France today contains the most confused, unstable and even perhaps insoluble conditions, both economically and politically. This confusion is greatly complicated by the great number of political parties and the fact that no single political party can ever dominate and control the government but must bargain and compromise with two or three other parties in order to achieve and maintain a majority. It was just such a situation which brought about the economic cancer of the Blum Popular Front government in which every sort of compromise was made with the Communists and extreme radicals. Indeed the tangle and confusion of France, both in internal and external politics, is today so vast and complex that at times it would seem that the only solution would be a violent revolution, such as de Gaulle has hinted at, in which everything was swept away and a new start undertaken. It would not be the first time that such a situation and such a solution has been a part of French history.

The situation which existed in 1940 when the whole nation collapsed into defeat still exists and in probably a more virulent form. It does not make of France either a potentially co-operative member of the European community or a source of strength as an ally. Nor does it tend to justify our intervention in Indo-China on France's behalf, an action which, as has been pointed out elsewhere, has had every kind of damaging repercussion for ourselves among the peoples of Asia. It is only one of the many instances in which we are giving vast financial and military support on the basis almost wholly of gambling. The situation in France is also direct evidence of the fact that no amount of external aid in any form whatever from cash to conscripted American boys can aid or change the general picture within nations who in the last analysis must solve their own problems and only resent increasingly American interference and meddling.

For this situation in France, French capitalism with its cartelism and monopoly conception, which bears little or no resemblance to American capitalism, must take a large share of responsibility.

One is accustomed to puzzled queries from Americans about why the Communist Party has from time to time become so powerful in France. The explanation is a complex one, although the fundamental reason is the closeness of the combinations of bourgeois capitalism and the avaricious determination of the cartelists to restrict and corner the wealth by almost every means possible. There are indeed other factors, including the peculiar form of the French government with the confusion and instability arising from a multi-party system in which sometimes a party consisting of not more than four or five members may determine a majority and hold out on a blackmail basis for the highest bid from right or left.

In probably no other nation in the world is the vote of frustration and disgust so proportionately and consistently heavy as in France. It is probable that as much as a third or more of the Communist vote is not Communist at all but merely a vote of protest against the frequent shabbiness, trickery and bargaining of the other parties and against the tight, closed avaricious operations of French capitalism and industry.

The Frenchman, neither by tradition nor inclination, leans toward

Communism and certainly not toward any Socialist doctrine which advocates the nationalization of his property, regardless of whether it is a half-acre suburban vegetable garden or a village *épicerie* or the huge Schneider-Creusot works. But occasionally, the French worker and white-collar class do rise up in indignation at the form and restrictions of French cartelist capitalism which is fundamentally designed and operates constantly to concentrate wealth and working capital in "rings" and frequently even in small family groups.

Capital in France has never belonged essentially to the people, as it has belonged to the people in the United States. And the situation is complicated and aggravated in France by the inadequacy of the tax laws and by the traditional French attitude toward them. Since the time of the Bourbon tax farmers the practice of evading taxes has been regarded as not necessarily dishonest; rather it is a well-founded convention in which everyone participates frequently as a gesture of protest against the government and against the bureaucratic tax collector personally. It is merely banal to point out again the intense individualism of the French and his fierce pride in thinking and acting as he sees fit.

The collapse of France in the Second World War arose not only from internal incompetence, confusion and division. The causes went far beyond that. In the political confusion and through the machinations of the Communist and extreme left parties, France had arrived at that ultimate point where it was every family and every citizen for himself. It is notable also that as a part of the same grand-scale greed which obsesses and has long obsessed French capitalism, great masses of capital move frantically out of France into foreign investments at the first sign of inflation or other political or economic upsets. In their fierce concentration upon economic control and power, French capitalists and industrialists not infrequently place that intense worship of concentrated wealth and power above the good of the country itself and above that of their fellow citizens.

10

England has neither friends or enemies nor policies. She has only interests.

LORD PALMERSTON

During the long period of the industrial revolution and the rise to great power of British capitalism, the British foreign economic policy was one of acquiring colonies by conquest and exploiting them both as markets and sources of raw materials, much in the fashion of the Spanish and Portuguese empires. It was only comparatively late in the history of the Empire that a policy of *development* rather than exploitation came into being.

This gradual alteration of policy brought about a dilemma which the Empire was never able to solve and which contributed greatly toward the gradual disintegration of the Empire itself. The very process of development, in colonies and in commonwealths and dominions, tended steadily to bring about in all of them a constantly increasing economic and political ferment and strength and consequently an increasing desire for independence.

In India, for example, two factors played great roles in her gradual separation from the Empire in virtually everything but name. One was simply the spread of education, begun by the British and carried on by the Indians themselves. It produced in time the core of Indian political unrest, resistance and actual rebellion which presently began to wrest right after right from the British as the old pattern of East India Company and colonial exploitation began to change. At length in the final few decades before the separation, the vast profits which accrued earlier for every pound invested began to diminish and at last vanished altogether, and India became a liability rather than an asset to the British capitalist and consequently to the British government and people. A ferment of religious feeling plus resentment brought about the Mutiny, but it was a ferment of education plus waning or vanished profits which produced the final separation.

At the end of World War II Britain was actually in debt to India for hundreds of millions of pounds. The development of industry and commodity production of various kinds financed by *Indian* rather than British capital made huge inroads into the British markets and, together with Japanese cheap labor, modern machinery and British industrial obsolescence combined, brought about the collapse of the cotton industry in Britain.

British capital and even the British government, aware perhaps of what Indian production had done to the cotton industry, resisted in every way, directly and clandestinely, the development of the steel industry in an India where there was abundant coal, water, high-grade iron ore and limestone. Eventually there came into being the great steel works at Jamshedpur-Tatanagar, one of the greatest in the world, entirely developed and financed by Indian capital and built and operated under the direction of American and German engineers. Eventually the American not only took over the operation for the Indians but trained Indian engineers to replace themselves, and in the end the great and expanding steel operation became wholly Indian—an immensely significant symbol of the profound changes taking place in a revolutionary world in which the old pattern of colonial imperialism is doomed.

Back of the new development policy toward the colonies, dominions and commonwealths lay another almost intangible factor, present in all Anglo-Saxon nations and one of those racial, human and national factors which frequently upset the operations of politics and even the rules of economics according to strict formula. This was the sentimental, liberal and reform ingredient which worked and still works today against the force of "closed" and sometimes ruthless European capitalism. This element has always been represented in parliament, at times very strongly (see Gladstone whom the superimperialist Victoria hated or in our own times Sir Stafford

Cripps), usually in liberal, radical and Socialist groups but at times even within the ranks of the conservatives and among the occasionally eccentric women of the long privileged capitalist class. It is this strong but intangible sentiment that has worked constantly and with missionary zeal for greater education, greater freedom, more and more rights for colonial peoples. As these were won or bestowed, the bonds of the Empire and consequently of the once dominant capitalists grew weaker and weaker. (In our own country at the present time this vaguely humanitarian, missionary Anglo-Saxon zeal is manifested among an element generally known by the cynical label of "do-gooders." Very often, as in the case of the British Webbs, the results of their unbalanced, emotional and illogical behavior create as much evil as good for the nation and the world.)

South Africa is today virtually an independent nation which acknowledges allegiance to the crown only on terms of convenience; and in many respects it cannot be counted upon for full loyalty. Canada likewise is virtually an independent nation with an economy and a capitalist system resembling much more closely that of the United States than that of Great Britain, a situation which is inevitable and which becomes increasingly true with the passing of each year. The rest of what remains of the British Empire, including the so-called sterling bloc, is maintained by artificial, emergency ties. And its pattern of controlled and regulated economics works primarily for the benefit of what remains of British capital and industry and only secondarily for the welfare of the bulk of British people. Sterling bloc manipulations, increasingly resented by all elements of the Empire (which are held together principally by a shadowy, intangible loyalty to the crown), cannot possibly continue indefinitely because of their artificiality and because of this resentment. Actually in many cases the working of the sterling bloc handicaps the welfare and advance of outlying sterling bloc members, and benefits primarily only Britain's closed industrial capitalism or what remains of it.[16]

The sterling bloc economy is of course a complete negation of the free trade which built the British Empire and which the United Kingdom can no longer afford. Actually and to a large extent the United Kingdom and its remaining capitalists are today drawing or feeding upon the economy of the dominions, commonwealths and colonies which remain in the sterling bloc. No nation with twenty million more population than it is able to feed, expending almost a third of its exchequer for imported food, can survive as a great power in a world in which more and more the nations are coalescing into self-sufficient economic units able to feed themselves, export food, and produce great masses of industrial commodities cheaply, while creating constantly higher wages and living standards.

In this picture the billions of dollars poured into Britain to prime its sagging economy have not even been mentioned. For the most part they have been swallowed up with little evidence of actually improving Britain's economy or even of stabilizing it upon any really lasting basis. Perhaps the best result is that the money bailed Britain out of bankruptcy. Nevertheless, her actual future remains largely unchanged, and the process cannot be continued indefinitely merely to maintain illusions and support pride.

It should also be pointed out that one of the great deceptions practiced by the pro-European and pro-British elements in this country is the effort to persuade the American people that "foreign" aid and "military" aid are different things, and that in cutting down or eliminating "foreign" aid we are freeing ourselves *wholly* from the vast burden of financing other nations. Actually, in terms of economic reality, "foreign" aid and "military" aid are exactly the same; for if we failed to bear the expense of arming other nations and providing them with supplies and troops, they would be forced to provide these things for themselves or sink eventually to the status of second- and third-rate nations. The complete withdrawal of both "foreign" and "military" aid might well be the most potent factor in bringing about the economic co-operation, and eventually political federation and union of a United Europe. By financing various European nations on a vast scale we have merely postponed this necessity and given them the illusion of false prosperity and recovery. Thus we have strengthened the position of nationalist and chauvinist politicians and prevented the awakening of the peoples of those nations to the grim realities of their situation, both in the present and the future.

So long as we continue to provide unlimited "foreign" *and* "military" aid and conscripted American troops, the solution of Europe's economic and political problems and the realization of a true European Union, will be delayed. If this pattern of American aid were carried too far and then suddenly withdrawn (which might occur with the changing temper of the average American citizen), the whole of Europe might be suddenly revealed in naked reality as a spectacle of Balkan-like confusion and an area of increasing menace in terms of disorder and war.

11

There is only one fair measurement of price for the individual in an economy. How long does it take him to earn his wife's clothes . . . a pair of shoes . . . a loaf of bread?

PAUL MAZUR

All the foregoing should serve to point up the differences between American and European capitalism, in development and actual practice. The differences do not end there. But again it should be emphasized that American capital represents first of all a dispersed and co-operative investment, including in the owners of shares and stocks alone many millions of the population. There still remain in the United States a few smaller industries and other enterprises operating on a closed capital basis with the ownership controlled by a family or a small ring. But under the American law, these holdings cannot constantly increase on a basis of inertia and concentration, since the burden of taxes becomes too great. Consequently much of this capital is channeled back in great blocks into the wealth of the nation through foundations, endowments of colleges and research and in countless other ways. No field of American industry operates openly upon a publicly accepted and approved cartel plan which regulates production and prices and limits free competition.

Most important of all, the driving economic impulse in the United States has been steadily and increasingly in the direction of competition rather than monopoly and cartelism. Small businesses are encouraged and frequently grow into large businesses. The antitrust laws operate constantly to break down combinations and monopolies which seek to control this industry or business or that one.

Not only the laws, but the deep-rooted sentiment of the people themselves operate constantly in this direction, so that competition, almost excluded under and by European capitalism and cartelism, is the very foundation of the American brand of capitalism. Profits of American industry as a whole are dispersed in the form of dividends to some millions of people, many of them stock and shareholding workers employed in the very factories which produce those profits. American industry does not belong to a few families, cartels and rings. In its essence it belongs to a nation of investors and through constant and open competition it is never subjected to the stultifying operations of monopoly and cartelism, regulated prices and *forced* buying. For some time there has been growing in the U.S. a kind of legend, promoted largely in New Deal circles, that the force of competition in the American economy is lessening and that mere bigness and monopoly are taking over. Actually the vitalizing forces of real competition have never been so strong or so stimulating, as economist Sumner Slichter has proven brilliantly in an article in the November, 1953, *Atlantic*.

Added to these factors is the element of machine efficiency and mass production operating upon the principle that the more that can be produced per man hour, per unit, per dollar invested or by whatever standard you may choose, the cheaper it can be sold. Small profits on mass products rather than high profits on expensive products is one of the vital differences between the operation of capital in Europe and in the United States.[17] It is connected with another dynamic wealth-creating factor—that of high wages and living standards. Such a system, with high industrial wages made possible by high production and efficient operation, enables all but a minority of American citizens to own automobiles, refrigerators, radios, television sets and all the "luxuries" which make the American standard of living seem almost fabulous to the citizens of other nations. It could be said indeed that many commodities regarded elsewhere in the world save Canada as luxuries are regarded in the U.S. by most citizens as necessities.[18]

All these are the reasons why the United States produces more industrial commodities than the rest of the world put together, commodities which, as a rule, are better and more efficient and cheaper, and to produce which the industrial worker is paid wages from ten to ninety per cent higher than the workers of most other nations.[19]

V

The World Failure and Decline of the
Marxian Illusion

1

Capitalism's big problem is not really political but economic . . . the problem of establishing itself as the arsenal, not only of production, but also of hope and meaningful freedom to the anonymous hundreds of millions who may otherwise take arms against us.

ROBERT L. HEILBRONER, *The Worldly Philosophers; The Lives, Times and Ideas of the Great Economic Thinkers*

ONE of the fundamental errors of our time, as pointed out in an excellent editorial in the *Freeman* magazine, is the assumption that democracy and Communism are opposites, that this opposition is political and that the basis of the real conflict tearing apart the world in which we live is a political or ideological one. The fact is that Marxian Communism is an economic rather than a political system and theory and that its opposite is not *democracy* but capitalism. Its absolute opposite is American capitalism, but not *European* capitalism with its cartelism, monopoly controls and class restrictions, all of which are also indeed an integral part of Marxian Communism both in theory and in practice. For the ultimate cartelism, with all its limitations, finds its concentrated essence in the Socialist state which owns and controls everything for the benefit *not* of a capitalist-industrialist minority, as under cartelism, but for the ruling oligarchy and upper bureaucracy as in Soviet Russia. Under a Socialist state the rewards are not dividends and increased capital gains, as under European capitalism, but privileges of every sort in the form of automobiles, apartments, country villas, expense accounts and countless other advantages limited to an even smaller minority than under the closed cartelist system of European capitalism.

There are many facets to this fundamental error, all of which give rise to countless blunders in opposing Communism in Russia, in the world and on the home ground of various nations. Recognition of this error and a new and different approach to the whole conception of Communism lies at the very root of any real success in combating its growth. In other words, it is impossible to base opposition to a hard inflexible and ruthless economic system such as Marxian Communism upon vague idealist talk of democracy, political systems or military alliances. The failure of much of the battle against Communism up to now arises from just those tactics, as does indeed the failure of the U.N. in attempting to settle world problems, political alliances (as against Red China) and "police actions" while ignoring all economic factors.

It must be borne in mind that the word "democracy" is extremely ephemeral and difficult to define, probably because in its essence it represents a vast amorphous generalization. You and I and the average citizen think we know what democracy is and we are likely to accept that meaning as definite and final although countless millions share interpretations of the word which are altogether different. In its root source and in practice, democracy means simply a system of government in which the people have or, as in the case of Russia and the satellite countries, are supposed to have a determining voice. In its most restricted sense it means direct participation in government by all the people, or in reality government by acclamation, and does *not* necessarily include government by representatives of the people chosen in free elections as we know democracy in the form of a republic. In fact democracy can mean almost anything and consequently its already vague meaning has been further distorted without scruple by Socialist propagandists all the way from the Webbs to Stalin and Malenkov.

In the case of countries such as Russia or the satellite nations it is true that citizens or comrades periodically go through the motions of visiting the polls and marking a ballot on which there is only one list of candidates (the candidates of an oligarchic dictatorial regime). Even though they might write in the name of some other candidate in presumable opposition, it is inconceivable that there would be enough identical "write-ins" to create even the faintest possibility of an opposition or the faintest evidence of any *real* manifestation of the people's wishes. Under such circumstances it is quite obvious that the people have no voice in their government. In this particular case, democracy is merely used as a "cover" word providing shadow but not substance and leaving the direction of the voiceless people wholly in the hands of a small organized minority, the so-called Communist Party, and more directly in the hands of the oligarchy or individual dictator dominating the party. Dictatorship by the "proletariat"—one of Communism's silliest phrases and especially meaningless in the U.S.—is *not* democracy.

In its constant use of the world "democracy" the Russian dictatorship has deformed its meaning even beyond the vague generality of its real significance. And it might be pointed out that much the same process has occurred in the word "Socialism" and even the word "Communism." No man in his right senses could believe or assert that the political philosophy and destructive expansionist-imperialist policies asserted and practiced under Stalin have much relation even to the original Communism of *Das Kapital*.

Soviet Russian Communism, still more or less pure under Lenin, became simply an instrument and a disguise to create world revolution, *not* for the sake of the working class or the proletariat of the world but to extend and realize the Soviet-Russian imperialist ambitions of the Kremlin oligarchy which are identical with the historic imperialist ambitions of Russia under the long period of Czarism.

The fundamental identity of aims in Czarist and "Communist" Russia is remarkable. It is manifested (1) by a constant striving for expansion's sake while neglecting or sacrificing the interior development of the nation both politically and economically, and (2) by an historic and traditional terror of invasion which both the Czars and Stalin constantly played upon in the noisiest possible fashion in order to alarm the Russian people and so maintain or at least encourage their support and loyalty.

Quite within the old Czarist Russian pattern of exploitation and expansion is the treatment of the satellite nations, especially Czechoslovakia, Poland, and East Germany, which have consistently been drained of the raw materials, labor and industrial commodities produced by their more efficient and already established industry and economy in order to bolster up the living standards and wealth of Russia herself. Even the rigid suppression of the working classes, which has existed from the very beginning, and the strikes, suppression and actual exile and slaughter of unhappy peasants and workers by secret police and military forces are in the old classic Czarist tradition and arise from the same causes, both economic and political.

It is a general pattern which has again and again, from the times of the Swedish wars through the Crimean, Japanese and Finnish wars, brought defeat and disaster to Russia and it may well do so again, if the existing pattern continues in force. It is like constantly extending the construction of a jerry-built house in which new wings are thrown up on foundations that are defective, without ever putting any siding or roofing on the structure, until the monstrosity eventually collapses in one part or another of its own weight. The gradually revealed fact of the weakness of this ramshackle structure has slowly destroyed the fabulous picture of Russia as a strong and irresistible power built up over a period of years by the

Communists themselves, the Pentagon generals and the American warmongering newspaper columnists in one of the greatest illusions and swindles of a whole people in history.

I repeat that the Russians have produced a system in which everything—philosophy, culture, political philosophy, science and what you will—is molded and dominated by economics rather than by political theory. This economic conception extends not only to internal affairs but to external and foreign relations, which will, of course, in Communist theory cease to exist once Communism has taken over the world.

Perhaps the greatest dupes in history are those who espoused "Communism" in the Stalinist manifestation and the "liberals" and Socialists who profess to find in it a doctrine which can bring peace and prosperity and "shared" wealth to all the world. They are doubly duped, not only in their delusion that "Communism" is a political ideology rather than an economic system but in the fact that they have merely been espousing and defending the centuries-old pattern of Russian fear of invasion, expansion, exploitation and imperialism, which has simply exchanged a Czar for a Stalin or a Malenkov.

In time there may arise in Russia a leadership or even a truly representative government which will understand that what Russia needs most, and has always needed for centuries, is at least a century of peace in which to develop her great natural resources, the roads and railroads which she needs so badly, her schools, her industry and countless other elements of the truly vast and solid potential that exists there and has never been realized. There may even arise leadership so wise that it will recognize the fact that if Russia were developed economically, culturally and in every way to the stature of which she is capable and for which she possesses all the natural materials, the satellite nations and even greater areas would, through economic dependence alone, fall under her economic influence, join her and co-operate willingly in a common greatness. Provided this influence were enlightened and benevolent, all would benefit, most particularly the smaller nations touching upon the vast perimeter of Russia.

This is a process which could never possibly be realized under Stalin's dictated sixteenth-century policies. It can never be realized through any policy based upon conquest and exploitation and a political expansion that is merely greedy, disorganized, disorderly, and that constantly consumes in arms production and the maintenance of huge armies, the very life's blood of Russian economy.

At the moment, the likelihood that Russia will develop an ordered, productive economy of benefit to *all* seems as remote as Utopia. It will, in the end, depend largely upon the gradual enlightenment, education and leadership of this vast and potentially great country within coming generations.

In the meanwhile Russia is in the position of a gourmand with a weak stomach who has swallowed everything in sight, is swollen and suffering, but still reaches out his hand for more. It is by no means impossible that under the strain of *real* war, the gourmand would finally blow up and burst into countless political fragments.

The fact remains that Marxian Communism, in its real, true and only sense, is not a political and certainly not a philosophical, spiritual or even a cultural doctrine, but the assertion of an economic doctrine in the most sordid materialist terms, and that its opposite is not "democracy," with its talk of freedom of speech and thought. Communism's appeal is primarily to the wretched and miserable and poverty-stricken in the purely economic sense and thus its most fertile ground is discovered in nations where great masses of people live under abominable conditions of poverty. These people are more concerned with whether they have shelter for the night and enough food to keep them alive until nightfall than with highfalutin talk of abstractions which they do not understand and in which they have little or no interest. A starving man in a tempest without shelter is not likely to be preoccupied primarily by thoughts of liberty and freedom of speech and the higher levels of spirituality. He is concerned first of all merely with the business of keeping alive.

The Communist appeal is a very shrewd one. It promises food, land, housing, tractors and the destruction of the more fortunate energetic and solid elements of society everywhere for the benefit of the less fortunate masses. Since the vast majority of people everywhere, especially in overpopulated countries that are short of food and employment and that have abysmal living standards, are *not* the richest, the most able or the most energetic, the Marxian doctrine has a great and wide appeal. It is Communist policy to create abysmal conditions and confusion where they do not exist or to spur the development of such conditions so that the materialist appeal of their promises will be proportionately increased.

2

. . . *There is strong internal pressure from the Soviet people who want a higher quality diet, particularly one including more meat and dairy products. Yet to produce one pound of meat requires on the average between five to ten pounds of grain for feed. At the same time the Soviet population is growing rapidly and each year there are more than three millions more persons to be fed. Yet the bulk of Russia's agriculturally usable land is already under cultivation, so that the greater part of any future increased food supply must come from higher production per acre, rather than from any major rise in the land area farmed. The need to shift from the present extensive Soviet agriculture . . . whose grain yields are among the lowest in the world . . . to an intensive agriculture using greater resources per acre to procure yields nearer those of the crowded lands of Western Europe has been recognized for some time in Moscow, and never so clearly as in the latest farm program.*

HARRY SCHWARTZ, reporting in 1953 on Soviet Russian food conditions for the *New York Times*

It is possible that the very materialist basis of the Communist philosophy and practice may in the end be its undoing; indeed, there is the evidence everywhere in the world that this undoing has already begun. The basic cause of the decline is the fact that nowhere has Communism or even Communism in the milder form of Socialism been able to turn its promises into reality or even to improve conditions. The Communist's first step, when they take over a country, is to divide and distribute the land among the landless people. It is a part of the wily Communist tactics to divide the lands into parcels so small that it is impossible for any peasant to work them on a practical basis, either in a national sense or in the sense of providing food and support for a single family. The next step—as a "solution" to this problem—is the nationalization of *all* land and the collectivization of all farms. The result nearly always is that the farmer finds that he is not only worse off in a material way but that he has lost as well his freedom and independence of action.

The final test of the Communist promises to raise living standards and provide every sort of material advantage has failed, not only in countries like Yugoslavia, which has broken away from the influence of Soviet Russia, but in satellite countries such as Poland, East Germany, Rumania, Bulgaria and Hungary, and finally in Soviet Russia itself. The Communist, collective system has *not* brought greater benefits either to the state or to the individual; both find themselves after a few years worse off with fewer material benefits even than under the old systems.

In this direction, the report of Nikita S. Kruschev, who at the time of writing shares apparently equal authority with Malenkov in the Kremlin, is an official record of the failure of the Communist program in Russia, where after nearly thirty years there is actually less livestock and less food per person than there was in the time of the Czars. It is significant that for nearly ten years Kruschev was in charge of the whole agricultural and collectivist program; and that it was impossible to reach the people and to attempt greater production of agricultural commodities without recourse to the Russian newspapers, *Pravda, Izvestia* and the *Red Star*. Through this necessity, the report, despite the Iron Curtain, has become available to the entire world and is evidence out of the horse's mouth of the utter failure in practice of Communist materialist promises.

It is equally significant that at the same time Kruschev's report was issued the people of the U.S., living under the American system of capitalism, had the best, the cleanest, the most nutritious and the *cheapest* food in the world, whether measured by the number of working hours required to buy that food (which is the only real standard) or whether in terms of the family budget. At the same time that Russia was failing to produce enough food to feed her people on a minimum diet of primitive foods, the U.S. was struggling with the problem of surpluses. The myth that the industrial worker, whom Communism with its vague bureaucratic inhuman liking for generalization terms the proletariat, lives in a "worker's Paradise" has long since been disproven by the facts available and again and again through the Communist press and published statements from Communists in high authority; but the myth was finally exploded with world-echoing violence in the disorders last year in East Germany, Poland and Czechoslovakia when the low wages, the long hours, the brutal exploitation and the starvation diet of workers within the "worker's Paradise" was revealed to every corner of the world. This revelation was followed by a second and even more violent explosion when the Communist authorities executed rebellious workers and shot them down in the streets of the Marxian Paradise.

An equally disastrous and disillusioning evidence of the utter failure of Communism as an economical *or* material doctrine or pattern occurred a few months later in Korea with the wholesale refusal of Chinese and North Korean war prisoners to return to a homeland under Communist rule, despite an absolute choice and all the blandishments of the professional Communist "persuaders." These colossal and spectacular evidences of failure could not be concealed from the whole world and contributed powerfully to the growing doubts of masses of people everywhere regarding the whole Socialist-Communist program. The evidence was especially forceful and unanswerable because, both in the satellite nations and in China, it came from the humbler masses of the so-called "proletariat" which Marxian Doctrine promises to benefit and glorify.

The opposite of Communism, both in fact and in appeal, is an *economic* system which produces actual results far beyond the most extravagant promises of Marx. Such a system exists. Under this system the vast majority of the people belong to the middle class which the Communists detest, thereby recognizing its force as a *real* undefeatable opponent. Under this system the rewards are not promises which have everywhere failed dismally to materialize, but promises that have been realized and that exist in fact. Such a system is American capitalism. This is the real and effective answer to Communist propaganda and promises.

We have lacked the realism and the courage to assert the virtues of this system and its real and tangible rewards, which exist for all the world to see. It is a system which needs no arguments for its defense, for it has already produced material standards of living far beyond those ever established before in the history of the world. That is a materialist boast but it is devastatingly effective when cited against the failure of another utterly materialist doctrine.

The Russian Communist propagandists have recognized from the very beginning the weakness of "democracy" as an appeal because in its meaning it is fundamentally amorphous and shadowy and can be distorted to suit any case or argument. They have sedulously avoided any reference, either in the original Marxian documents or in later propaganda, to the larger refinements of human existence and have concentrated wholly upon very definite and even sordid materialist promises and rewards, so simplified, so definite and so sordid as to have a great appeal to the illiterate, the childish and the ignorant. The obvious procedure and winning tactic is to attack them on their own ground—the materialist one—which does not give them a foothold anywhere.

The odd and shameful thing is that under the pressure of

propaganda from the Communists, the fellow travelers and the "liberals," there has come into being a strange impression that American capitalism (which has produced not only the greatest material welfare in the world, but has also served to preserve the liberties of the people from the tyranny of both the dictator and the bureaucracy) is something to be ashamed of. This is one of the great absurdities of history.

Highfalutin, idealistic talk is a meaningless weapon against Communism especially when directed toward peoples living perpetually on the borders of starvation. We have in the U.S. a much better system than European capitalism and certainly an infinitely better system than Communism or Socialism in any of their manifestations anywhere in the world.

"Democracy" obligingly spreads a tent over all sorts of contradictions and absurdities, including the phony "voice of the people" in Soviet Russia, and is meaningless to hundreds of millions of Asiatics. When the opponents of Russian Communism seek to use "democracy" as a weapon against Communism, Russia and the Cominform, they are using a sword of lead which Russia and the Communists promptly seize from their hands at the very beginning of the conflict—a sword indeed which the Communists and the Kremlin rejected for themselves from the very beginning.

Communism in essence is a system in which free will, initiative and rewards are, either for the large or small investor, landowner or businessman, or even the worker, completely destroyed and an all-powerful state and an overwhelming mediocre bureaucracy determine everything, and always on an *economic* basis. Through their power they may even destroy the labor unions, transfer whole masses of workers from one area to another, send others into political-economic exile, and dictate to the individual what kind of work or career he may choose. The real rewards, both material and in terms of power and privilege, go entirely to those skilled in bureaucratic politics and intrigue, and very rarely to the most efficient or able in the objective creative sense. While the theoretical and dialectical emphasis is upon economics and welfare, the rewards go most frequently, as in Soviet Russia, not to the men who serve best the interests of the state and the people but to those individuals and cliques most skilled in intrigue and the struggle for political power or even for survival. Everything is subject to the theoretical economic good of the state, the theoretical benefits in turn to be distributed by the state to the individual citizens. These benefits in any state, Socialist or Communist, in our time have been extremely small or nonexistent, and much liberty and human dignity has been lost. In the Communist state politics do not exist for the people but only on a mad and intense basis within the ruling bureaucracy.

Marx and Marxian Communist dogma have always said, "This is entirely a materialistic world, and control by the state of *all* the economic factors in the lives of individuals will solve all of man's ills." We should say in return, "Very well then, this *is* a completely materialistic world, but you have espoused the wrong system. You have espoused a system that does *not* produce the fair distribution of wealth and the material benefits which you have promised through the control of men's lives by a materialist state. Your system has failed wherever it has been tried. It has failed all the way from the case of the British workingman, who must pay steadily increasing taxes, to the case of the Soviet workers, shot down or exiled by Russian Communist armed forces. Under your system not a single goal or promise has been achieved, and meanwhile you have lost or destroyed completely such *un*material values as freedom, dignity, originality, genius and many other things without which man cannot live."

If we had consistently opposed Communism upon a basis of material welfare rather than complicated and weakened the struggle by every sort of political, philosophical, military and idealistic argument, we should have made much greater progress. The weakness of the whole Voice of America program lies in the failure to adopt such a propaganda program. When we simply repeat that Americans have more of everything than any other people on earth, we merely arouse resentment, but when we explain *how* and under what system Americans came to have more of everything than any other people on earth we weaken the materialist foundations of Communism in Russia and everywhere, for we are explaining an economic system (American capitalism) which works brilliantly in practice where the Marxian system, in every degree from mild Socialism through brutal Communist dictatorship, has failed dismally on the record itself.

3

Never have I met a man of such offensive, insupportable arrogance. No opinion which differed essentially from his own was accorded the honor of even a halfway respectful consideration. Everyone who disagreed with him was treated with scarcely veiled contempt. He answered all arguments which displeased him with a biting scorn for the pitiable ignorance of those who advanced them or with a libelous questioning of their motives. I still remember the cutting, scornful tone with which he uttered—I might almost say "spat"—the word "bourgeois"; and he denounced as "bourgeois"—that is to say, as an unmistakable example of the lowest moral and spiritual stagnation—everyone who dared to oppose his opinions.

CARL SCHURZ, *Lebenserinnerungen*, p. 143

The record of the results of the Communist system becomes clearer each day, and more devastating; even the average citizen and the worker everywhere is becoming aware of Communism's failure to "produce the goods." The record of Russian Communism, not only in the satellite countries where Russian soldiers and police suppress the "workers" by force and compel them to "norms" which are virtual slave labor without reward, but even within Russia itself, is the clearest and most brutal evidence of the failure of Communist goals.

In the actions represented by our foreign policy and in our propaganda, we have again and again missed the opportunity to emphasize and clarify the failure of the materialist and economic base on which Communism is founded, or we have been too late and too weak and confused in our attack. It is probable that Communism is on the wane as a doctrine and an economic system throughout the world, but it is being weakened by its own obvious failure and not through any propagandist skill or even military pressure on our part. Allow me to emphasize again the point that lofty and exaggerated talk and propaganda concerning vague abstractions such as democracy, liberty, freedom, etc., etc., is ineffectual and even meaningless to the Chinese or Indian Coolie or the bewildered half-savage African Bush Negro, who represent the most fertile ground for Communist propaganda and whose principal interest in existence is to find enough to eat from day to day. The Cominform never bothers with these promises of abstractions; it promises food, houses, shoes, land, better wages, etc., etc., although it has failed everywhere to realize any of the benefits it promises.[1]

The Communists—even the Russian Communists—have been shrewd enough either consciously or by accident, to confuse us and the fundamental issues. They have been able to do this because, in many respects, their cold and calculating fanaticism has given them a clearer vision of the economic realities of the world today than we have been able to display. And they have never been handicapped, as we have been, by veritable armies of fuzzy thinkers, sentimentalists, eggheads, fellow travelers and cynical political leaders who have at times actually played the Communist and the Soviet and Russian game when it seemed to be to their own selfish advantage. They have not hesitated to move in upon the intense nationalist movements and the strivings for independence of small and undeveloped nations everywhere and to make many of these movements *seem* to be stimulated and controlled by Russian Communist direction and pressures. They have done this in Indo-China and even in China and are attempting it now in Bolivia, in Guatemala, in Egypt, in Iran, even in Argentina and elsewhere. If we had recognized these strivings for independence and national dignity as what they are and *not what the Communists wished us to believe them*, if we had faced the reality that all of these restless uprisings were only a part of the disintegration of the old colonial empires, and if we had used sympathetic tactics toward these nations in both our foreign and economic policy instead of siding with the colonial powers in an attempt to prop them up in the illusion that their former power and wealth can be restored, the history of our times would be utterly different and we should be much nearer to world peace and prosperity.

We left these awakening peoples, struggling toward national entity, dignity and freedom, with no choice but in many cases to be against us, especially since Communism and the Kremlin gave them, as in the case of China, material assistance and promised them everything. We even became involved in the disastrous and unnecessary Korean disaster, in which we furnished ninety-five per cent of the money, supplies and armed forces, thus enabling Britain to keep Hong Kong as a crown colony while she assumed a role of moderation and friendliness toward Red China and became her advocate for admission to the United Nations. The U.S. meanwhile through the tragic farce of its "police action" for the U.N., was made to appear as China's enemy and the enemy of all Asiatic peoples.

Much of the blundering and disaster arose from the ignorance of other nations, of history in general and of the psychology and even the living conditions of other people, which characterized many of the prominent figures who conducted our foreign policy during the past ten years. If they were not ignorant, then the blunders, the confusion and the victimization can only be ascribed to the undue friendliness of powerful figures high in our government toward

Europe, the old colonial empires, especially Britain, and even perhaps toward Soviet Russia itself.

In such a climate it was extremely easy for the Russian Communists to make hay and to appear constantly, in a false face, as the defender of liberties and the independence of small peoples. All of this was, of course, complicated by the ignorance of the American people as a whole regarding even the simplest facts of the times in which we live, and by the American "idealism" that has consistently and tragically muddled our participation in world affairs for nearly a generation.

The presentation of *American* capitalism as the opposite of Communism and the presentation of the doctrine of economic co-operation for the benefit of all (both large and small nations) have been consistently confused and weakened by the fact that the proponents of capitalism have allowed themselves to be pushed into the position of *defending* it (a situation for which we may well thank the so-called "liberals" and "intellectuals" within our own ranks) and by the fact that we have never taken the trouble or possessed the foresight to make clear that there are two kinds of capitalism, extremely different in origin, theory and practice—one American and the other European. We need to make clear that the one is based upon economic co-operation, free competition and dispersed participation, and the other upon the remnants of feudalism, colonial imperialism, cartelism and economic inertia rather than dynamism; that American capitalism offers a pattern for international co-operation—which has already been put into practice in certain limited areas by American overseas industrial operations—that under European capitalism is nonexistent and indeed impossible.

We need to make it plain that American capitalism is completely opposed to the exploiting, closed colonial capitalism of European origin and practice. All this is scarcely understood abroad. Indeed, American capitalism came into being spontaneously and without planning or theory or ideology, as in the case of the steadily closer relationships between the U.S., Canada and Mexico, as well as in minor manifestations in such areas as Peru and Saudi Arabia. This extension of *American* capitalism is not understood because it is a wholly new thing in the world and in the whole field of international economic relations. It is based upon principles of sharing, development and co-operation hitherto virtually unknown in the world save perhaps centuries ago in certain aspects and operations of the Roman Empire.

Because this vital difference between the two kinds of capitalism, or rather one might say between economic co-operation and old-fashioned colonial capitalist exploitation, has never been made clear, Communist propagandists have been able to charge American capitalism with all the evils of the very European capitalism that brought about the whole Socialist-Communist movement—a burden of misconduct and evil of which American capitalism is almost wholly innocent.

Many of the arguments of the Socialists and Communists against European capitalism with its "closed" rings, cartelism and restricted family ownerships, and against the consistently shabby and oppressive treatment of workers, were valid in the past and to a large extent are still valid. They are not valid against American capitalism which is so dispersed that actually it is in *the hands of the people*, who in reality hire the skilled executives who run their businesses and manage their properties or the investment of their money for them. The numerous stockholders pay these executives from time to time out of the profits on the money that has been put to work to create more and more employment, cheaper and better and more abundant goods of all sorts, and higher wages. It is a chain action that produces a dynamic growing economy and a kind of capitalism which, in conjunction with a steadily increasing population and a constantly astonishing technical advance in all fields, seems to assure a solid, prosperous and *self-sustaining* future for the U.S.

4

In both these countries [France and Italy], Washington has done little to change the popular mood, neither pressing reforms on the conservatives nor giving a minimal amount of blessing to anti-Communist radicals. The result has been a polarization of opinion in which, tragically, the forces of reform have become intertwined with the forces of neutralism, while the groups associated with U.S. policy are identified with those either hesitant or unwilling to undertake measures of social improvement.

THE NEW LEADER

Very few of the elements or practices listed above exist in most European countries, the only possible exceptions being in Holland, Denmark and Sweden, where some of the forces are in a mild form of operation.

The capitalist system in France and England and in the old Germany was and is fundamentally and structurally very different from the American system, and its operations have varied or changed very little since the period preceding World War I. Nor are they changing much even today despite vast new political, social and economic pressures. The basis for the accusations and criticisms of the Communists and the Russian "Communists" has been created by the operation of the European capitalist system with its closed, monopolist and cartelist pattern. It is a system which has worn itself out and in its present and past form cannot continue to exist in the world of tomorrow.

The crisis for the European capitalist system is doubly serious in a country such as Britain, where not only an outdated form of capitalism but even world economic and political policies belonging to another age continue to be pursued in a world in which they cannot possibly work and on the false and determinedly self-deceptive assumption that Britain, in terms of economic wealth and domination, is still a great power or at least can recover the power and prestige she once knew.

European and in particular French and British capitalism can be altered and reformed and shaped into a modern pattern such as exists in the United States. However, this can only be done by radical and in some respects revolutionary changes—much higher industrial wages, a dispersal of wealth through far more widespread investment and ownership of banks and industry, the modernization of industry, increased efficiency, the free exchange of goods over a larger area, a broader general consumption of commodities of all sorts, and a general increase in purchasing power. Cartels, which at present limit trade by artificial "mark-ups" and lower the quality and desirability of commodities, must be abandoned in favor of free competitive production. And the narrow frontiers and nationalist ideas that limit not only the free exchange of raw materials and manufactured commodities but inhibit in every possible way any degree of European economic prosperity and stability or self-sufficiency, will also have to go. This is especially true of an area in which a constantly rising population creates steadily increasing strains upon declining supplies of food, raw materials and foreign exchange. In existing conditions, under growing population pressures, living standards and even wages must in the long run be forced constantly downward, regardless of the political regime in operation.

Each of the changes mentioned is in itself revolutionary and all are interdependent in the general pattern of change. They are nevertheless changes that have begun to come about here and there, for example in new methods of mass production at lowered costs and in the formation of the Schuman Plan and the steps toward economic alliance in Holland, Belgium and Luxembourg. But all of them must come about in one form or another if the capitalist industrialist economy of Europe is to survive and prosper in this vastly changed world.

The reform, if it comes about, will be inevitably toward the incorporation of the European nations into larger and larger co-operative economic units. The ideal, for the nations and people of Europe, would be the eventual formation of a large and rich state federated at least economically and centered about the heartland of the geo-politicians. It would be a unit in which there would be freedom to move about and stretch economic elbows, a unit largely self-sufficient, as is the U.S. (especially in conjunction with Canada and Mexico), in terms of markets, raw materials, production of in-dustrial commodities, labor and food, operating as a single economic bloc so far as interchange of goods with the rest of the world is concerned. Eventually a common currency would be necessary and would contribute a stability which European nations have not known in nearly a generation and which is unlikely to be established ever again under existing conditions.

The strongest opposition to the development of such a pattern will come and has already come from the industrial-capitalist minority which in the past profited by cornering the wealth and the means of producing wealth under the cartelist, closed ring system of capitalism. This opposition still hopes desperately, especially in France and Italy, to maintain all the advantages and privileges which existed under the old pattern now in the process of disintegration. In a changing world which moves ahead with small regard for the interest of so minute a group, the choice of this small capitalist minority becomes more and more clearly defined as one between such a revolution as is outlined above and eventual nationalization of their wealth and the means of producing wealth. In the meanwhile the operations of this minority upon the old selfish pattern offers constant and even increasing comfort to the Communist-Socialist elements and fuel and substance to their arguments against capital-ism—arguments in which the U.S. suffers under the general head of being a capitalist country, although its capitalism bears little resemblance to that of Europe.

To a very large extent the foreign aid program and the so-called Marshall Plan, in all its gibberish alphabetical manifestations, have operated not to bring about an economically, and eventually a politically, united Europe but in exactly the opposite fashion. They have bolstered up the selfish interests of the small industrial-capitalist minority through financing the improvement and the enlargement of their tightly owned industrial activities and production without in any way guaranteeing that the benefits would be passed along to the working class in higher wages and purchasing power, and to the people in general. Indeed, in many cases the foreign aid program has merely saved the old system from complete bankruptcy. By keeping it alive, it has delayed the revolutionary changes which must come about in one form or another, either through gradual reform and modification or through nationalization and revolution. Here again, by the mismanagement of foreign aid and the failure to demand in return reforms of the European capitalist system, we have been made to appear actually as the friend of the monopoly-cartelists and the enemy of great masses of people, especially in France and Italy, who have received small benefit or none at all.

This situation lies at the root of the fact that all the billions poured out in European aid have not lessened the strength of the Communists among the industrial workers and lower middle class in France and Italy and have affected very little the strength of the Labor-Socialist group in Britain.

It might be said that the foreign aid funds have served to increase employment. They have expanded the base of employment but only at a level of wages which, especially under inflationary conditions (and in Britain an increased tax burden), permits the worker and his family merely to exist without any margin for the savings or for the widespread purchase of industrial commodities which the pattern of American capitalism makes possible.

In some countries, notably France and Italy, the small but immensely rich minority that has been the chief beneficiary of foreign aid fails to make its fair contribution in the form of taxes toward the expenses of government, either because the necessary legislation does not exist or because of the widely popular habit of tax evasion. In many cases the favored and even pampered position of the industrialist-banker-capitalist group in Europe is something Americans, even of the same category, cannot imagine. In fact, much of the foreign aid money, as the Senate Committee to Investigate Foreign Aid pointed out, is simply taken from the American people in taxes to pay the taxes of people in European countries, especially in France and Italy, who refuse to tax themselves adequately.

The fact is that the money poured into Europe by the American people has been for the great part like water poured to prime a pump which will not prime until it is repaired—or, in other words, until economic co-operation becomes a fact on the European continent and until the European system of capitalism undergoes a broad and revolutionary reform which disperses ownership and profits and consequently purchasing power over an immensely greater base.

European capitalism is no longer dealing with a world of *controlled* sources of raw material or of *controlled* and even *forced* colonial markets, as in the past. Nor can it continue to exist on the medieval level where villages exchanged commodities manufactured within the limits of their territories under a guild system. Modern conditions of transport and communication, the modern operations of economics on a vast scale, have made economically impossible the existence of a great number of small independent countries shrunken to the relative status of the medieval villages. The smaller over-populated nations, without great interior markets, without cheap and abundant sources of raw materials, and without in many cases enough food to supply their basic needs, simply cannot remain nationalistic, unco-operative worshipers of the god of sovereignty, except at a vast cost to themselves and at the price of constantly endangering the stability and peace of the world in general.

The cartelism of certain large industries in Europe, notably the steel and oil industries, came into being largely through recognition of the fact that uncontrolled and openly competitive industry among a great number of small nations, mostly overpopulated (comprising in all a land mass only a fraction the size of Brazil, Canada, Russia or the United States), simply could not even exist economically save through close co-operation in a *controlled* and *closed* market. This artificial cartelism crossed national frontiers everywhere, but in no way affected the well-being of the mass of people. With the profits going continually back into industries and enterprises and the pockets of a single family or "closed ring" of owners, it turned out in the end to be no solution at all, but only productive of greater, more intensified evils and concentrations of wealth and profits.

Indeed this cartelism was and, if fully revived, will again be one of the principal assets of national and world Communist propaganda, just as in France it was the principal force behind the wholly disastrous "Popular Front" movement in the thirties.

The odd thing is that although industrial cartels, representing closed and limited individual capital industrial investments, operated continually in Europe regardless of frontiers or national antagonisms, even in extreme cases in time of war, the nations and peoples themselves were never able to co-operate in a similar fashion.[2]

Britain's indifference and even opposition to economic, political and military co-operation with other members of the European family is largely based upon the assumption that the United Kingdom is still or can be again the heart of a vast and rich empire, in spite of the fact that it has disintegrated and can never be re-established. The illusion is propped up by vast contributions in money and military equipment from the United States and by the artificialities of the sterling bloc economy, neither of which can continue indefinitely. This illusion and consequent refusal of Britain to co-operate with the other small nations on the continent is dangerous not only to the future well-being of all Europe and the British Isles but to the future existence and maintenance of what remains of the commonwealth, domininons and colonies. They are sharply aware that development and freedom in their own areas are being handicapped

for the sake of the United Kingdom and in particular for the benefit of British industry and the obsolete pattern of capitalism, cartelism and minority interests upon which it is founded.[3]

Recently in Brazil I came upon one of the final liquidations of
British capital overseas. It was a huge plantation owned by capital
in London, one of the best industrial-agricultural operations I have
ever seen. It was up for sale either to a Brazilian buyer or to one of
those roving syndicates made up of European and Levantine capitalists without loyalties or much nationality. The reason? Although it
had once been a great money-maker and actually is producing high
profits today, Brazil's temporary restrictions on exporting profits and
high taxes in Britain made the operation no longer profitable. So one
more fundamentally profitable British investment overseas was being
liquidated. If taxes in the United States continue to increase under
the strain of foreign aid programs, government ownership and management of public utilities, increasing bureaucracy, wholesale overseas military commitments, etc., it is by no means inconceivable that
the whole immense and prosperous economic system existing under
the name of capitalism (even in the American sense) could come in
time to the same tragic end. We are in fact engaged at the moment
in every kind of overseas commitment and at times in actual war, as
in Korea. The sum total of all these activities, many of them meaningless, useless, muddled and extravagant, represents virtually the
same drain during two world wars that wrecked the economy of
Britain and caused the slow dissolution of the Empire, the Socialist
revolution and the nationalization of industry which accompanied
it. Even American capitalism, with all its dynamism and dispersal,
cannot survive indefinitely such a monstrous drain. Today many a
dividend held by small income investors is simply turned over to
government to pay for these huge expenditures, thus nullifying the
benefits and advantages of American capitalism over the European
variety. It is by no means impossible that if this immense drain con-

tinues, especially if it is accompanied by inflation, we shall arrive at the ultimate point of repudiation of government bonds.

During World War II the writer participated in the selling of great quantities of U.S. War Bonds and employed before large rallies of citizens the common slogan that "government bonds were the best investment in the world" and that in ten years an $18.75 bond would be worth $25. In uttering such statements he felt constantly like the traditional snake oil merchant, for out of his long experience with European currencies under conditions of war, inflation, socialized bureaucracy, civil strife and vast governmental expenditures, he knew that government bonds were *not* always the best investment in the world and that they could actually be repudiated when governments became bankrupt and inflation took over. He also suspected in his heart that in ten years the value and purchasing power of the $18.75 bonds would *not* be worth $25 and perhaps not even worth the $18.75 paid for them. This was exactly what happened. Actual repudiation of government bonds *could* happen here under perpetual government deficit financing and a constantly increasing monstrous national debt. It is terrifying to contemplate what would happen in this country and in the world if an uncontrollable depression occurred under existing conditions of government expenditure, military expansion, debt and deficit financing. Such an event would mean the end of the way of living as Americans know it and delivering the whole world over to Communism and even anarchy.

5

Our relations with Western Europe have seen the revival of a new type of Washington isolationism, in which we provide money and pep-talks but withhold any type of leadership.

THE NEW LEADER

From the time of Marx onward, Communists and Socialists have always been aware that their worst enemies and the most powerful forces operating against them, were not the small minority of very rich capitalists, estate owners, bankers and industrialists, or even the conservative politicians or "intellectuals." These could, if necessary, be liquidated quickly one way or another or driven into exile, once a revolutionary movement, either violent as in the French and Russian Revolutions, or peaceful as in Socialist-Labor Britain, was started and on its way. Their strongest and most potent and indestructible opposition came from the middle class, representing those benighted members of society who liked owning their own homes and gardens, owning and operating small factories and farms, managing their own lives or businesses and sharing fairly in the general wealth of a nation. This backward class included frequently great numbers of professional people and even some "intellectuals" of the weak "liberal" type.

The most prolonged and vicious persecution in Russia has been directed consistently against this class, reaching its peak in the wholesale liquidation of the Kulaks or prosperous landowning peasants, always the most stubborn resisters of Socialism or Communism wherever these backward ideologies come into practice. Actually there was no real middle class in Russia. The bourgeoisie consisted of a few small shopkeepers, some intellectuals, professional people and clerks and a considerable faction of landowning peasants. The great rich landowners, bankers, industrialists and privileged aristocracy were liquidated by death or exile almost overnight; but even the small army of the middle class put up a stubborn resistance which in the end was subdued only by their virtual extermination. Except for this obstinate group the Russian Marxian Revolution was easy going, what with the wretched condition of the people and the vast promises of the Bolsheviks.

It should never be forgotten that the middle class which owns something and shares in the benefits and general wealth of a nation are the greatest champions of freedom, economic, political and spiritual. France, with all its characteristic individualist political vagaries, is still essentially a solid nation, and resists and survives crisis after crisis, wars and occupations of territory because so many Frenchmen have little shops and villas and small bits of land. Countless Frenchmen voting for Communist Party candidates in protest against the imbecilities and compromises of the other political parties would desert the Communist group overnight and turn archresisters if the prospect arose that real or Russian Communism might seize their property and throw it into a common pool. Fundamentally, for this reason, the Communist Party in France is one of the most unstable in Europe, especially since many a Frenchman began to discover that Communism of the Russian variety dominated from Moscow was not even Communism, but only a variety of Russian imperialist expansion which made a dupe of him. With this realization, party membership began to shrink at a rapid rate and in 1952-53 the Communist press had largely to go out of existence for lack of support and funds.

6

Communist parties remained, but they ceased to constitute in most countries any immediate revolutionary threat; they came more and more to be a sort of traditional fixture of the Western state—a curious receptacle into which there could be poured, decade after decade, all that fringe of the human species that tended by nature to turn against its human environment and to seek fulfillment of its own ego in the defiance of all that others believed and cherished. (Such people always exist; they are a mutation of the species. The presence of real grievances and hardships has only a remote relation to their state of mind. Their trouble is subjective; and if it arises originally in environmental factors, as I suppose it often does, these factors are never—but really never—the ones of which they are conscious, of which they complain and against which they inveigh.)

GEORGE F. KENNAN in the *New Leader*

Indeed the very simplicity and crudity of the Communist appeal is working toward the defeat of Communism throughout the world and tending more and more to reduce the leadership of Marxian Communism to the proportions of a sinister world-wide psycho-pathic cult. A truly balanced and informed and reasonable mind cannot accept intelligently the Marxian doctrine in terms of the human race alone. Those apparently *intelligent* individuals who have accepted and even espoused the doctrines sooner or later reveal, as in the cases equally of Chambers and Hiss, some unbalanced psychopathic quirk or influence which deforms the intelligence as well as the judgment.

The broken promises of Marxism and the failure anywhere and everywhere to get results disillusions in time the simple-minded and uneducated, especially when this failure is coupled, as it always is, with abysmal living standards, exile, imprisonment, torture and every possible restraint upon individual liberty. As this disillusion-ment increases—and it is increasing rapidly—the appeal and promises of the Marxian doctrine die out. Presently there is left only the *hard core* of Communists, which as time and experience reveal, consists largely of psychopaths, downright crooks and gangsters or individuals who regard the Communist Revolution as a short and easy pathway to power over their fellow men (in itself a manifesta-tion of psychopathic personality).

The root of Communism's attraction for apparently educated and even so-called "intellectual" persons lies almost invariably in (1) a "revenge" complex for some injury, real or fancied, for some handi-cap or injury suffered early in life, (2) in an unstable emotional make-up, (3) in outright delusions bordering upon insanity, (4) in the practice of "intellectualism" to the point where the human race or even individual man is forgotten and ignored and both become merely the inert and dead materials employed in a chemistry experi-ment to support or elaborate a theory.

A wretched childhood and a disturbed, overemotional nature contributed, by Chambers' own confession, to his original conver-sion to Communism. In the case of Alger Hiss, every word of evidence at hearings and trials revealed the tragedy of a man trapped by delusions . . . He believed that he was cleverer than everyone else in the world. What he was seeking in reality was power, and he saw Communism as a means of gratifying a natural taste for conspiracy and as a quick pathway to this power.

No test illustrates more profoundly the essential difference between the "intelligent man" and the "intellectual" in the generally accepted sense of the word. The balanced *intelligent* individual could not and does not succumb to reactionary Marxian dogma, since he has not become intellectualized to the point at which humanity and common sense are sacrificed to dialectics and formula and calculation without balance. It is not impossible for an "intelligent man" to possess intellectual qualities and have intellectual achievements to his credit. But countless intellectuals, and almost all of them associated with the Communist movement, have reached the point of deviation from the human race in general and true intelligence (which implies balance, logic and common sense) in particular. It is such a difference which perhaps explains "intellectuals" of the type of Joliot-Curie, Pontecorvo, Fuchs and a considerable number of our own people. Whatever the reasons or distinctions, it is slowly growing apparent that at least the leadership of the Communist movement everywhere is becoming increasingly a "cult" leadership in which sadists, "intellectuals," psychopaths, gangsters and cranks co-operate to promote the reactionary doctrines of Karl Marx and the distorted imperialist "Communism" of the Kremlin.

The Comintern has had its toughest fight to make headway in the United States. Even in the depths of a colossal economic depression, party membership represented only a tiny minority of the total population. Its membership today is infinitesimal in relation to the total population. At times, through the sympathy and support of a "liberal" fringe—the same fringe which is the first element to be liquidated once the Communists take over—it has had an appearance of greater strength than existed in fact. The only force the party has even been able to exert in government was clandestine and secret, through the activities of men like Alger Hiss, Lee Pressman and the fringe "liberals" who were never quite sure what they were doing, where they were going or what they had let themselves in for.[4]

The progress of Communism in the United States, save among the fringe liberals, a few college professors and teachers and psychopaths with grudges against society, has been rocky going because the hated bourgeoisie under the American system of capitalism is so numerous and under the system of free elections is so powerful. Even today, if the Congressional investigating committees attempted to go out of business, they would be forced back into operation through the violent protests of millions of middle class citizens. There is no better evidence that capitalism—but decidedly the American variety—and not "democracy" is the direct opposite of Communism. Nor is there any better evidence that the soundest bulwark of such abstractions as "liberty" and "human dignity" is an economic one—high living standards, high wages and dispersed ownership of wealth in terms of "working money."

The fact is that no nation in the world, with the possible exception of a few small nations like Switzerland, Denmark and Sweden, has so large a middle class as the United States, and on the basis of ratio and proportion, the United States is still very likely *the* middle class nation of the world. Allowing for a small minority of the poor of the sort whom Christ observed we shall have ever with us and an equally small minority of very rich who will have so difficult a time with the eye of the needle, the entire American population is middle class.

How can the average industrial worker, with wages from ten to ninety per cent higher than those of any other workers in the world, with his car, his home, his garden, his refrigerator, his radio, his television set, protected by his powerful union organization, be called oppressed and sunk in slavery? The picture which the average Communist paints merely becomes ludicrous. The fact is that the proletariat of Marxism (the class of the oppressed industrial worker) simply does not exist in the United States. Nor do the conditions which produce a proletariat and fresh ground for the Communist to cultivate, although such conditions still *do* exist under the closed system of European capitalism. It is unlikely that the U.S. would ever develop the conditions that would create masses of Communists. The United States has already passed through that test in the thirties and today its economy is far more securely shored up and reinforced than it was a generation ago.

The great and fundamental weakness of Russia, whether Czarist or Soviet, has always been the lack of dispersed wealth of which the middle class is the foundation.

The fact that the actual capital and material wealth of a small clique in Czarist Russia has been translated under the Soviet pattern into special privilege, free motors, elegant housing and other less tangible rewards for a tiny minority, does not alter the condition itself—that of having no large, secure, independent middle class possessing *in toto* by far the biggest share of the nation's wealth.

Countries with wealth dispersed through a middle class and especially those with a democratic-republican form of government, do not move toward dictatorships on either the Nazi or the Communist pattern. Chaos, tyranny and war in both Germany and Italy began with the ruinous inflation following World War I, when, under Nazi-Fascist doctrines, the middle class was persistently persecuted and its wealth destroyed. Somewhat the same process is actually under way today in Argentina, where very rapidly the whole middle class is becoming extinct, coincidentally with the inflation of currency, a severe decline in production of goods of all sorts, the virtual disappearance of the export trade and shortages of credits not only of dollars but of all foreign currencies.

One might almost say that nations react toward radical or reactionary doctrines (and these as in the case of Nazism and Communism are frequently identical) in an almost exact ratio to the degree of the existence or nonexistence of a large and secure middle class. The impulse toward Socialism in England arose largely from the fact that great industries were almost exclusively the properties, not of middle class stockholders dispersed over the whole of the nation, as in the United States, but of a few immensely rich families or small closed upper middle class groups. When this impulse toward radicalism or reaction begins, it gains almost immediately the support of the so-called "white collar" and "intellectual elements" both of which, through experience and greater education, contribute far more than mere numbers to the rapidity of the change.

The vast wealth, productivity and general stability of the United States is based fundamentally upon the fact of *dispersed* wealth and an immense and solid middle class. The average worker in the United States and especially the skilled worker, knows an income, a diet and living standards much higher than those of most European citizens commonly considered as the "bourgeoisie," a factor which makes it extremely difficult or impossible to organize politically a "labor party" as it is known in England and in many European countries. As has been pointed out before, the same condition has made the growth of Communism virtually impossible. Even the bitter years of the Great Depression brought eventually not the expected chaos and revolution but only legislation and the acceptance of new principles which served to distribute wealth still further and to provide safeguards against the repetition of such a calamity, thus spiking even more effectively the Communist guns.[5]

It could be said indeed that in the United States at least ninety per cent of the population, judging by income, purchasing power and the ownership of such commodities as electric refrigerators, radios, automobiles, etc. (regarded in virtually every other nation in the world as luxuries), belongs to the solid middle class.

7

The generous heart wins friends, but a bought friendship is a prostitute friendship. One Eisenhower or one Stevenson is worth more in terms of affection than the whole Marshall Plan.

GEORGE CATLIN in *The New Leader*

Reforms in the cartelist closed capitalism of Europe can not only bring the continent a greater permanent security but can meet and check once and for all the possibility of Communism's rise to power. What these reforms are has been outlined earlier—briefly, heavier and more fairly distributed taxes and a greater distribution of wealth and economic opportunity in terms of higher wages, savings, investment, purchasing power and wider participation through investment of savings in the operations of capitalism itself.

By now the results of Communist-Socialist adventures into government have been established and proven here and there throughout the world. A simple analysis, of which any moderately informed person is capable, cannot fail to show that they are not good in terms of freedom, of economic security, of living standards and diet, of civilization or in any other terms you may wish to list. Certainly they do not come within miles of the attainments in general welfare and living standards of American free, dispersed capitalism.

Government in the form of a republic or a limited monarchy under complete control of the people and operating under a sound capitalist economy based upon dispersed wealth still represents the farthest political advance yet made by man. The very operations and results of Socialist-Communist theory and practice merely prove what should have been apparent all along—that both are in general principle merely reactionary. They are a return to the primitive communal patterns of prehistoric man or the few savage tribes that still lead a jungle or desert life in the midst of this incredibly complex, unevenly developed and complicated world. Communal, Communist or Socialist principles are simply unworkable in such a world.

Primarily they can produce dubious benefits only in small tribal communities or in small nations with a high degree of poverty, ignorance and illiteracy. Otherwise the system produces lowered living standards and encroachment of liberty on all sides.

The fact is that too many Americans take for granted what they have and assume that their welfare, security, prosperity and high living standards, the roads, the communications, the schools, the research, the opportunities, exist elsewhere and everywhere. All of these things simply do *not* exist everywhere and few of them exist elsewhere in any remotely similar degree, save perhaps in Canada whose economy so closely resembles that of the United States as to be almost indistinguishable. The sturdy American drugstore, frequently the butt of jokes, but a kind of symbol both as a community center and a mountain of reasonably priced necessities and commodities looked upon in many countries as luxuries, represents a living standard and shared abundance which cartelist capitalism, Socialism and Communism have never produced and never will.

This is an aspect of American capitalism with its capacity to generate wealth and a dynamic economy which has never been properly developed or explained in all the opposition to the Communist-Socialist dialectic. Its explanation and use in propaganda (even through the example of the ordinary drugstore) is the most important weapon in combating Communism. However, it is important *not* to emphasize simply the fact that Americans have all this abundance and even luxury (as is done all too frequently by the Voice of America) but *why* they have it and how the system works which produces such abundance and material well-being. The evidence of the failure of Communism and even of mild Socialist plans is all about us—from Britain, through Argentina to Moscow and the satellite countries—and can no longer be disguised or concealed. It has been a painful, devastating and tragic trial which, after death, wholesale starvation, wars and immense misery of all sorts, has finally ended in disillusionment, not only in a strictly material sense but in every other sense touching upon man's spiritual and intellectual well-being.

The accusation may be made (and it frequently is by apologists for the failure of Socialist dogma) that the arguments listed above are almost entirely material and so they are; but the original thesis of the chapter was that Marxian Communism and Socialism is in reality neither a political nor a cultural theory or plan of government but rather an *economic system* and that in opposing it we weaken the whole argument by assuming that it is primarily concerned with politics and government or spiritual values rather than with economics. The real, unanswerable and strongest argument against Marxian theory is not the example of democratic or free government but a contrary economic system which produces infinitely greater material benefits.

The perfect opposite to Communism is capitalism in the dispersed *American* form. Marxian Socialism, in any manifestation, is essentially and brutally economic both in promises and theory. Nowhere in the writings of Marx or in Communist or even Socialist propaganda are there genuine evidences of concern with the spiritual or the cultural. These appear spasmodically in later manifestations concerned with mass schools, nurseries, state theaters, etc. As a rule all of these are better managed and more productive and certainly more widespread when spontaneously created by a free and prosperous people than they are when conceived and *imposed* by a state bureaucracy.

But the important point is that Marxian theory and practice have failed badly in the very field upon which their advocates place the greatest emphasis—that of a completely materialistic economic system which produces a more evenly distributed wealth, better living standards and an increase in well-being for all the people. The record in practice, whether in Hitler's National Socialist Germany, Mussolini's Italy, Stalin's Russia, Peron's Argentina or Cripps' Britain, is ludicrous by comparison with the achievement of American dispersed capitalism in full operation.[6]

8

The whole foreign-aid program from the beginning has rested on a false diagnosis of the ills of Europe and the "underdeveloped" countries and a false conception of the remedy. In practice, instead of inducing the beneficiary countries to return more quickly to sound policies and free enterprise, our aid has subsidized socialism and encouraged these countries to continue statist controls far longer than otherwise.

HENRY HAZLITT in *Newsweek*

At the same time that disillusionment regarding Communism increases everywhere, the rebellious colonies and the smaller independent nations find themselves in a weakened economic condition which permits them in neither a political nor a military nor an economic sense to remain *wholly* independent and dominant, as many have attempted to be in the past. In this rapidly changing world, nations and especially small nations must not only practice economic co-operation but accept to some degree the fact of economic *dependence* upon larger richer nations. Total independence and even *actual*, isolated independence, such as existed here and there in the world before modern means of communication had shrunk and contracted it everywhere, have become impossibilities.

It is such a world revolution, political and economic, that is actually taking place and that is the cause of so much disorder and confusion and war. One of the great blunders of our times is the determination of Western governments, politicians and diplomats (particularly our own) to confuse this revolution with both Russian and world Communism and to blame or credit Communism for the general world disorder. This revolution and the breakup of the old colonial-imperialist world would have occurred if Lenin, Stalin and the Cominform had never existed. The Communists horn in wherever they can and endeavor to take credit wherever there is disorder and revolution. By giving them credit and using them as an excuse for the occupation of Korea or the defense of Indo-China, the West, and especially the U.S., merely defeats its own case and strengthens the reputation and actual achievements of Communism and Russia. It also makes enemies of peoples everywhere who are struggling toward independence and dignity. It is this confusion of analysis and understanding that makes us appear to the peoples of Asia, the Near East and even some Latin-American peoples as supporters of the dying colonial powers, of imperialism, and not at all, as "liberators" and "defenders against aggression."[7]

This confusion is in evidence throughout the world—in Iran, in Egypt, in certain small Latin-American nations and even in China. What thoughtful person can believe that China will remain indefinitely a subject and satellite nation wholly dominated by Russia or even by Communism? Egypt is the very nearly perfect example of a nation struggling for independence and dignity in which a revolution has taken place with which the Communists and Russia have had nothing whatever to do, although they have made every possible attempt to infiltrate both the old government and the new and to claim credit for the revolutionary changes. Iran is a similar case. Here too the Communists moved in *after* the event, and at the time of writing still have not managed to make Iranian resistance and revolution appear to be the result of Communist activity. In both nations, as in Indo-China, the disorders and revolution are the last manifestation of a struggle for freedom from domination and exploitation by the old colonial-imperialist powers. The pattern has repeated itself in various forms almost everywhere. In the cases of the satellite nations, it is doubtful whether the Communists would ever have succeeded in taking over without the aid of the "intellectuals," the "liberals" and the mild Socialists. But these and similar elements held the door open for them and by collaborating with them, opened the way for invasion and occupation. Again and again the revolutionary changes were not caused or even cultivated by the minority Communist group, which merely moved into the vacuum largely created by the so-called "liberal" politicians.

The small nations which are gradually achieving a state of independence and self-government find themselves in an impossible position economically. For in an intensely industrial world shrunken by modern means of transportation and communication the small independent nation becomes an anomaly. In the world of today there are three great nuclei about which eventually other smaller less fortunate nations must group themselves economically. These are Soviet Russia, the United States and, potentially at least, Brazil.

The almost cosmic drive behind this political and economic nuclear process is virtually irresistible. It sparked the spontaneous and increasingly powerful impulse toward economic union of the countries of Europe which, as individual, isolated nations with customs and trade barriers of all sorts, become steadily more insecure and insignificant. The same force lies at least partly behind the Russian drives both eastward into Asia and westward into Europe and partly behind the impulse of China to turn toward Russia.

In the intensely economic age in which we live complete sovereignty and even *real* democracy (particularly in its aspect of free enterprise and distribution) become actual luxuries permitted only to the great, self-contained and self-sufficient nations which are not forced by economic circumstances either to bargain, appease or make deals in order to survive. In overpopulated countries with poor or unbalanced supplies of food and raw materials, some system of government intervention and control of distribution becomes the only means of preventing squalor and actual starvation. Only economic co-operation on a mutually beneficial basis with larger, richer and more fortunate land-mass nations, can meet and solve the problems of small or backward nations.

From a strictly economic point of view, countries such as Bolivia or Iran or even the Central American and Near East nations have no real excuse for existence and cannot exist in the future on a completely independent basis. The attempt or determination to do so implies subsidies on a friendly basis from more fortunate nations

(American aid) or appalling conditions of living and education and a viciously bad internal distribution of wealth, which can lead only to revolution and disorder and open the door to Communist agitation. Such a condition actually faces some European nations today. It will grow worse if economic co-operation and actual political federation are not accomplished, and if the large land mass of Western Europe and the geopolitician's heartland are not permitted to function as a trade area with the potential stability of the great underpopulated self-sufficient areas like United States, Canada, Russia and Brazil.

As the once great colonial powers such as France, Great Britain and Holland disintegrate and lose their farspread overseas colonies, either as the colonies achieve independence, or come under the economic influence of the great land-mass nations (as is happening today to many parts of the British Commonwealth) the importance, force and economic drag of the great self-contained nations become steadily more irresistible even to the once powerful European colonial nations themselves.

For example, many consider that the future economy of the United Kingdom is tied into that of her dominions and commonwealths and the United States and eventually cannot be maintained upon any basis other than one which leaves Britain actually in a dependent role. In fact the various loans, gifts and subsidies by the United States to the once rich colonial powers of Europe are merely a makeshift and hidden recognition of this condition carried out upon a dishonest and unrealistic basis by agencies operating under various alphabetical names. This process and deceit merely prolong the agony and prevent a sound and realistic settlement of the world's vast economic muddle.

The only possible alternative for these small overpopulated European nations poor in markets, raw materials and food, lies in economic union and eventually political federation. Unfortunately such a union is crippled in advance by the fact that a large and rich part of Germany, all of Czechoslovakia, Poland, Austria and the Balkan states are at present mere satellites of Soviet Russia and in many economic senses almost wholly isolated from the rest of Europe, to whose economy and trade they are vitally important.

Western Europe plus the Russian satellite nations is the heartland of the geopoliticians and rightly so. Its center is the area in which the Rhine, the Danube and the Elbe have their origins, for here lies the rich nucleus of agricultural wealth, natural resources, food, industry and markets, especially under a dynamic wealth-increasing economy on the American pattern. This heartland should by every economic, geographical and physical law, provide a great, united and self-sufficient land mass to form the nucleus of great economic power and attraction; but at the moment it is divided into many small overpopulated nations and cut almost in half by the Iron Curtain. Even if the nations of Western Europe achieved eventual economic federation, the whole group would still be handicapped so long as the vital satellite nations with their rich resources of food and raw materials lay behind the Iron Curtain, because it would still not be big enough and rich enough, either in food or raw materials or even markets to take care of its great and increasing population.

Tragically the whole of Europe is divided and interdivided, not only in Western but Eastern Europe, by every manner of trade and customs barrier, by differences of language and vast differences in custom, tradition and civilization. Some of the people still live on a level which is almost tribal. Who can doubt that if this large area from the Atlantic Ocean into and including the Ukraine could be united and established as a free trade economic unit, it would be an area of immense wealth, power and importance and one in which the well-being of the people as a whole would be improved to a degree which is almost inconceivable.[8]

Soviet Russia's move westward has been prompted by more than the deep traditional and national desire for buffer states. Part of the motivation has been a cloudy and half-conscious realization that the very heart of economic Europe does not lie now or ever will lie in Russia proper but in great areas where the three rivers, the Rhine, the Danube and the Elbe, have their sources. Even with her expansion westward, Russia is still far off base among the deserts, tundras and mountains of the East, and it is possible that there will be no peace and no more prosperity in the whole of Europe until this area is united and permitted to function as a single great economic unit.

In view of all this, it is a significant and interesting fact that the doctrine of the self-determination of small nations advocated by Woodrow Wilson and imposed by him on the Versailles Treaty over the greater, more realistic wisdom of Clemenceau and the canny, opportunist shrewdness of Lloyd George, has turned out, in the light of our times, to have been a disastrous doctrine and one which in large part brought about the Second World War. It was a doctrine based upon a nineteenth-century sentimental liberalism rather than upon the economic realities of a modern world. It served only to increase the already disastrous fragmentation of Europe, to create new barriers to trade, food and economic prosperity as well as in the end to heighten rather than to diminish the intense almost tribal nationalism and feuding of individual small peoples and nations.

Here a highly emotional and unrealistic theorist, supported by similar qualities in the nation he represented, forced upon the world a doctrine and a plan which ran directly counter to the irresistible mechanical and economic forces already at work. For even then the disintegration of colonial empires had set in and the eventual unification of large self-sufficient economic areas upon a basis of economic nuclear attraction had become inevitable.

9

"Men everywhere look to us for guidance," writes Mr. Markel [in the N. Y. Times Magazine]. This is, of course, not true. There is no wide-spread anti-Americanism in Britain, and what there is, is as vocal on the extreme Right as on the extreme Left. But, far from a disposition to look

to America for guidance, there is a widespread belief that the chief characteristic of American foreign policy is inexperience (if, indeed, there is any consistent American foreign policy at all) and that it is America which needs guidance.

GEORGE CATLIN in the *New Leader*

Our present foreign policy (if indeed it has any consistent pattern which gives it the right to be called a policy) is largely based upon a similar old-fashioned nineteenth-century liberalism and conceivably can bring about equally disastrous results. The only difference today is in the expressions used to define what is essentially the same fatal error. Our policy with its "nonaggression" pacts and its insistence on the attempt to guarantee the independence of small countries in every part of the world, is all part and parcel of the same pattern, and continues to fragment the world and create constant and increasing disorder rather than to unite it. Of this fact the whole tragic history of the Korean mess is ample proof.

The United Nations, already so costly to the United States in money, lives and material, operates only on the political level and as in Korea, only serves to disrupt any possibility of a sound economic pattern and the establishment of real peace. In all of this, the vital questions of the free-flowing exchange of goods, union rather than fragmentation of self-contained and contiguous trade areas, proper distribution of food, raw materials and markets, are wholly overlooked. In many ways our foreign policy is as anachronistic and out of date in the world as the Ivan the Terrible policy of Stalin was in a Russia which liked to think of herself as a modern nation.

The freedom and independence of Korea, surrounded by Russia, China and Japan, cannot possibly be maintained save by the permanent presence of large and vastly expensive deployments and installations of the American Army, Navy and Air Forces. It would be much better for the Koreans, the world and the United States if Korea made a co-operative economic treaty with Japan or with Japan, China and Russia, even if it meant the economic absorption of Korea into larger economies. The Korean people would be far better off than they are today or conceivably can be in a future which holds little but the prospect of continued wars, raids, devastation and misery. But that is their hopeless prospect, unless the U.S. guarantees Korea's security in perpetuity at a vast expense in money, material and lives—something which the American people will in the long run be unwilling to accept.

Korea is a first-class example of the fact that the American government, acting independently or as a kind of universally unpopular stooge for the U.N., cannot possibly run the whole world and dictate the policies of nations everywhere, without eventually ruining her economy and, through vast military operations, even losing her vaunted freedoms at home. Permanent conscription, drafting millions of unwilling and resentful young Americans to follow a stupid and confused policy everywhere in the world, is the first dangerous step in losing those freedoms.

The Wilsonian doctrine of self-determination sought to break up such economic combinations as that of the Austrian empire. This empire had already proved its profound economic soundness, although politically, because of its traditions, culture and the curse of the Hapsburg dynasty, it remained in a sixteenth-century state of development.

The explosive conditions created by the monstrosities of the Polish Corridor, the isolation of Vienna, and the Sudetenland in Czechoslovakia, and by the restrictions upon nations such as Germany, bursting with interior pressures arising from population and food shortages and constantly declining living standards, were the result of attempting under an impractical "idealism" to fight the vast nuclear economic forces and to split the world into smaller and smaller independent and largely isolated units. The end could only be disaster, chaos, anarchy and finally a huge and destructive war. And so it turned out. The result was inevitable, simply because every explosive economic force in a shrinking world was operating in an exactly opposite direction. Every economic force today is operating again in exactly the same fashion—against virtually the whole of our international policy. Winston Churchill and many other wise Europeans are well aware of this. Much of the growing resentment against the United States throughout the world arises from the conviction that we are trying to force the rest of the world to follow a policy that is a muddle of fear, sentimentality and blundering, complicated by the hysteria of the "Russian menace," and that runs counter to every force at work. Indeed, we foster European economic federation in theory while we espouse further fragmentation in Korea and in Asia generally. Undoubtedly, one of the greatest initial appeals of Comintern propaganda, however phony, is that of the *United* Soviet Republics. The same idea gives at least a superficial appeal and reality to Russia's "peace campaign."

Save possibly in the case of Russia, these irresistible economic forces are not imperialist in the old-fashioned sense, but fundamentally co-operative for the good of all. Upon their recognition and realization depends not only the eventual freedom of some nations but the economic welfare, security and living standards of *all* smaller nations. It is obvious that a gradual and voluntary development toward complete economic and political union is a better course than the outdated process of semimilitary domination now being practiced by Russia, or indeed than our own course of military intervention and meddling everywhere in the world.

In other words, the gradual union of adjacent smaller states within the orbit of a central great nuclear state can best be accomplished by the lowering of trade barriers, the free exchange of goods, food and raw materials, and finally a common citizenship and currency among all the nations within the group, with economic union eventually becoming political union.

Such obvious nuclei already exist either actually or potentially in the world—the United States (and Canada), Soviet Russia, and in South America the great state of Brazil. A fourth nucleus, as I have pointed out—and a far more natural one than Russia—could possibly one day come into spontaneous being in the heartland of Europe; but the complications and difficulties are so tremendous that such an occurrence within the life of anyone now alive seems highly unlikely. Both Asia and Africa remain still in a state of turmoil, revolution and flux almost like that of the world before creation when no proper solidified nucleus had yet emerged. All our efforts to crystallize political form out of Asiatic chaos have been, from China through Korea, wretched failures and only operated against the immense forces of inevitable economic co-operation. And any future efforts based solely upon the enmity and threat of Soviet Russia and "Communism" are doomed to the same end.

The partition of India into Moslem and Hindu states reduced greatly the potential of India as an economic nucleus. To date it has produced many of the same confusions, limitations and economic maladjustments that complicate to an apparently hopeless degree the economic union of the European states upon any plan comprehensive enough to produce genuine economic stability, enduring prosperity or permanent peace.[9]

One of the extraordinary progressions of our times is the decline in importance and influence of individual European countries (which together, only a short time ago, represented the very center of the civilized and economic world) and the shift of that power and importance into Asia, the Western Hemisphere and even to still half-barbaric Africa. Three elements are responsible for the shift—the disintegration of colonialism, the simultaneous rise of nationalism and, above all, the irresistible force of the wealth represented by the undeveloped natural resources of these areas—a wealth far greater than that of all Europe taken together.

All of these forces, tending to unify large areas around a single rich nucleus, have been confused and hindered and here and there checked completely for the time being by the chaos of revolution and the burden of past hatreds, traditions, illiteracy and many other factors from which man, however eager, cannot wholly liberate himself overnight. And it is in this confusion that the doctrinaire Communists and to some extent the Russian imperialist-Communists make hay on all sides.

10

Unlike western Europe, the United States was born modern. The sum of the characteristics of the modern age—capitalist enterprise, representative government, and unprecedented growth of production, exchange, and consumption—are congenital with the United States. They are the modalities of its existence, peculiarities of its nature. In contrast, when these characteristics appeared in Europe, it was a Europe that had been adult for a long time. For western Europe the birth of the modern world was an upheaval and a subversion. The United States belongs much more intimately to the modern world, and indeed symbolizes it to European eyes. The industrial revolution, the very spirit of modern times, found in the New World virgin soil which had not been worked over as in Europe. Nothing makes adaptation to new conditions more difficult than the perfection with which older conditions have been fulfilled. In Europe, modernity was a revolution which took place within a society that already had its own norms, its own civilization, its own ways of life.

JULES MONNEROT in *The Freeman*

We in the United States, as a nation, have the means of counterbalancing this Communist advantage in at least two ways: (1) By stating clearly the virtues and benefits of the American system of capitalism, which has certainly produced by far the greatest material benefits mankind has ever known and is certainly not lacking on the side of freedom of action and thought for the individual. (Indeed where else in the world do such things exist at the moment in a greater or indeed even a similar degree?) The evidence of the benefits of such an economic system is abundant, but we have permitted it to be identified with a pernicious and outworn European capitalism and have failed to emphasize or clarify it as a proper alternative to both the European system and to Communism. (2) By offering and practicing full economic co-operation with smaller, less fortunate nations on a fair basis, profitable to them as well as to ourselves. It is a pattern that already exists between us and several other countries, notably Peru and is presently being forged between us and Brazil, and toward which many of our foreign enterprises overseas—notably the oil companies operating in Arabia, in Venezuela and elsewhere—have already pointed the way. It is quite the opposite of the old pattern of exploitation practiced by British oil interests in Iran, which has ended in calamity for all, and probably for the Iranians most of all.

Such a nuclear pattern does not mean that the smaller nations are either *absorbed* by the nucleus nation or that they lose their independence and become mere colonies. It is a question of co-operation and common action, which will benefit citizens of the smaller nations, in terms of political and economic security, far more than the citizens of the larger nuclear nations, who have infinitely less to gain.

In the federal union of the United States, made up of forty-eight units of every size and with a great variety of wealth and population, and even of racial and religious origins, it is the smaller and poorer states which gain enormously through sharing the wealth, manpower and security of the larger, richer and more populated states.

Canada and Mexico in their relation to the United States have been steadily approaching this sort of nuclear economic union in which there is a free interchange of manpower and capital and to a large extent freedom of trade. The next step will inevitably be a common currency, uniting, equalizing and stabilizing the value of all three currencies—Mexican, Canadian and American. Since there are in the world, save in the United States, very few large sources of exportable capital for foreign investment, it will be the United States that supplies the capital, either from private sources or through government, for the development of the two less wealthy nations. The process is already in operation, as manifested by the spontaneous flow of more than four billions of American dollars—largely investment dollars of the people—into Canada within less than two years.

The failure of the Mexican government, after the nationalization of American oil company holdings, to carry on oil operations efficiently or profitably is evidence of the reverse of this picture. Today American capital is again invested in Mexican oil and the profits are much greater, while Mexican wages, living standards, purchasing power and general national wealth have increased steadily out of all proportion to the money profits, which are not reinvested in Mexico but exported to the United States. Under complete co-operation even these exported profits would actually cease to be "exports" and would become part of the common wealth and economy shared by the citizens of both nations. And who can question the effect of *complete* co-operation upon the stability of the currency of the smaller nation?

If there were a common currency, with no trade barriers, and complete economic and political union, the benefits to the Mexican people as a whole would be infinitely greater in every way.

Let us suppose that some of the Central American and some of the smaller, less developed South American nations became part of such a pattern of economic federation and co-operation. The results could only be political stability, internal peace and order, and greater national wealth for the countries themselves, as well as infinitely better living standards, a higher literacy, greater opportunity and personal freedom for the vast majority of individuals. It would also end the domination and exploitation of the people now practiced by political cliques and military dictatorships, and the accumulation of vast fortunes by a few families whose intrigues in many small Latin-American nations perpetuate political unrest, economic insecurity and a fairly constant state of chaos. Most important of all, such a federation and co-operation would bring about rapidly the formation of a solid middle class—upon which all real freedom and stability depends in any nation.

Communist agents, sympathizers and propagandists have cultivated enthusiastically and forcefully the intense nationalism that has flared up here and there in small nations throughout the world and which exercises a destructive force away from permanent peace and stability in the direction of still further economic fragmentation. They promote this nationalism, either through design or instinct, because, like the doctrine of the self-determination of peoples, it is in this modern world and in the face of the consolidating economic forces of co-operation, essentially a *destructive* doctrine because the modern world cannot advance save by *increasing* rather than diminishing the areas of free trade, co-operation and eventual confederation. But nationalism ignores co-operation and refuses to accept foreign capital investment, skills, knowledge and financial backing, and thus increases still further the destructive force of fragmentation. The first result is increased poverty, unemployment and unrest, and the final result is chaos—a condition which the Communists seek to create everywhere in the world and the only one under which Communist and Soviet Communist doctrines can make real headway.

Even in Brazil, much of the intensity of nationalist feeling can be traced directly to Communists or their sympathizers, who quickly fasten like limpets to a rock onto any violently nationalist plan or policy. The very *last* thing the Communists wish to see is a strong developing Brazilian nation, working in co-operation with her neighbors in North and South America and possessed of a sturdy growing middle class. An intense and exclusive nationalism would cripple this development and create in Brazil the exact conditions the Communists seek constantly to create in all nations. The more fanatic the nationalists the more support they receive from the Communists and the more they aid Communist infiltration and domination. Indeed at times the fanatic nationalist serves Communism, wittingly or not, better than the Communist himself.

The condition of Iran, engulfed today in the flames of an intense and self-destructive nationalism, is a perfect illustration of the process. It is not strange that an outburst of nationalism should have been provoked to a great extent by the remnants of the old and dying doctrines of colonialism practiced by the British oil interests. A more generous program would have brought greater wealth and stability to Iran herself and in the long run would have produced greater profits for the British shareholders and prevented the catastrophic nationalization of their interests. Today, as confusion, poverty, bankruptcy and chaos increase under a fanatic nationalist regime, Iran still lies wide open and ripe for Communist invasion, both ideological and perhaps physical.

Britain's old-fashioned and somewhat greedy policy toward Iran was in direct opposition to the whole irresistible principle of the nuclear economic pattern. It was a remnant of nineteenth-century exploiting colonialism which has nothing whatever in common with the consolidating co-operatives economic forces now making themselves felt throughout the world. Indeed it seems likely that in one way or another, either through imperialism and military force or economic co-operation, Iran will inevitably fall within the orbit of Russia, whether under the present government or a greatly changed one, coming into existence in the future. I doubt whether any amount of diplomacy or actual intervention can do more than delay such a development. In the sense of nuclear economics, the attraction of Russia for Iran is irresistible—provided always that revolution and political and economic disintegration within Russia do not delay or prevent the process. In reality the same strong attraction exists for the whole of the Middle East and will continue. Who can doubt that under a stable and progressive government, creating wealth and developing the whole nation, rather than destroying its economy continually by vast military expenditures, Russia would influence immensely and in time dominate quietly the whole economy of the Middle East? The failure of Soviet Russia in this area as elsewhere is that she has attempted to impose such a domination by intrigue and by political and military means rather than through economic co-operation. Under Russia's present government and policies the latter method is impractical and beyond achievement. For despite her vast size and resources, she is still a weak nation economically and will be so as long as vast expenditures for armament continue to cripple her economic development, production and living standards.

Throughout the awakening parts of the world today, the urge for independence, intense nationalism and Communism are in almost every case part of the general picture of unrest and confusion accompanying the breakup of the great colonial empires. This confusion plays directly into the hands of the Communists everywhere, and in the process the intense nationalists become as great or greater dupes than the "intellectual liberals" who hold open the door for Communist infiltration. The intense nationalist is himself working counter to forces against which he is in the end powerless and which frequently make him appear an unbalanced fanatic. He is working against the immense tidal economic impulse toward union, federation, co-operation or whatever you wish to call it, to which the only alternative is further fragmentation, disintegration, international chaos and regional wars. Let me point out again that one of the attractions of Comintern propaganda is the idea of the union and co-operation of small, independent or semi-independent nations within the *Union* of Soviet Republics. However disastrous such a union has turned out to be in fact, the idea still has great appeal and is one manifestation of an impulse and movement operating everywhere in the world today.

This impulse is and will be increasingly irresistible, whether it takes the form of American co-operation or Russian conquest and exploitation or simply the sensible union of smaller states into larger and more workable federations. The urge of the intense nationalist is to draw a Chinese wall about his own particular nation and to resent and resist all economic and political co-operation outside the borders of his own country, though by doing so, he handicaps his own nation in a hundred ways, and creates precisely the conditions the Communist desires most—depression, unrest, poverty, inflation and unemployment—and into which he can enter with his specious promises of abundance. The Iranian nationalists have created just such a picture.

This increasing fragmentation and nationalism follow almost exactly one of the main principles of Soviet Russian Communist doctrine. This is first to give the land to the peasants in such small and inefficient, impractical parcels that only lowered living conditions, confusion and hardship can result, and then to take it away again in the form of collective farms on the pretense that allowing the peasants to own the land is inefficient, unproductive and cannot be afforded by the proletariat and the rest of the nation. This has been the Russian pattern of dealing with the mass peasantry, whether in Russia, Hungary, Poland, Czechoslovakia or any Communist Russian satellite country you wish to name.

It is this same progression through intense nationalism, economic depression, distribution of land into small impractical units, and finally to a Communist state that is taking form at the moment in Guatemala, in the old now threadbare belief of the duped nationalists and "intellectual liberals" everywhere in the world that you can do business with the Communists, make bargains and be rid of them whenever you wish. In fact the intense nationalist, however profound his blind and frequently stupid patriotism, is not only the dupe but actually the best ally of the Communists, who when the time arrives will ruthlessly liquidate him and introduce the very form of government, oppression and misery which perhaps he has most abhorred. But by that time it will be too late and if he is still alive and out of prison or concentration camp, he will find his country subject to a bureaucratic tyranny, and exploitation and servitude far more detestable than anything he had ever imagined under the name of imperialism, colonialism, or any of the other shibboleths Communists use to beat a horse which is long since dead.

This now familiar delusion is cherished particularly by many Latin-American nationalists and political leaders and by the intense nationalists in Brazil. Among smaller nations the most extreme and absurd example is that of Bolivia which by any standard of economics, culture, tradition, politics or by any measure whatever, should never have become an independent nation and cannot possibly survive economically as such. Bolivia is merely a chip detached during a typical Latin-American political feud from the geographic and economic massif of Peru. It has no seaport, no wealth but its now nationalized tin, and no middle class; it is unable to feed itself on any but the lowest levels of nutrition; and its general living standards are among the lowest in the world. Bolivia may nationalize its tin, distribute its infertile soil in small fragments among the people and finally follow the general Communist pattern and still achieve nothing save greater economic and political confusion, illiteracy and misery for the people themselves. Even if Bolivia's tin became indispensable to richer nations and a bargain were made at high prices, this would not solve the fundamental, varied and basic problems. These will remain insoluble so long as Bolivia insists upon intense nationalism and detachment from larger more economically fortunate nations.

The fact is that Bolivia should never have become detached from Peru and that its people have little future except as the nation integrates its economy with that of larger and richer nations such as Brazil or Peru. The worst sufferers of the present policy are the poor and wretched *people* of Bolivia. This is the very dilemma faced at the moment by other nations such as Iran and Guatemala.

The problem of the intense nationalists in Brazil is not different in principle from the dilemma of the Bolivian nationalists, but only in degree; and it is less dangerous only because Brazil herself is so immense and her potential wealth and food production so vast. But what a prize this would be for the Communists and their Russian imperialist friends!

VI
Summary

I

The West is no longer gullible. It is no longer weak. It is no longer wholly on the defensive. The Communist power is no longer monolithic, it shows cracks in the Far East, in Europe, in the Middle East, even in Russia itself. The Kremlin can no longer expect to demand something save as it yields something.

WALL STREET JOURNAL, December 3, 1953

The whole period following the end of hostilities—if indeed there has been any real end to hostilities since 1918—has been one of the utmost confusion. It has been a period of revolutions of every kind, caused variously by the mechanical factors which have greatly shrunken the world, by the dubious accomplishments of the United Nations, by the disintegration of the old colonial empires and the accompanying struggle for independence of small nations and by the activities of the Cominform. There has been much loose and addled talk concerning the "world responsibility" of the United States, mostly among the same Utopians who have again and again confused every issue and created actual obstacles to the settlement of the world's difficulties.

Even if this talk of "world responsibility" had much validity, we have certainly failed in almost every manifestation of our leadership, and in many ways, by our muddled policies and general interference in every part of the world, have only maintained the confusion and even agumented it. The truth is that though the world has shrunk, it has not become so small that one nation, even so rich and powerful a one as the U.S., is capable either of accepting and practicing "world responsibility" or even of attempting it, without further confusing the world and bringing ruin upon itself. About the whole of this "world responsibility" school of thought and action there is an alarming miasma of megalomania.

The whole pattern of our interference and of our policies has

233

included little but the old nineteenth-century political ideas which brought about two world wars and are perhaps in the process of bringing about a third, which could easily mean the end of civilization or even of life upon this planet. The whole progression has been based not upon an effort to bring about agreement and co-operation in terms of sound economics, free access to markets and raw materials and food, and the free circulation of populations, but upon the old *political* patterns of world "power politics," "balances of power," "containment," "resistance to aggression," "self-determination," "military defense and alliance" and other shibboleths and practices which have in the past been disastrous to the whole world and make world peace upon any lasting basis impossible. In other words, the whole development of events, in which this country has played the most prominent part, is essentially destructive rather than constructive, reactionary rather than progressive or even revolutionary.

We wish to win the friendship of Asia and make much propaganda about this; but at the same time we support and aid the old disintegrating colonial empires which have exploited the Asiatic people for centuries and are hated by them. We pour billions of dollars into the nations of Europe, which has perhaps saved them from temporary bankruptcy but has done nothing to solve the real and inevitable economic ills constituting the *real* causes of their decline. These same ills also constitute the basis for new disorders, wars and revolutions which serve in the end only to strengthen the advance of Communist doctrine. Our indiscriminate aid has merely obscured the necessity of economic union in Western Europe and has created the illusion that Europe is recovering and need not make any effort of its own toward economic co-operation. The tragedy here is that economic co-operation is the only means of preventing the whole area of Western Europe from either succumbing eventually to the power of Russia or perhaps even Germany or becoming merely another Balkan area with all the evils which the Balkans have long brought to the rest of the world.

We seek to dominate all Asia and to determine its course in history, even to its alliances and the forms of its governments. We sought to prevent the domination of Asia by an Asiatic power and engaged ourselves in a disastrous war to prevent Japan's program of "Asia for Asiatics" only to defeat Japan temporarily and leave the threat of new dominance to Red China and remotely to Soviet

Russia. We have intervened disastrously and in the long run futilely in Korea. This attempt to dominate and direct the whole course, not only of Asia but of the world, is a policy of insanity which can only cause war after war and the eventual ruin of this nation. The future of Asia will be determined, not by a few men in Washington on the opposite side of the world but as it should be, by Asiatics; and if the people of Asia choose to involve themselves in the disastrous experiment of Communism, from which it will take them generations to emerge, that is Asia's problem and not our own. We can do nothing, in any case, to check or to alter that vast rising wave of desire for independence, for dignity, for power that is sweeping the whole of the enormous Asiatic area. How much wiser would we be to follow a policy of detachment, offering encouragement and aid when necessary and when asked for, and to co-operate in the re-establishment of the trade and exchange of food that lies at the root of all the troubles of the world. But instead we seek to restrict trade, to force the countries of Asia into a mold of politics and government which may be suitable in the rich U.S. but is meaningless and even destructive under existing conditions in many Asiatic nations. Democracy in the form of a Republic was attempted in China and produced only warlords, confusion, misery, dictatorship and finally Communist domination. The problem of China's form of government is not our problem but that of the Chinese people. We could help China and the Chinese people far more by opening up all trade, by co-operating with her in the field of knowhow and even perhaps capital investment. Whatever we have done in the direction of China or by our intervention in Korea since the fall of China to Communism has served only to harm the interests of the huge and suffering population of China and to strengthen the hold of the Communist masters. And it has made us no friends anywhere in Asia. Our intervention in behalf of France in the Indo-Chinese area has been merely disastrous on all sides of the picture. It is an intervention and a battle which in the long run can never be won by either France or the U.S. even though we pour more millions and more lives into the debacle for years to come. Even military victory would solve nothing, for it could only bring years of expensive "occupation" and "protection" which can only be futile in the end.

We have intervened everywhere it was possible to intervene, not necessarily for good or for future progress and peace, and frequently with disastrous results, since almost invariably our intervention has had political and military rather than economic motives. The only exception has been the dubious "foreign aid" program, which history begins to show has for the most part operated to bring about exactly the opposite of a unified, co-operating, prosperous world based on sound economic practices. We have largely thrown Asia and South America into the discard for the sake of shoring up the dying colonial imperialist nations of Europe. We have established extravagant military installations in forty-nine countries of the world and have many others, undisclosed, elsewhere. We are conscripting our young men to send them into every part of the world in order to defend peoples who in some cases are indifferent to their own defense.[1] We are supplying not only billions in foreign aid, but more billions in military supplies and in the support of conscripted American forces all over the world.

In most cases our own young men are conscripted for longer periods of service than those of other nations and in some cases our armed forces are larger than those of the nations we are "occupying." We have attempted to impose trade restrictions on half the nations of the world, and by doing so have not prevented the importation of valuable materials into the Iron Curtain nations but have only checked the free flow of raw materials, food, industrial commodities and even poplations, which is the very foundation of any sensible or enduring peace. We are attempting to maintain frontiers in nearly every nation of Europe and Asia. The arrogant assertion that Korea, lying in the very midst of the Russo-Chinese-Japanese orbit, is our frontier is an idiotic assumption which cannot be maintained save at huge expense or the prospect of a third World War and economic ruin. If Korea is our frontier, so then is every nation in the world, and we are tempted to ask whether our future policy will be one of maintaining military installations and conscripted armies in *every* nation of the world. Already the partial application of that policy, together with our interference in world trade and the pressures we have put upon other governments in the battle "to save the world from Communism," have earned and are increasingly earning us the dislike and resentment of peoples everywhere.

The *reductio ad absurdum* came recently with the announcement that the U.S. would co-operate in the establishment of a Japanese defense army of 300,000 men. In Japan, an almost unanimous outcry and real opposition arose on the basis that such an army would necessitate conscription, which was highly unpopular. Presumably, under present conditions, we are expected to conscript young Americans in order to defend not only Korea but Japan. The tentative figure of 300,000 Japanese soldiers seems negligible in comparison to the 3,500,000 Americans now serving in the Armed Forces in all parts of the world. Conceivably we could eventually arrive at the point at which a considerable part of our population would be conscripted not only to guarantee the defense of all other nations, but to fight their wars for them, as we have been doing in Korea.

More recently the Chief of Staff, Admiral Radford, made a speech in which he advocated no reduction whatever in our Armed Forces, while at the same time employing the usual Armed Forces "Trial Balloon" technique of hinting at actual military and naval intervention in behalf of the French in Indo-China.

The "neutralism" of a large element of the European population has a sound, reasonable and logical basis, for in essence the U.S. is seeking to use the European nations partly as a shield in case of war with Russia, much as an invading army might push women and children in front of them to save themselves from the fire of the enemy. Europeans, who would be the greatest sufferers in any conflict between Russia and the U.S., are becoming aware of their position, and are orienting that position more upon the assumption of peace and economic co-operation with Soviet Russia than upon expectation of and preparation for war, which has been consistently our own policy, despite all our talk of peace. This attitude on our part, largely espoused and kept alive by the Pentagon, certain hysterical columnists and certain demagogic politicians, gives perpetual substance and reality to the Soviet charge of warmongering.

2

There is in fact an opinion in Europe, which has begun to carry great weight, holding that in ideological conflicts, it is only after tension has been relaxed that specific issues can be settled.

In any event I am convinced from what I learned in Europe that a principal cause of the divergence and the friction between European and American opinion is over the attitude toward relaxation of the tension. Our official actions are based upon a fear that if the tension is relaxed, the great projects of NATO and of European unity to which we are committed will collapse.

There is a kind of fear that there will not be enough fear to make these projects go forward. This attitude is founded on experience in the long struggle in Congress and in the European parliaments over the Marshall Plan, rearmament, restrictions of trade between East and West and the like. In the last analysis it reflects a belief that the democracies will not make the necessary sacrifices to save themselves unless they are perpetually scared to death.

This is a fragile foundation for great policy. The trouble with relying on fear is that one becomes dependent upon the adversary to keep on supplying the fear in order to make the policy come through. Now it is reasonably certain that whatever else has or has not changed inside the Soviet Union since Stalin's death, the new Soviet rulers have made up their minds to deprive the West of the stimulant of fear, to reduce the tensions which originally evoked the policies and on which they have become for so long dependent.

This kind of tactics could be ruinous to the whole structure of our alliances if we continue to make the main postulate of our policy the fear of Soviet military aggression in Europe. The purposes of our great policies are sound. But they cannot succeed, and they are in fact failing, because they are based on a premise which none of our allies any longer accepts—namely, that we are preparing for a hot European war in the fairly near future.

WALTER LIPPMANN, December 3, 1953

The attitude that another war is inevitable and that we must ruin ourselves by undertaking not only to guarantee the safety of the whole world, but to finance the world and to provide all nations outside the Russian orbit with military materials and conscripted American troops, has been and is consistently being built up in this country through a deliberate terror campaign. But the people, fortunately, are tiring of government "from crisis to crisis," and are beginning to see that many of them actually are contrived or created by actions of our own Pentagon and our own State Departmcnt. The propaganda of terror and war and defense preparations has at times reached proportions in this country, which resemble strongly some of the methods of the practiced and organized propaganda used under the Nazi government in Germany, and for much of it the Armed Forces and the presence everywhere in government of the military brass are responsible.

It is doubtful whether history will ever record how near this nation has come to being taken over by militarism, and the danger is not yet past. In no country in the world, including Soviet Russia, does the brass of the Armed Forces play so great a role in government and policy or so affect the lives of the people. They have resisted bitterly every attempt at reform, at economy or even the reconsideration of our military needs in terms of modern warfare and the Atomic Age. Throughout history in all nations the military forces never make a concession, an economy or a reform until they are forced to do so. They maintain all the old abuses, obsolete principles and practices, and extravagances, and constantly ask for larger appropriations, more power and more conscripts. Tradition, reaction and greed for power of the military have wrecked more than one great nation. One would think it would be enough to finance other nations or even to provide them with military equipment; but the Armed Forces also insist on providing them with conscripted American troops in increasing numbers and fight to prevent any reduction of the number of American troops (now seven divisions) in Europe or elsewhere overseas. The same brass is now preparing to fasten upon the American people a pattern of universal military training, regarded for a couple of centuries by embattled European nations as an evil blight which they would willingly abandon if it were possible. If we did not have a program of intervention everywhere in the world, with division after division stationed from one end of the earth to the other, the necessity of conscripting troops would greatly diminish or disappear entirely and the chances for peace would be greatly augmented. As Clausewitz, quoted earlier in this book, stated, "A nation constantly preparing for war will get war." One might also add, with the complete support of all history, that any government dominated by the military has small hope of ever negotiating a sound and lasting peace and is, on the contrary, inevitably headed for war.

The presence and influence of the military everywhere in our government are dangerous principally for the reason that military men are, by training, experience and mentality, specialists who have been trained for the specialty not of peace but of war. Their presence and influence in government must of necessity be a dangerous one, whether they are known as the Chiefs of Staff in the U.S. or the General Staff under Kaiser Wilhelm II or Adolf Hitler. Only the greatest of military men—the Caesars and Napoleons—ever attained the rank of statesmen, concerned as much with peace, stability and law as with the practice of war; and even the records of these men are clouded by the suffering they inflicted in the achievement of their larger ends. The encroachment of the Armed Forces brass on government and the field of general policy has been on the increase since the beginning of World War II, imperceptible at times but *always* on the increase . . . an increase measured also by steadily mounting demands upon the American people for appropriations, for power and for conscripted troops. The exception voted by Congress permitting General Marshall to serve as Secretary of Defense was one serious indication of this encroachment and was contrary to the wise determination of the founding fathers, who even invested the President with the title of Commander-in-Chief, that the government should be operated by civilians. The results of this concession are regarded by many honest and informed citizens as extremely dubious, and today it is probable that the great majority of Americans favor the nullification of this Congressional concession as rapidly as possible.

The resistance of the Armed Forces of any genuine unification economy, loss of authority or concession for the sake of greater efficiency has been notably discrediting and even sordid. The Navy clings to outmoded machines of naval warfare and resists every effort at economy and efficiency. The Army clings to great masses of foot soldiers which are as obsolete as the crossbowmen of Agincourt save to do police duty for the United Nations or to serve as "occupation" troops. The Air Force, despite its curious record of extravagance and inefficiency, not only resists violently any program which would reduce costs and increase efficiency but even puts out, like a squid, a cloud of misrepresentation. At the time of writing, a Congressional committee is investigating the "incredible" accounting methods of the Armed Forces. Although Congress ordered them to change these muddled methods years earlier, there is little evidence that any notice was ever taken of the order. Even Truman's Secretary of Defense, Mr. Lovett, who rarely questioned any proposal of the Armed Forces for increased power and appropriations, has testified to this complete disregard of the will of the people expressed through their elected representatives.[2]

Many of the arrogances, abuses and extravagances of the Armed Forces came into being during the Truman administration when a President and Commander-in-Chief, who might justly be said to suffer from a toy-soldier-professional-veteran complex, gave the military anything and everything it desired. Under the Truman regime the civilian heads of the various defense departments were little more than the puppets of the Armed Forces.

But the greatest danger has come from the wholesale military propaganda spread through "public relations" officers, over television and radio and in the movie theaters and through the lavish entertainment of newspaper and magazine editors and owners, and in dozens of other less ostentatious ways, all designed to make the American people believe that they are in imminent danger of extermination or at best of invasion. It is doubtful whether Hitler and Goebbels ever attempted a more thorough job than the Armed Forces lobbies of "conditioning" the people to their ends. This all out campaign of propaganda, paid for by the very taxpayers at whom it was directed, has been a tower of strength in securing popular support for these lobbies, unquestionably the most powerful lobbies today in the U.S. government. Both the propaganda machine and the lobbies have been operating at full force since the arrival of the Eisenhower administration and a cabinet of civilian officials who, for the first time in nearly ten years, have made an effort to check the increasing demands of the Armed Forces and to investigate the waste, extravagance and inefficiency within their ranks. These efforts have been met with every possible obstruction, opposition and resistance by the Armed Forces brass both openly and below ground. The worst effect of their propaganda and lobbying has been to make American public opinion as a whole sound warlike to the rest of the world, thus giving substance and reason and comfort to the Soviet accusation of warmongering. By constantly alarming the Russian people and providing the evil men of the Kremlin with concrete and quotable evidence, not only for their own people but for the millions everywhere in the world, that the American government and people are determined to have war, the propaganda of the Armed Forces and the color that it imparts to American public opinion and policy has undoubtedly complicated immensely all progress toward peace and diplomatic negotiations with Russia or even resistance and reform *within* the borders of Soviet Russia.

This factor, taken together with the obvious absurdities of the "containment" policy, our far-flung military installations and occupation troops, and the assumption that we are prepared at any time to send money, men and military materials to support any small nation or tribe which gets into trouble, cannot but produce before the world the general picture of what seems to countless people everywhere the biggest "aggressor nation" of them all. So vast and irresistible has been this pressure from the brass of the Armed Forces that few have dared to speak out against it or to define it as what it actually is.

General Ridgway, Chief of Staff, recently complained of the lack of respect toward the Armed Forces and in particular of the use of the word "brass" to denote the generals, admirals and the Pentagon—again a word which has come into common use because there was a need for it and because it has a real meaning. I would suggest that General Ridgway attempt some small degree of objectivity; he would find that the Armed Forces have asked for what they got.

The fact is that of the nations of the world, from Soviet Russia to the small Latin American military republics, none is so dominated by its military forces in government and in their interference with the lives of citizens. Their influence has been strongly evident in all the operations of our foreign policy everywhere but notably in Europe where responsibility has been almost entirely in the hands of generals, while the status of official ambassadors has sunk at times to the level of that of office boys of the President and the generals. The situation recalls the methods of Napoleon and at times those of the Germany of the General Staff under the Kaiser. The determination to *force* a European alliance against Soviet Russia, regardless of indifference and even resistance, likewise resembles the Napoleonic pattern, but we must never forget that Napoleon was actually conquered in the end. It is scarcely a situation contrived to promote peace either directly or in the reactions of other nations to such a condition.

One other factor which has at times implications which are terrifying is the actual *ignorance* of many individuals high in government and in the Armed Forces, not only of history, economics or any other field beyond their narrow range of training and interests but even of contemporary events and conditions which could have been learned merely from a casual reading of the daily newspapers or the weekly and monthly magazines. Evidence of their ignorance and comparative lack of contacts with the realities of the world in which they are living has come to light again and again, even in the case of the highest executive of the nation.

It is these men who determine to a great extent what our taxes shall be, whether our sons, husbands and nephews shall be sent into some remote army of occupation or intervention to be killed, maimed and tortured. Among these men are many who make incessant and increasing demands not only for more conscripts and for more power and money but also for more and more of the precious raw materials in the form of minerals, oil, and countless other items of real wealth, that are the very foundation of our strength and well being. It is almost impossible to estimate the amounts of these precious resources which in the form of tanks, ships, planes, guns, etc. were poured into World War II and have rusted and rotted away in swamps and deserts in every part of the world, abandoned either by ourselves or by the allies whom we supplied with such a lavish hand.

The greatest fortune of Britain has been until quite recently the quality, the knowledge, the education of the men who have managed her destinies both at home and in the world. Of these men Churchill stands as a brilliant symbol. It was and is not only his character and his courage which make him a great leader and perhaps the only truly great statesman of our time; it is also his wisdom, his knowledge, his information gained not only from experience but from *reading*. The man is a university in himself and possibly no one matches him in the variety and the depth of his knowledge, for it includes not merely information, in which any college don might match him, but an understanding of people, events and even humanity together with the ability to make sound judgments and to act.

One of the tragedies of our time, not only for ourselves but for the whole world, is the fact that the U.S. came into a position of world dominance ill-equipped in able, informed and wise men competent to cope with the responsibilities of so great a position. Many of those in power and authority have been ill-educated men, even in terms of universities or self-education, whose entire experience and point of view has been limited by the borders of the U.S. (which is quite unlike any other country in the world). Or they have been specialists in banking, in industry or in military affairs, with the circumscribed points of view and interests that result from intense specialization in limited fields. There are also men who for years seem not to have read books at all and who seem scarcely able to find time to read the daily newspapers. We are frequently told that they relax by reading detective fiction and murder stories, as if there were some virtue in this.

World citizens, world statesmen, even world politicians with any thorough knowledge of the humanities, of the world, or of history have been rare indeed in the time of our responsibility and in numbers wholly insufficient for the crying need. We have certainly not produced a Churchill or anyone approaching his stature and understanding. Specialization does not produce such men and specialization is very possibly the worst fault of our American education and the greatest handicap to our capacity to assume world leadership and responsibility or to work toward any sound solution of the problems of the world and of peace.

The failures of the Labor government in Britain have arisen largely from the same limitations of education, knowledge and experience. The leaders, with the exception of Aneurin Bevan, have mostly been dull, gray, uninspired mediocrities, whose specialized education and experience has been confined to labor unions. In this respect even Bevan himself approaches world problems as if they were the problems of trade union politics.

Soviet Russia suffers worst of all through the self-imposed limitations of a whole educational policy which distorts history and even day-by-day events, and sets up barriers that prevent the people and even the government officials from acquiring knowledge, learning and wisdom regarding the outside world. She has consistently produced, since the death of Lenin, the most provincial set of politicians the world has known since the Middle Ages. In the affairs of the world today, world statesmen or even men equipped to become world statesmen are rare indeed. We must first produce men with "world minds," not only leaders but minor officials and citizens, before we shall begin to solve our human problems or to set up world government or United Nations organizations.

3

Militarism in every age has destroyed itself.

ARNOLD TOYNBEE

Virtually every manifestation of military activity is a drain upon the lives and well being of our people and upon our whole economy in every possible way. It is obvious that in times of conflict waste cannot be wholly avoided, but when it is constantly snow-balled by widespread intervention, inefficiency and blundering to a size which is unjustified save in the reckless periods of actual war, the drain becomes as dangerous to the nation as any foreign infiltration or influence or treasonable internal activity. Equally costly to the nation in the long run is the unwillingness of the Armed Forces brass to co-operate in the unification program. It is conceivable— and there is plenty of evidence throughout history to support such a conception—that militarism and the domination of government by the military can be more destructive than any external force.

It is ironical that exaggerated expansion of military expenditures and powers is always based upon the argument of defense. Even in Germany under both the Kaiser and Hitler, when constant military expansion resulted in an explosion of aggression against other nations, the excuse and "justification" was that of defense *against* aggression. These are points not to be overlooked in the rapid and uncontrolled expansion of our military air and naval forces.

The waste in money, natural resources and manpower arising from *all* non-productive and frequently destructive military expansion is evil enough in time of real peril and war when we are compelled to look upon these things as necessities; it becomes doubly evil when it exists and continues to grow in time of peace or in such a period as that described as the "cold war."

The evil of this pattern is not confined within the borders of the nation itself but creates a climate of tension, alarm and suspicion throughout the entire world and serves more than any other factor to obstruct permanent peace and even the possibility of reasonable negotiation of international difficulties.

Perhaps no problem confronting us today deserves so thorough an examination as the great power of the Armed Forces lobby in Washington and the steady and unbroken progression of free government in the direction of militarism. But such an examination will be exceedingly difficult to achieve so long as the lobby itself operates in Congress, so long as an unmodified propaganda of terror continues and so long as the influence of the military pervades the executive branch of our government. Their determined resistance to reform is revealed in their constant and at times unscrupulous efforts to thwart the plans of Eisenhower's civilian appointees to restrain or curtail their steadily increasing power. The courage of these civilian officers of government and their determination to carry through their plans in behalf of the people in the face of all manner of pressures and tactics deserves the fullest appreciation from the nation itself.

Again, these words are perhaps unpalatable in certain restricted quarters but I doubt that they are unpopular with the people as a whole and they have long needed to be spoken and written.

Not long ago Bertrand Russell, writing in the *New York Times Magazine*, observed, "People everywhere are deeply troubled by what seems like a fated and predetermined march toward ever greater disaster. Many have come to feel that nothing can be done to avert the plunge toward ruin. They see mankind driven on by *angry gods*, no longer master of its fate.

"I think this view is lazy and superstitious. The misfortunes of the human race since 1914 and those much greater misfortunes with which it is now threatened, have been brought on not by fate but by human volition, by the passions of the many and the decisions of the few."

Whether or not Lord Russell's assumptions are true, it is certainly true that the military powers within this nation are doing little to change such a condition and such a delusion. In no other nation in the world today have the military forces such power in government. They might well be classified as the "angry gods" to whom Lord Russell refers.

4

Men and women get together and create as a sop to their conscience a mass of words. One such mass of words is the charter of the United Nations . . .

We don't cry at the charter any more—we laugh at it. It has been interpreted, misinterpreted and explained. It is the one thing all of us can hide behind when we do not want to fulfill our obligations, and that is not the way to peace.

We talk of peace, we discuss peace, we read and lecture, write books on all the disasters that will follow from a third World War. And yet what do we do to create that climate in which these words can find the right soil in which to grow? What do we do to plant this tree? And my answer is, just nothing.

MADAME VIJAYA LAKSHMI PANDIT,
President of the United Nations Assembly

In October of 1953 the United Nations organization had a birthday. Great efforts and much money were expended by its advocates and the various editors and paid executive secretaries of U.N. propaganda organizations to whip up enthusiasm and publicity. The effort aroused little interest or notice and it is probable that not 10 per cent of the American people were aware of the occasion. The lack of response was universal and indicative at least of an abysmal lack of interest. It was as if the nation regarded the U.N. as a minor debating Society.

This attitude would seem perhaps harmless and logical but for the vast expense, confusion, dissension and tragedy which the organization has already caused, and the troubles which it may cause in the future. If it were merely a harmless debating society, it would never have developed the active opposition that it encounters with almost every action it takes. The assertion that it has brought peace and settled disputes is manifestly absurd. On the contrary it has served to *create* difficulties and ill feeling, and to make large troubles out of small ones that would otherwise have been settled peacefully on a local basis, or which were in their essence entirely outside the limits of U.N. functions as established in the Charter.

As has been pointed out elsewhere, the U.N. was founded to deal with world troubles of a political nature while ignoring completely the economic causes of these troubles—a process which might be illustrated by the case of a doctor treating the patient for symptoms while he dies of the disease. In itself this factor would have crippled the U.N., either dooming it to futility or making it certain that it could only enlarge and distort the world's troubles. Bad as that would have been, in action the U.N. has compounded the evil, and has degenerated into a stage for the struggle between two power blocs, one supporting Russia and the other the U.S. The existence of the veto has paralyzed the U.N. and made any enforceable decision on the basis of world government impossible in any case where there is a dispute between these two power blocs. Thus, the very nature of the way the U.N. operates has tended to create increasing tensions and enmities and to make any real settlement between the two blocs or the two nations themselves more difficult than it would have been if the U.N. had not existed.

It is highly probable that but for the existence of the U.N. we should not be involved today in the insoluble mess in Korea and fifteen thousand conscripted young Americans would not have been killed in battle and another six thousand would not have been tortured to death, and another 130,000 wounded or injured. And the taxpayers would have been spared a vast burden. If the U.N. did not exist we should not today be engaged in a dispute over the admission of Red China to a seat in the organization, a dispute which grows increasingly bitter and which may cost us the friendship and co-operation of many of our existing friends and allies. Russo-American relations could scarcely be worse than they are today and I think it reasonable to suppose that if the U.N. had not existed to provide a platform and loud-speaker for Russian insults and propaganda and for open face-to-face abuse and accusations between the diplomats of both nations, the situation would be infinitely less grave. Certainly in no sense whatever could the U.N. be said to have prevented open warfare. It has served largely to maintain and continue an atmosphere of hatred, accusation and general hostility between the two nations and in doing so has created an atmosphere of hatred and disagreement among smaller nations supporting one power bloc or the other.

The U.N. was fundamentally the conception of the Utopians and was designed and set up, as Secretary of State Dulles has pointed out, on the assumption that the conditions under which the war was fought would not change, and that the world would continue under the domination of three men, who apparently considered themselves immortal. Two are already dead and the third cannot survive forever. And meanwhile world conditions have not only changed but become increasingly complex and difficult so that, as Secretary Dulles has again pointed out, the Charter of the U.N. has become obsolete, almost before it was born.

The assumption that the U.N. would protect the rights and interests of smaller nations has proven equally invalid. As in the League, the smaller nations have no real authority or force in major decisions, but are forced to cluster around the two great power blocs. At the same time the existence of the U.N. has made it possible for the smaller nations to make every sort of appeal for their own selfish and sometimes insignificant ends and to magnify any small dispute or border war that occurs into a matter of world importance. Moreover, there has been a consistent tendency for the U.N. to intervene in the internal affairs of individual nations, over issues that are quite properly the internal concern of those nations alone.

One example of this has been the appeals made from time to time by radical Arab elements for intervention in the affairs of France's colonial empire. One might as well expect Alaska or Hawaii to appeal to the U.N. because they have not already been given statehood. The unwarranted and blundering intervention of our own State Department into the Moroccan situation (later repudiated) is evidence of the degree to which the U.N. may involve this and other nations in a backhanded way in matters which are not properly their concern, save in the minds of the Utopian do-gooders who are the strongest supporters of the U.N.

In a similar fashion the U.N. has displayed a steady inclination to intervene in the internal affairs of South Africa. The internal affairs of the French Colonial Empire, South Africa or any other nation down to the Bantu tribes may be going badly or in a fashion to earn the disapproval of certain lofty minded individuals and factions, but the fact is that these internal procedures are not the affair of any other nation or of the U.N. itself. Intervention either by act or implication or lofty statement will not modify or change these internal actions but will only create resentment and magnify

differences among nations that otherwise would have been insignificant matters of routine.

The tendency to meddle in the internal problems of individual
nations extends even to the affairs of this nation and can be extremely dangerous, owing to an existing clause of the U.S. Constitution which asserts that the provisions of any treaty shall supersede
and if necessary nullify any existing law which is in conflict with
the treaty. The situation is obviously one that menaces the welfare
and the right of the American people to govern themselves and
could bring about a considerable loss of sovereignty. It is especially
dangerous in view of the usurpation of powers by the President
which took place during the Roosevelt and Truman Administrations,
when by tricky methods in order to avoid difficulties with ratification in the Senate (as required by the Constitution) both Roosevelt
and Truman made many binding agreements without ratification
by the Senate, without the consent and even without the knowledge
of the people. These unratified and unapproved and sometimes
secret treaties were defined as "executive agreements." It was this
usurpation of power by trickery that made possible the tragic and
muddled agreements of Yalta, Teheran and Potsdam. The will of
one man, the President, without the approval or even the knowledge
of the Senate or the American people, committed the U.S. to a
whole series of agreements which have since proven to be ill-advised,
blundering and disastrous. It is to correct this situation and confine
the powers of the Chief Executive to the limits prescribed by the
Constitution and the fundamental principles of representative government that the so-called Bricker amendment has been proposed in
Congress. The existence of the U.N. plus the usurpation of power
by the President in terms of "executive agreements" provides a situation of great and constant danger to the people of the U.S.

It is obvious, I think, that the United Nations' power to meddle in
every international crisis as well as the internal affairs of individual
nations without the power to enforce its decisions, or with at best
a power dependent wholly upon the voluntary co-operation of
nations in a kind of international police force, reduces the organization to a level of the ludicrous. Or it would if it were not for the mischievous and tragic possibilities involved.

Few evidences of the absurdity of the do-gooder Utopians are clearer than those exposed in the so-called Human Rights Declaration. A committee of the U.N. spent years wrangling over an agreement to impose willy-nilly on all the nations of the world the implied standards of freedom and equal rights enjoyed by only a few. As the Utopians seek to bestow or even impose representative government upon small nations which are unprepared for it and where it could only be a disaster, so the U.N. sought to impose "advanced" ideas upon all nations regardless of whether their populations were literate or even had words in their languages to define the abstractions set forth with such airy irresponsibility in the Human Rights document. It is interesting to observe that no sooner was the document completed than it was promptly forgotten and thrown into the ash can of international politics.

On the record it is extremely dubious whether the U.N. has made any contributions worth consideration toward establishing political stability or peace in the world. Its capacity for creating mischief and for immensely complicating the grave difficulties of a troubled world is abundantly evident. In the whole matter the U.S. has emerged as the stooge of the U.N. operation. Leaving the vast expense and loss of life incurred by the Korean tragedy to one side, consider the fact that although the U.N. comprises nearly sixty nations, the U.S. pays more than 60 per cent of its costs.

The very presence of the U.N. within the borders of the U.S. has not only provided Soviet Russia with the finest sounding board in the world for her propaganda but unquestionably it has also served her as a base for her espionage operations and the dissemination of propaganda within the borders of the U.S. The action of the U.N. special committee in regard to the suspension and dismissal of U.S. employes of the U.N. who were found to be disloyal or who took refuge in the fifth amendment was an ominous example of the power and will of the organization to intervene in the affairs of individual nations. Not only did this committee, made up of four aliens meeting in Geneva, decide that the U.S. should reinstate dismissed and suspect employes (many of them hired on the recommendation of Alger Hiss); it ordered also that they should be paid very large compensations for their dismissal or suspension. Under such conditions not only would this nation be forced to maintain in its employment individuals of suspect loyalty but in this case would be required as well to pay them substantial damages. Of the compensation demanded by the U.N. committee, the U.S. would be paying more than 60 per cent. Again, there is a situation that would be absurd but for its ominous and dangerous implications for the future. Even ex-Senator Lodge, one of our representatives in the U.N. and himself a supporter in the past of the organization, referred to the situation as "shocking and outrageous."

It is already abundantly evident that in any grave matter of international politics, the nations within the U.N. simply by-pass and ignore it and operate unilaterally or in terms of power alliances. Of this process NATO is the perfect example. Here a group of nations *within* the U.N. formed a frankly admitted power alliance against another nation or group within the same organization (Soviet Russia and the satellite nations), thus nullifying in the most outright and cynical fashion the declared fundamental purposes of the organization.

Again, we have the spectacle of a member of the U.N. (Soviet Russia) making war and aiding the belligerents (Red China and North Korea) who are engaged in war against the other members of the U.N. At the same time Soviet Russia seeks to be placed upon the U.N. "peace" commission as a *neutral* nation. This, as someone has pointed out, is like placing on the bench beside the judge the gangster who is on trial. One is tempted to ask how idiotic and how pompous the human race can become.

But, as I have pointed out earlier, the U.N. was foredoomed by at least a half-dozen major factors. It concerns itself only with the political aspects of world troubles and almost never with the economic inequalities and strains that are the root causes of these troubles. It gives equal representation to all nations regardless of their size, populations, literacy or actual or potential powers. By the very nature of its setup it provides internal government and decision by an oligarchy of four powerful nations who are constantly at odds in one way or another, thus involving in these differences *every* nation that is a member and some that are not. Incident after incident that might have been settled unilaterally between the contending powers themselves is thereby magnified. Under such conditions the U.N. must inevitably degenerate, as did the League, into a struggle between two powerful nations or two powerful groups of nations around which the other smaller and less powerful nations must cluster in self-defense. The veto power held by the four great nations, paralyzing and nullifying any real decision or action, is another factor making for inevitable failure. Finally, the organization has no power to enforce its decisions save as it can depend upon the power of the U.S. or Soviet Russia, possibly the only two nations in the world which today could afford a "police action" of even the feeblest sort.

The fact is that in a world where nations exist on every possible level of enlightenment, literacy, self-government, ideology, economic condition and living standards, there is as yet no place for so-called world government or federation. In such a world an organization like the U.N. can serve only to distort, magnify and increase difficulties and disagreements, all the way from the difficulties between such great powers as the U.S. and Soviet Russia down to the differences between half-civilized tribes on opposite sides of a frontier.

5

It makes no sense to export our manpower now to nations that collectively have far more manpower than ourselves. It makes no sense to pour our military supplies into a Europe that could turn out to be a mere "warehouse" for Soviet Russia. The greatest deterrent to an attack by the Communists on Europe is the knowledge of our certain participation in its defense. It is our immediate use of air power, rather than our immediate use of any token manpower, that would really count. It is Europe itself that must be prepared to meet the first shock of an attack wholly with its own land power. If it cannot do this, it is hopelessly lost.

One of our fundamental mistakes was our well-meant effort to "assume world leadership." Though European politicians urged us to do this, they were not sincere. What they wanted us to do was to implement—i.e., to pay for—the policy that they thought we should follow. Our effort to decide European policy ourselves, and particularly our effort to push Europe into defending itself more than it thinks it needs to, has merely been resented, and has led to much of the anti-American feeling that now exists.

Our real role in Europe was not to lead there, but to follow—literally, to offer to "back it up." What we should have said is something like this. "You and we may not agree regarding the extent of the danger of a

Soviet attack on you. We'll have to leave that to you to decide. But if you fellows will pledge to support each other, we will pledge to come to your defense in the event of any attack which you yourselves decide to repel by armed force. Otherwise we won't try to interfere in your affairs or tell you what to do."

There is still time to follow such a policy. It will mean the termination of our economic aid and arms aid programs, which seem to have earned us only ill-will. As the example of France so outstandingly proves, our aid has been completely futile in trying to prop up a country that does not wish to take the measures necessary for its own recovery. There is more than one indication, in fact, that it is precisely our aid program that has delayed the self-reform and the self-defense that is Europe's only hope for survival.

THE FREEMAN, September 7, 1953

The development and the *use* by Truman of the atomic bomb, under particularly irresponsible and revolting circumstances, have created a whole new problem for the world, perhaps the mightiest problem with which the world has ever been faced. We have only begun to explore the full impact of its implications, not only in the direct and tragic physical sense but in the world of diplomacy and international relations and on the whole picture of military equipment, operations and conceptions. In the U.S. to date little or no effort has been made to adjust the structure of military operations and concepts to the situation, save only to add vast expenditures for atomic warfare in the form of new atomic and guided missiles, while still clinging to the old concepts of huge armies of foot soldiers, obsolete naval weapons and all the old paraphernalia of World War I. No adaptations or adjustments have been made, but only additions; so that the burden of expense increases steadily and destructively without progress either toward economy or efficiency.

The primary consequences of the creation of the atomic, the hydrogen and eventually perhaps the far more devastating cobalt bomb are, I think, obvious. If they are employed in a wholesale fashion, the process means the end of civilization as we know it and possibly the virtual extinction of mankind. We hear much talk of a "shrunken" world but atomic warfare, with the means of spreading its destruction anywhere, has shrunk the world to a degree unconceived of even as short a time as ten years ago. The argument has been made that the bomb is merely an extension of all the weapons that have been becoming increasingly terrible since the invention of gunpowder. This argument is not valid for a number of reasons, and primarily because there has never before existed a weapon that could exterminate whole cities and industrial centers and virtually win a war within twenty-four hours.

Perhaps the primary consequence of the invention and use of the various nuclear bombs is to present us with definite choice of disasters. These are three: (1) that we continue in an arms race between Soviet Russia and the U.S. which wrecks the economy of both nations (2) that we base our defense upon the atomic bombs, continue the arms race into eventual war and destroy each other overnight, with ruin for Europe and perhaps the rest of the world. There is a third choice which, as Adlai Stevenson has pointed out soundly, lies through the door of the conference room. But—and this is a very large but—a conference concerned merely with geographic and national borders and political alliances, with defensive and offensive alliances, with all the old political shibboleths and maneuvers of the nineteenth century, will solve nothing. Although such a conference might bring about a state of eased tensions and temporary peace it would, in the long run, merely lay foundations for future stresses and eventual war.

The primary purpose of any conference must be to establish the free exchange of raw materials, of food, of manufactured commodities, and even if possible wholesale immigration to relieve population pressures. It is quite evident, I think, that such a conference must not undertake to solve *all* the political problems of the world at one sitting or even the economic ones. It should set up a nucleus of understanding and aim for the construction of a sound and workable program that will put the individual countries of the world on a reasonable economic basis and thus alleviate fundamental stresses and strains wherever they exist. Such a conference should be a beginning and the very first step would certainly be for this nation to abandon its policy of containment or encirclement of Soviet Russia. As a second step it could abandon its attempt to impose trade limitations for its own purposes upon other nations, and could aid in the opening of frontiers everywhere to the free extension of trade and the free passage of individual citizens from one nation to another. These agreements *must* be made and this progress must be guided by the strong and powerful nations without the muddling influence of countless small satellites and backward nations or nations wholly without sound economic bases and potentialities sufficient to support their political desires, however passionate, for independence.

The element of *power* is one that has been overlooked on our own side and abused on the Communist side. If one believes as all anarchists believe (and anarchists are merely intense individualists) that the best government is no government at all then I am an individualist to the point of being an anarchist; but my reason tells me that a community with *no* government is out of the question in man's present state of development, whether the community be a great modern state or any of the small Utopian Socialist communities which have failed again and again here and in Europe. Law cannot function nor order be established without power. A world in which countless irresponsible, backward and cantankerous small nations, subject to dictators and demagogues, would be able to keep us all in turmoil and in constant danger of becoming embroiled in their feuds is obviously as nonsensical as a small town in which law, order and administration was given over to the most irresponsible, ignorant and even criminal elements.

Since order cannot be maintained without *power*, in any world in which there is peace, the responsibility for keeping it in order and in peace must rest upon the *great nations possessing power*. It is therefore necessary to concentrate upon agreement, understanding and peace among these great nations without troubling ourselves too much for the moment about aggressions and tribal disorders among all the small and undeveloped nations whose very existence, economic or otherwise, is dependent upon the great nations. We as a nation, have scampered here and there, in recent years all around the circumference of the world, intervening, encircling, creating new tensions and troubles until we threaten to transform the whole world into one large Balkan area. These difficulties cannot be solved so long as our methods and policies constantly run counter to the inevitable forces at work, both politically and economically, to produce *larger* and *larger* nations or combinations of nations rather than smaller and smaller ones. Instead of trying to bring about union on a sensible, workable and economically sound basis we have operated since the establishment of the disastrous "self-determination" philosophy of the doctrinaire Utopian, Woodrow Wilson, only to fragment the world into smaller and smaller, disorderly units, which cannot support themselves and consequently are constantly threatened either by Communism or aggression. In the U.S. there has arisen an unreasonable, sentimental and wholly impractical cult which hysterically sees "independence," without qualification, as the answer to all the ills of the world. Independence in small and backward nations may well bring merely disorder, corruption and tyranny *inside* the nation itself and incalculable troubles for the rest of the world outside.

Aggression may be morally wrong *in theory*, but in practice it can in the long run provide the greatest possible security and benefits for the world, for the smaller nations and an opportunity for lasting peace. There are times when the arrest of a criminal or an imbecile by a policeman might be termed "aggression," but it is none the less necessary. The Roman Peace, the most enduring and profitable the world has ever known, was created and maintained through *power* and *aggression*; and the Roman citizen, whether he was Scythian, African, Gaul or Arab, was much better off in every sense under a powerful, prosperous and orderly state than as an exploited slave of his own small, half-civilized and disorderly community before Rome established order, economic co-operation, prosperity and a sound judicial system.

Neither peace nor civilization has ever been advanced or developed in a world filled with the brawling of small tribes and irresponsible small nations, but only in times of peace, prosperity and order, maintained by one or more powerful nations. We shall have such peace and we shall make progress toward such a goal only when the nations of the world and particularly the small nations espouse co-operation and evolution toward larger and larger economic and political units, until in the remote future we shall indeed have One World. We in the U.S. are contributing little or nothing in that direction.

With the disintegration of the peace and order maintained by the old European colonial empires, even on the basis of power and

exploitation, the world has fallen into utter confusion and revolution which our present muddled and contradictory policies tend to
aggravate and confuse still further. Our main and primary objective
should be to settle the difficulties among the U.S., Soviet Russia and
Western Europe and to establish a basis, however frail in the
beginning, for co-operation and understanding. When that is accomplished it will be time enough to deal with the small, backward and undeveloped peoples, tribes and nations, with the status
of the satellite countries, with "aggression" in Korea and Indo-China.
We cannot work in both directions at the same time, especially in
the atmosphere of tension which the policies of this nation, under
militarist influence, and the policies of Soviet Russia under the
dictator Stalin (who was quite possibly a madman), continue to
create and maintain.

The Europeans of good will are quite right when they assert that
only when this atmosphere of tension is relaxed can we hope to
establish any real basis for reasonable and productive negotiation.
In the meanwhile power must once again maintain order, as Britain
has wisely seen fit to do in British Guiana.

Quite obviously the best way to begin easing tension and restoring the world to some degree of sanity is to open up trade and
permit a free flow of the raw materials, food and manufactured
commodities upon which the prosperity and well-being of all
nations are and must be founded. The effect would not be economic
alone and confined to improved living standards, a better diet and
general prosperity: these improvements would in turn produce a
relaxation of the harsh political conditions within such nations as
Soviet Russia and Red China. For with the relaxing of tensions, these
governments would be able to modify much of their political harsh-
ness, and in general permit the process of evolution to soften Marxian
doctrine and practices within their borders. At the moment there
is little prospect of the relaxation of an arms program which consumes by far the greater part of Soviet income, and under the
present tensions, this circumstance is not likely to change. The
Moscow government is faced by two serious problems (1) the
necessity for vast expenditures on arms, created by the tensions of
the moment and the armament race in which she is engaged with
the U.S. (2) the discontent—not only in the satellite nations but

among the Russian peoples themselves—with the high costs of living
and the inadequate amounts and quality of civilian commodities.
Both of these problems account to a great extent for the belligerency
and intransigeance of the Moscow government.

We have chosen as a policy to seek to strangle trade with Russia
and Red China in an attempt to bring about a steady deterioration
of living conditions and a proportionate increase in discontent
within the borders of both nations. At best, this is a policy of gamble
in which the cards are stacked against us; and by restricting trade
and prosperity, we are simply creating discontent and dislike of us
among the other nations of the world. Very shortly we shall be
faced with the dilemma of either permitting Japan to trade freely
with Russia, China and other Asiatic areas or of subsidizing Japan
with American taxpayers' money and conscripting American youth
to provide her with a defense army. The second horn of the dilemma
is about as destructive a condition as it is possible to imagine, not
only for ourselves but for the whole of the Asiatic world. It could
not be carried through without ruin, and in the process we should
earn the increasing enmity of Japan as well as of China and Russia.
In such a situation, in which China, Japan, Russia and ourselves are
all involved—and indeed all the world—the fate of Korea, if she
does not choose to co-operate, seems reasonably and even in a
humane sense, of little importance. It is a choice between bringing
down a whole world into ruin for the sake of a small, stubborn and
unco-operative Korean leadership or of forcing co-operation from
a people who independently can have no economic excuse for
existence.

Our present policy of attempting to throttle the internal welfare
of such great and potentially great areas and nations as Russia and
China while at the same time "encircling" them is a policy of ruin.
And it is a policy which becomes increasingly intolerable not only
to these two nations but to Japan, to India, to Ceylon, to the
European nations and all the others that for reasons of overpopulation, insufficient resources and actual and real problems of food
must trade in order to live. Not only do we weaken these nations
but we shall in the end alienate all of them and lose whatever
degree of co-operation still remains. It places us in the position of
the hog lying in the manger so that none of his fellows may eat. It

is primarily a destructive, self-defeating and militarist conception and in its operation a policy as detrimental to any hopes of peace as it is possible to conceive.

As has been pointed out earlier in this book, true Democracy is a luxury which is compounded of many things. It must be earned by the people who enjoy it. It is the product of literacy, of intelligence, of education; but it is also the product of prosperity and well-being. In the U.S. we have been fortunate in being still underpopulated and in possessing vast internal wealth in the form of natural resources. Countries lacking in these advantages must manufacture and trade in order to create or maintain good living standards and diets. Where there is not enough of anything or everything, true Democracy has small chance and every sort of Communism, Nazism and dictatorship takes over, if for no other reason than because when there is not enough things must be shared and an absolute state must manage the distribution. (A condition with which the American people themselves are familiar through the sacrifices of freedom and the rationing, price regulations and other totalitarian measures forced upon them in time of war scarcities.) Communism flourishes and spreads where there are poverty and scarcity and the most effective possible way to ensure the spread and the *maintenance* of Communism where it is already established is to apply the pressures and impose the handicaps that produce poverty—which is exactly what we are doing today in many areas of the world. As has been pointed out elsewhere, we have in effect been saying to half the world, "You may not trade with the other half of the world and if you are, in consequence, faced with bankruptcy and near starvation, we will subsidize you in order to prevent your utter ruin and final submission to Communism."

It is indeed a strange policy. Not only is it hurtful to the pride of other peoples and encouraging to Communism but it keeps the world in a state of tension fatal to its peace.

A prosperous Russia, a prosperous China and Japan, a prosperous Europe are the best guarantors not only of peace but of the eventual slow destruction of the Marxian theory (which in practice fails to produce either prosperity, freedom or food) anywhere in the world, including Soviet Russia itself.

6

Certainly Britain, and other Commonwealth countries, want to trade with China. Why not? By blocking this trade—and by backing the Japanese invasion of other former British markets in Asia—the Americans are destroying British and Commonwealth prosperity. As a socialist, I am an anti-imperialist: but the new imperialism of the dollar seems to me at least as harmful as the old imperialism; I know that our small, over-crowded, over-industrialized island must trade to live, and we do not want to live mainly on dollar handouts, grateful as we have been for them. If all that Mr. Dulles and other American spokesmen have said is true, they want a strong British and Commonwealth alliance; yet American actions in recent years—the insistence on an impossibly large defense program for Britain as well as the disruption of British overseas trade—have tended steadily to weaken Britain economically.

Tom Driberg, British Labor M. P. in *Time* Magazine

It is obviously impossible to establish overnight wholesale free trade, but a beginning could be made, let us say, within certain areas where the difficulties would not be too great and where the natural geographical limitations and potential balances of agriculture and raw materials against industry obviously exist already.

These areas are obviously (1) the Western Hemisphere, (2) Western Europe including as much as possible of the European Heartland of the geopoliticians, (3) Russia, China and Japan, (4) possibly India and Pakistan with the rest of Asia.

Each of these areas has the materials, real or potential, for pros-perous, solid economic and human development, and to a large degree is potentially self-sufficient in trade, manufactured com-modities and even food, despite the immense populations which exist in some cases. Who can deny, for example, that if the frictions, closed frontiers and trade restrictions of the Russo-Sino-Japanese area were removed, all three nations would benefit immensely in terms of prosperity, food, general living standards and eventually even free government? Who can deny that in such a vast trading area, unified and co-operating, there would be a very rapid expansion of prosperity and an immense easing of tensions of every kind?

But such an economic union and co-operation cannot come about so long as the old and dying colonial powers, abetted by the U.S., seek constantly to set up in that area political enmities and alliances, and intervene to prevent such co-operation, prosperity and peace. The Japanese idea of Asia for the Asiatics was and is fundamentally a sound idea and one that, if permitted realization, would have by now contributed greatly to the peace and stability of the world. Its economic base was wholly sound and in material terms it could only have *improved* the condition of millions and even of hundreds of millions of Asiatics, regardless of whether or not they maintained that costly and increasingly impossible thing known as "sovereignty." In the case of Japan it was not economic policy or the economic principle of Asiatic union which brought war but the disastrous dominance within Japan of the military forces and the war party and the determination of the Western colonial and industrial powers to maintain and if possible increase their markets within the Asiatic orbit. Inevitably the two conditions met in conflict, with the U.S., having comparatively small trading or economic interests in the vast area caught in between and bearing by far the greatest burden of the cost in money, men and material. This determination by the colonial empires to maintain and even expand colonies and trading centers throughout the Asiatic territory in the end only served further to retard the development of the Asiatic nations, and, on the principle of the vicious circle, to strengthen the intense national-ism and military domination inside Japan and in other Asiatic countries. It also pushed all of Asia more and more rapidly into a state of resentment and rebellion against the West and fertilized the soil for the advance and growth of Communist doctrine.

The ensuing war broke the economic and military power of the European colonial and industrial nations thoughout the whole area so that they are no longer able to *enforce* their domination in a crisis but are being steadily pushed out as Asia wakens in revolution, shakes herself and begins the slow and difficult business of advancing into the realm of modern industrial nations. The fact is that, although at a huge cost, mostly to the U.S. the West won a technical victory over Japan it lost the war. For the Western nations lost colonies, trade and influence and emerged greatly weakened in every way. Power in the area merely shifted, perhaps temporarily, from Japan to Red China, with Russia conniving in the background. As historical perspective becomes clearer, it will be evident that Asia was lost not to Communism but to the peoples of Asia.

In attempting to thwart the powerful surge of economic and political forces, we merely paid a great cost for defeat. If Roosevelt had not chosen to espouse the cause of the European colonial empires in this area—which did not belong there on any grounds, moral, economic, sociological, cultural or otherwise—it is quite possible that Pearl Harbor would never have occurred and Asia would not today stand wide open to the influence of Communism and, secondarily and temporarily, to the influence of Russia. Our intervention in behalf of France in the Indo-Chinese area is merely the last extended gasp of a generation-old policy of backing the past to the neglect of the dynamic rising forces of the future.

The hopeless, bloody, wretched struggle in Indo-China is the last vestige of waning European power in the East and in the end the struggle must be lost as many intelligent Frenchmen already understand. The intervention in Korea, of which we were the dupes, cannot be maintained in the long run as China slowly finds her feet, Russia develops and Japan, like Germany, again rises from the dust of defeat. The world would today be much nearer to a lasting and perhaps a permanent peace if the Western nations, and most of all the U.S., had sought to aid economic understanding and co-operation among China, Russia and Japan instead of seeking to complicate their problems by intervention and to maintain or re-establish for the Western powers, and particularly Britain, the old trade domination of the past. We in the U.S. have been the pawns in the whole affair. We have gained nothing and lost much, including the respect, trust and friendship of millions of Asiatics. The tragedy is that the battle is a losing one which can never be won by the waning powers of a day and world which has gone forever. The insistence of Britain upon the possession of Hong Kong as an "outpost of Empire" must also end in defeat the moment British possession and management of the port ceases to be of advantage to the Chinese and their allies, as it is today and has been throughout the whole of the Korean War.

It is obvious that to destroy or abandon overnight all tariffs and barriers which protect certain minority and frequently selfish elements in individual countries throughout the world would produce for a time confusion and perhaps bedlam, although much less than many people believe. Even adjustment at a moderate rate of speed would produce some dislocations. It is obvious that the dairy industry in the U.S. cannot prosper if great quantities of dairy products from Denmark, where wage scales and taxes are about a third of those in the U.S. are admitted freely and in wholesale lots. This same dislocation would occur with dozens of other industries and agricultural enterprises, but only so long as the U.S. and Denmark remained two *separate* nations. With customs unions, free trade, a common economy and eventually a common currency, the difficulties would quickly be eased, to the immediate and large benefit of the smaller country and with no appreciable long-run damage to the dairy industry of the U.S. There would even be some benefits in so far as the American consumer is concerned. In Denmark a rising scale of wages, resulting from economic union with the U.S., would in time enable countless Danes who cannot afford today to buy quantities of butter to indulge themselves in the purchase not only of butter but of many other commodities, both agricultural and industrial, as well. The difficulties with regard to shortage of dollars would vanish overnight.

Denmark is not the perfect example since geographically it is remote from the U.S., but I have taken Denmark and the dairy industry because the case is so simple and uncomplicated. One might well expand the idea and return to the case of Canada and the U.S. Here there is geographical contingency and an economy which by force of circumstances becomes steadily more and more a common economy. The tariffs that exist on either side are not in the real sense protective or antagonistic tariffs; in Canada their purpose is chiefly to produce government revenue. In many cases American companies which were forced through export into Canada to submit to Canadian tariffs on their products have set up factories within the Canadian borders and in turn have done much to promote Canadian prosperity and employment. The abolition overnight of all tariffs on both sides, a customs union and eventually and inevitably a common currency, would cause few dislocations save in the case of a few bureaucrats and of a few minor agricultural products, difficulties that would adjust themselves quickly enough. The wealth, the power, the well-being of both nations would be enhanced by such an economic union and the possibilities of genuine economic stability greatly improved; and again the greater benefits would be on the side of the less developed nation, although both sides could only benefit in the end.

The principles are simple enough. They are merely these—that the larger the trading area, the greater the internal consumers' market for both agricultural and industrial commodities, and the sounder the indispensable balance between industry and agriculture. The larger the pool of natural resources, raw materials and real wealth, the greater the prosperity and the security of the individual nations and individual citizens. The larger the economic area involved, the less are the chances of friction, either minor or to the point of war. The larger the area, the richer it must inevitably become and the more self-sufficient and secure in all senses of the word, even in matters of defense if the occasion arises.

The reciprocal trade program is a step in the right direction toward free circulation of food, raw materials and manufactured commodities, but it is too scattered, too diffuse and for countless reasons can never be wholly counted upon as permanent. It is a little like an assembly of nations acting as market place merchants bargaining with each other, always upon the basis of the best and the sharpest deal. And, as has been abundantly proven in these times, it is constantly subject to the difficulties, the temporary legislation and the political and economic crises of the various nations involved in the treaty arrangements. It is subject also to vagaries of Socialist governments and their complex bureaucratic regulations and, most of all, to the absurdities of pegged currencies in which the government gives a purely arbitrary value to its currency, usually in terms of dollars, a value which may, as in France and Italy within recent times, be wildly out of line and serve to throttle all trade. The operations of the reciprocal trade policy must at best always be a changing, temporary, patchwork pattern.

Britain has attempted to produce a kind of common economy among the crown colonies, commonwealths and dominions but it has never wholly succeeded because the economies of Canada, South Africa and India are no longer controlled by Britain nor are their currencies truly common currencies. Only in the cases of the crown colonies and Australia and New Zealand has Britain been able to establish any sort of common economy and common currency and here the problem has been immensely complicated and harmed by the sterling bloc principles and by the attempt of the British government to fix or peg the value of the pound sterling at an unrealistic level. Both processes have worked considerable hardship for the people of Australia, New Zealand and the crown colonies while benefiting the home islands, especially the minority represented by British capital and industry. The system is in virtually no way the kind of true economic union suggested and advocated here. Nor is it anything more than a temporary patchwork program, like nearly all the proposals of Lord Keynes, born of crisis and near desperation.

Such a program of economic geographic union as is suggested here must proceed gradually and it must be built from a logical nucleus and upon a sound base. The world reformers would perhaps attempt to set it up overnight, producing the same disastrous confusion and futility that has been produced by the United Nations. The logical nuclei around which to build such a plan have been mentioned earlier in this book—the United States together with Canada and Mexico; Soviet Russia; a federated Western Europe, preferably including the Central European nations. But it need not all be as exact as this. It might be that China, India and Japan would provide an excellent opening pattern of free trade and currency and the exchange of food, raw materials and manufactured commodities, with the smaller Asiatic nations falling inevitably within their orbit.

Brazil, if properly developed, represents a nucleus for an economic union of the Latin-American nations, from which all would benefit. As has been suggested earlier, economic union and common currency among all the nations of the Western Hemisphere could produce a growth not only of common prosperity and power but of civilization and power such as the world has never seen.

I repeat for emphasis that this pattern should develop slowly and solidly, that it should rest preferably upon a compact geographic basis and that it should develop from a nucleus, growing constantly outward.

It is the sole process by which all the world may attain security and prosperity. It is the sole reasonable basis for the advance of education and living standards everywhere. In the end it is the *only* basis for permanent peace, which even the domination of the world by one powerful nation cannot provide since such a world would still be in a constant state of smoldering rebellion.

Let us look far into the future, perhaps too far for most of us to see clearly. As each of these nuclear economic areas grew, spread and prospered there would inevitably come a time when two or three of these areas would see the huge advantages of merging and further increasing trade, distribution of food, raw materials and all commodities to create a still vaster area of security and self-sufficiency. And so the process might continue until there existed in reality One World, founded upon reason, intelligence, economic common sense and reality, with all the real reasons for war eliminated, with living standards leveled off at a high plane and a decent diet for everyone. Until that time, the existence of these large, geographically sound, self-sufficient economic units could only serve to improve constantly the standards of living and civilization for all concerned.

Such a pattern of world peace and stability will never come into being so long as small individual nations refuse to co-operate economically, or so long as the political patterns and practices of the nineteenth century and even earlier still prevail, as they prevail today. A new world cannot come into being so long as Soviet Russia and the U.S. continue to involve the whole world in their enmities, bickerings and mutual interference in each other's problems.

A fresh start is needed and it cannot be even attempted so long as the military tactics and the policies of the Generals dominate international relations. There is something degrading to the whole human race in the fact that supposedly civilized people still continue to operate in the field of foreign relations and negotiation on the basis of military force and under the influence and even the direction of the professional military mind.

We have discussed the case for the vast and rich self-contained economic orbit which lies within the Western Hemisphere. The case for the economic union and eventual political federation of the nations of Western Europe has been discussed so thoroughly by statesmen, politicians, press and experienced writers that anything that might be written here would only be a repetition of familiar arguments. There seems to be universal acceptance of the idea, with

opposition arising here and there only from chauvinistic or opportunist politicians and old-fashioned cartellist capitalism. The greatest
obstacle lies in the intransigent attitude of Britain, both from the
Labor and the Conservative parties. Their opposition is based upon
two assumptions: (1) that a united Europe would provide an over-
whelmingly strong trade competition for the industry of the British
Isles, (2) that Britain will again attain the great wealth and power
that she knew in the immediate past.

The first objection has validity, as has been shown in the past
and is being shown now by the rising world competition of a re-
viving Germany alone, especially under the impetus of free enterprise principles. It is highly possible that Britain as part of a United
States of Europe, participating in the advantages of such a union
rather than attempting competition, under a semi-Socialized state,
would be far more prosperous and in the future far more important
in world politics than she is today.

The other path for Britain would be to attempt to maintain the
artificial trade areas among the commonwealths, dominions and
colonies which exist within the artificial sterling bloc economy, but
the situation is extremely unstable and cannot be maintained once
the components realize, as they have already begun to do, the great
economic handicaps and complications affecting themselves. Such
an artificial union and co-operation could only become stabilized
and permanent within the borders of a thoroughly co-operative
economy, operating not for the principal benefit of Britain alone
but on a basis of complete equality, and including all the remaining
portions of the Empire and possibly even the U.S. and the Western
Hemisphere. This would establish an enormous, prosperous, self-
contained and stable economic orbit, but in it Great Britain would
be forced to play a minor role, a sacrifice which as yet she is quite
unwilling to make. Indeed, the problem of the future of Britain is
one of the most difficult and complex faced by any nation in the
world today. It can eventually be solved for the good of the British
people only upon the principle of equality of co-operation with
richer, more fortunate, younger nations rather than upon the old
basis of economic and colonial dominance which has been shattered
and cannot be restored.

The condition of France at the moment is not an encouraging

one, nor calculated to hasten European federation. Handicapped
as always by the multiparty system of republican government and
the inherent individualism of the French character, she represents
a state of economic instability in which the evils of cartellism are
balanced against the Socialism which it is largely responsible for creating. What happened in France illustrates brilliantly how Socialism
and bureaucracy make their creeping advance—a development feared
by many in the U.S. There the people are saddled by a steadily growing, burdensome and expensive bureaucracy, while the government
finds itself, without quite understanding how or why, in every kind
of business and trade activity once assumed to belong to the field
of private enterprise. The result is economic confusion, inflation,
high taxes and general loose ends. And it all came about almost
without the realization of the French people. A bit here and a bit
there, and France discovers that she is close to being a Socialist
nation with all the handicaps in taxes, living standards, restrictions
of energy and initiative which have become the obvious signs of
Socialist government everywhere.

In the general European picture and in relation to our own aggressive policies in Europe, she does not represent what could be called
an ally of great potential stability. As was pointed out earlier, it is
possible indeed that only a genuine revolution, perhaps even of
violence, can alter the paralyzing form of her multiparty government and free her from the mass of economic and political evils
which have been mounting slowly and steadily since the end of
World War I, and which received a great impetus during the
Popular Front government of the thirties. The old fear of Germany
and the traditional antagonisms of culture and character are still
operating strongly in France and have managed at the time of
writing not only to slow up economic progress but virtually to
paralyze the whole plan of joint European defense and European
economic federation. At the same time, the French government
continues to demand *increasing* financial and military aid from the
U.S. and the maintenance in Europe of a huge army of nearly eight
divisions of conscripted American troops for her defense, though
almost overnight, she might fall into violent revolution and emerge
as an ally of Russia.

France and in some respects Britain offer the extraordinary picture of old-fashioned, cartelist monopoly. Capitalism operating within the frame of Socialism—a situation which can produce only the utmost political, economic and social confusion.

Other great obstacles to a world-wide plan of economic reorganization and progress lie in the area of Central Europe, now split neatly in half by the Iron Curtain. The sources of food and raw materials within the area comprising East Germany, Poland, Czechoslovakia, Austria, Hungary and the Balkan states are of enormous and indeed fundamental value to the establishment of a permanent, stable and prosperous European federation and economic orbit. It is here that negotiation with Soviet Russia upon some free trade basis becomes indispensable to the whole European plan, but such arrangements can never be established in the present atmosphere of military threat, political juggling and general confusion to which our own foreign and military policies have contributed and are continuing to contribute so much.

7

The way to Peace is through the door of the conference room.

ADLAI STEVENSON

It seems clear to me and to many more experienced observers that the foundation of any real peace, or merely the beginning of negotiations in that direction, must be based upon expanding and freer trade of all sorts. I am not suggesting that it be undertaken on any world-wide scale all at once, which would only create economic chaos and a political confusion like that created by the United Nations' attempt to set up world government overnight. What I am urging is the expansion of free trade within given large orbits where it might well go into operation at once to the benefit of all concerned. The irresistible trade and economic attraction of Soviet Russia and the Western European nations was immensely evident in Czarist times, and until World War II, and it is still evident today in the tentative and increasingly strong efforts in that direction from both sides of the Iron Curtain. To put it crudely, Western Russia and Eastern Europe, now behind the Iron Curtain, have what Western Europe needs and vice versa, and a free flow of food, raw materials and manufactured commodities between the two areas is inevitable, whether it comes about through economic co-operation or through domination and conquest by war. Not the least evidence of their irresistible attraction for each other is the constant flow of smuggled contraband materials from Western Europe and the smuggling of gold (recently becoming a legitimate flow) in large quantities from the East to the West. Yet consistently U.S. action has attempted to block and throttle that trade in raw materials, machine tools and other products. Our own policy has been to bring pressure on Western European nations to hamper that trade on the grounds that they must not supply possible war materials to a nation that is a fellow member of the United Nations and with which we were and are ostensibly at peace!

I repeat that in effect our general policy in this situation is to say to Europe and even to some Asiatic nations (notably Japan and Ceylon), "You must not trade with Russia or any of her satellites or allies and the American taxpayer will reimburse you in cash for the losses incurred by this restriction." This might conceivably be a tenable if somewhat reckless policy if it were buying us security and if it made unnecessary vast investments in military installations and the conscription of millions of young Americans to "defend" these same nations which we handicap by such a policy. But the fact is that it does none of these things. We not only pay the deficit we create by attempting to regulate the trade of other nations but we also furnish unlimited quantities of military supplies and conscripted troops— all without achieving much, if anything, in the way of "defense." Worst of all, such a policy serves to disrupt and delay the expansion and development of trade everywhere and so to delay and inhibit the establishment of any real peace and stability.

It is obvious that these restrictive measures are of military origin and certainly do not produce an atmosphere in which world conferences for peace can have any validity or even be attempted with any reasonable degree of success. This is especially so when they are coupled with a policy of "containment" and "encirclement" which involves the constant threat of military installations almost everywhere in the world, many of them virtually upon the frontiers of Soviet Russia. These are perhaps unpalatable and unpopular words to be written at this time but their truth is undeniable.

At the same time that trade restrictions in Western Europe were set up at our insistence, the same policy was undertaken, and without success, in the entire Eastern Asiatic area. Having engaged ourselves needlessly and foolishly in the Korean mess, we then sought to arrest or at least restrict the free flow of trade within the surrounding area. Many politicians and generals advocated an attempt to shut off not only contraband and war materials but *all* trade, a policy which would have created the greatest difficulties and embroiled us in every kind of dangerous complication. The evil effects upon the world in general of such a policy were exemplified by the situation of Ceylon, where we attempted to prevent Ceylon from exchanging raw rubber with China in return for the vital rice supply necessary to feed the people of Ceylon. Again we simply created ill-feeling toward ourselves in Ceylon, India and the whole nearby Asiatic area.

The ironic fact in this Eastern situation was, as has been pointed out earlier, that while we actually fought the Korean War against our traditional friend and ally China, Britain and the British shipping trade carried on a lively business with the Manchurian, Chinese and Russian ports, recognized China's Red government and even supported her claims to a seat in the United Nations! Thus, after all the bitter sacrifices of the Korean blunder in which we were *apparently* defending a small Asiatic nation from aggression, we emerged as the enemy of China and aroused suspicions and hostility throughout Asia, while Britain emerged in the role, however false, of China's and Asia's friend. It sometimes appears that we never win, no matter what we do.

The fact is that intervention by a large and powerful nation which has a concerted policy, either good or bad, can be effective; but intervention here and there and everywhere with no policy at all, and certainly no really constructive policy, can only create new tensions and confusions and chaos throughout the entire world. Certainly our policy of intervention, from the secret agreements made at Teheran, Yalta and Potsdam onward, has been one of confusion and cross purposes, aggravated constantly by the presence and influence everywhere in government of the generals who not only conceived of virtually every problem solely in military terms but actually brawled among themselves over the conduct of the Korean campaign and the entire Asian policy.

In short, our whole international policy since the end of the war has been based upon military and political intervention, never upon any real plan of easing the economic stresses of the world. The results of our actions remain dubious; they may have served only to aggravate the world situation by saving some nations from temporary bankruptcy and thus preventing the more rapid development of co-operation and federation in Europe.

All our pressure upon a reluctant Europe to establish a strong united military force as a "defense" against Russia seems likely to end in failure or at most in an indifferent result. In the meanwhile, it has made constantly more remote the chances of negotiation and peace. The reluctance of the European nations to assume immediately after the end of the war new and destructive military burdens has a peculiar significance. It indicates that the European nations (certainly as well informed as ourselves, and perhaps better, concerning the weaknesses and internal troubles of Russia) have never taken the attitude of terror and alarm which has so carefully been built up in this country by the Pentagon and certain newspapers and politicians.

None of this is written with any intent of justifying or even condoning the behavior of the evil men of the Kremlin. Stalin was perhaps the greatest monster in history, but such a monster is as difficult to replace as is a great and noble leader of mankind, and it is unlikely that Soviet Russia will find the means of replacing him. Again and again he broke his word—a characteristic apparent from the moment he drove Trotsky from power but used as an *excuse* by the men who negotiated the blunders of Yalta. His successors are not, by Western standards, noble or trustworthy men and they still attempt to use the doctrines of Communism to create confusion and general bedlam for their own nationalist-imperialist purposes. In this tactic they have been greatly aided by small groups of psychopathic and power-hungry dupes among the native citizens in almost every country of the world, citizens guilty of a treason far more effective in promoting the interests of the men in the Kremlin and of Soviet Russia than the ideology of Communism, or the Russian duration of the Cominform itself. They have been aided as well by a great soft mass of "Socialists" and "liberal" dupes and by the fanatic nationalists in almost every nation. They have never needed to hire or import special agents, save to direct the activities of the volunteer traitors existing among the "liberals" and "intellectuals" in every country.

The men of the Kremlin are frightened men, frightened not only of each other, but of conditions inside Russia and throughout the satellite nations and the world. They come from a nation which again and again has been invaded and plundered by the nations of Western Europe and only a short time ago was betrayed and invaded by the armies of Hitler and Germany. They are aware by now that—as the recent statements of Kruschev revealed—Russia has made little if any real economic progress since the time of the Russian Revolution and that the Communist system itself must be at fault. They and the Marxian system are responsible for the fact that according to Kruschev himself, there is actually less food per capita in Russia than in Czarist times. They have provided for the people of Russia one of the lowest living standards in the world, unaccompanied by the freedom and dignity which is known even to the humblest Burmese or Javanese. The possibility of providing anything better is obviously remote or unattainable so long as the greater part of Russian economy is absorbed by military production and conscription. The evil men of the Kremlin do not sleep well and they, more than any of us, are aware that Soviet Russia is *not* a united and solid nation.

It has been said again and again *even* by the Pentagon generals that Soviet Russia does not want war and will never deliberately precipitate a condition of war. For the men of the Kremlin, the strongest argument with the people of Russia, their strongest hold upon them, is the threat of attack and invasion, something the Russian people have dreaded continuously for centuries. Our policies of "containment" and "encirclement," our military installations everywhere in the world, our insistence upon a European army of "defense," our constant brandishing of the atom bomb as a weapon serve only to convince the *people* of Russia of the warlike intent not only of Western Europe but especially of this country and thus to strengthen the hold of the Kremlin upon them. Even worse is the fact that such tactics not only strengthen the hold of the men in the Kremlin over the Russian people, but over millions elsewhere throughout the world, and so increase the fear and dislike of the U.S. as a warmonger nation. It would be difficult to conceive any tactics more effective in promoting the cause of world Communism.

At the time of writing, when Churchill has just said that the situation is less menacing but more obscure, we have reached that ludicrous and tragic point in the affairs of nations at which negotiation and conference seem wholly blocked and we are reduced to the level of two gangs of children facing each other on opposite sides of a chalk line shouting at each other, "I dare you to cross the line!" We cannot evade our share of the responsibility for such a humiliating and uncivilized situation. Nor can we escape the fact that the whole military policy of the U.S. and the influence of the generals is largely responsible.

The men of the Kremlin were and are evil and Stalin was a true historic monster but their activity alone could not have brought about so rapid and terrifying a degeneration of relations between this country and a nation which only a few years ago was a friend and ally. There has been a constant piling up of misunderstandings, of deliberate deceptions, of insults and accusations. Country has been incited against country. We are not guiltless, nor is Britain, but the United Nations and on our side the Armed Forces generals, together with a few politicians, have been elements responsible for this tragic degeneration of world relations. Nations have short memories, as history has proven, but no memory has been quite so short as that of the U.S. Here we have already forgotten the brutality and viciousness of the attack, only yesterday, of Hitler and the German people, upon Europe, Russia and the civilized world. We have forgotten Belsen and Buchenwald with lightning speed, and we have forgotten that *both* Russia and France live next door to a nation which twice within a generation, plunged the whole world into war, invaded and desolated both France and Russia and slaughtered their people by the thousand. This fact makes some of our tactics seem not only tragic but cheap and trivial.

8

Many Europeans and Asians mistrust the tendency to dragoon the whole world into two big-power blocs, each professing the noblest intentions and emitting, alternately, highfalutin slogans about democracy and Tarzanlike boasts of invincible might. We have seen this tendency in American and Soviet policy alike. We believe that it is wrong in itself, and likelier to lead to war than to peace.

TOM DRIBERG, British Labor M. P. in *Time* Magazine

What is needed is a new conception and a fresh start. The peoples of the world want nothing so much as peace, a peace in which they can go back to work and live decent lives once more. The nations of the world need peace and no nation needs it so badly as Soviet Russia. She needs peace to consolidate her internal economy and to make some real and lasting advances which will build up the living standards of her people. She needs it if for no other reason than the cynical one of consolidating the territorial gains she has already made and of achieving some peaceful and enduring compromise which will remove the threat of trouble throughout the satellite nations. She needs it as some assurance that she will not again and quickly be invaded by Western Europe. The evidences of her weaknesses in every way increase from day to day, yet the legend of her invincible strength and its ominous threat- which have been sedulously built up in this country and other parts of the world, plus the military policies founded upon these legends and propaganda, make it virtually impossible for her to take any but an attitude of defense, suspicion, bluff and threat.

Let us be honest . . . painfully so perhaps.

President Eisenhower, ostensibly representing the American people, asked for acts rather than words from Malenkov's Russia, before any conferences or negotiations were undertaken. A few gestures were forthcoming from Russia but no act or policy statement of any real significance. But let us look at it another way. Which nation is it that has surrounded the other with political alliances, with military installations, with troops, with fleets? Which nation is it that occupied and created a war on the very frontiers of the Manchuria that was delivered over to Russia by Roosevelt at Yalta? Let us suppose, as I have suggested before, that there were Russian troops and military installations in Mexico and Alaska and Central America and that Russia was marshaling the nations and military forces of the Western Hemisphere against us. Let us suppose that a Russian fleet dominated the Caribbean. Let us suppose that, *under these circumstances*, Russia also had great stocks of atomic bombs and her military men carried on constantly a propaganda of terror, aggression and war. Let us suppose also that our government was a bureaucratic tyranny, and torn with jealousies, rivalries, intrigues and assassinations, and that wholesale assassination by purge was a part of our political system. Let us be honest and ask whether any of these circumstances would induce us, a presumably proud people, to make concessions? Let us also ask how great a threat or menace we would actually be under such conditions.

Let us go a step further and look at the whole European situation in the light of history and of the laws of compensation and retribution. Let us consider the undeniable fact that Germany has arrived at her present humiliating condition because she asked for it, not once but twice within the memories of men and women still middle-aged. Let us remember that the Germany of Hitler was guilty of brutalities, of crimes, of oppressions quite as great or greater than anything in the long list of Soviet evils, not only in viciousness but in number and extent. Let us go back still further and regard the spectacle of Europe itself, a comparatively small area of the earth's surface, which in its rivalries, its intrigues, its jealousies and hatreds has kept the whole world in turmoil for centuries and has twice embroiled this nation in devastating wars.

If we are decently honest we cannot on the one hand charge Soviet Russia with immorality, with persecution, with trouble-making, with tyranny while we absolve the worst offender, Germany, and take her suddenly to our bosom less than ten years after the horrors of Belsen were opened up for all the world to see. Some of the war-mongers have short memories indeed.

These considerations and reflections may be unpalatable and unpopular but they are based upon truth, logic and reason, and not upon the hypocrisy of recent years. Hypocrisy, vast military expenditures, threats, great conscripted land armies, jet planes and atomic bombs will not bring us peace, any more than the confused and futile gestures of the Utopians who would solve all the trouble of the world overnight by wishing on a penny and putting it under the pillow to sleep upon. Peace will be forged out of honesty, out of brutal truth, out of the recognition of the economic facts of life. It will not be achieved by military threats and force and the complicated meanderings and shifting alliances of the nineteenth-century power politics. Nor will it be achieved by intervening in the affairs of other peoples with the pompous statement that it is for their own good when actually we are thinking of ourselves and our "defense." We deceive no one nor do we gain friendships. By now we know that friendship cannot be bought, and one small Asiatic country, Burma, has flung our money back in our faces.

Earlier in these pages I quoted de Tocqueville's nineteenth-century prophecy that there would one day be only two great and first-class powers in the world: Russia and the United States. One of these *is* undeniably a great power. The other is great with vast potentialities which have not yet been realized. Only one of the two among all the nations of the world could now carry on another war without utter ruin. Britain, France, Japan and Germany are no longer great powers, and we indulge in a hypocritical politeness when we treat them as such. We are behaving like the old countess who put on a shabby frock to receive the vicar's wife for tea at the castle. Some of them may achieve great power again, but the chances are small. All of them wish only for peace and an opportunity to work and live decently. The men of the Kremlin are actually afraid and they know, better than any of us, that war might bring them to the same bitter end to which Hitler came in the sordid *Gotterdämmerung* of an underground cave in the heart of Berlin.

We have been talked to death by the hypocrites, the pretentious, the pompous, the Utopians on the subject of our "world responsibility" and the "obligations of world leadership." To date we have made a sorry mess of both principally because in our attempt at leadership we have ignored the very principles that made the U.S. the richest, the freest and most powerful nation in the world. Instead we have persistently followed the old political patterns of a Europe which has finally ruined itself. We have succumbed to the primitive policies of militarism and become dominated by professional generals. We could lead the world but we have certainly not done so. We have merely compounded its already great confusion. Let us recognize our great power and act accordingly, rather than threaten and intrigue and meddle everywhere.

9

Human beings can alter their lives by altering their attitude of mind.

WILLIAM JAMES

Up to now this book has been concerned almost entirely with the material side of world problems because the writer believes profoundly that out of material welfare are born such beneficial things as representative government, education, liberty and dignity. As

Churchill has said, "Democracy is not a harlot to be picked up in the streets." Neither can she be disposed of in a forced and brutal marriage nor be given away to the first passer-by. Above all democracy in the sense of responsible representative government must be earned, and no people can earn it and give it to another. As the wisest of men, Voltaire, remarked "any nation gets the government it deserves."

But beyond democracy, or more precisely, beyond representative government, there are still higher values: those concerned with decent living and the peace which walks side by side with the pleasures of the family, the intellect, with freedom from the brutalizing influences of forced military service (the very first surrender of freedom), with culture and civilization itself. Even under representative government these higher values are damaged or annihilated in time of war or in the Orwellian state of "war in peace" in which we are living. They are seriously damaged and inhibited under any government dominated by the military.

It is curious that all the Utopians, all the eggheads, all the false "liberals" confuse freedom and civilization with plumbing. They would *buy* democracy and friendship. They would *impose* freedom and dignity by armed force. They would give every man in the world a quart of milk or an automobile, even though, as Secretary of State Hull snorted profanely at Henry Wallace's weird statement, "————!!! The Chinese don't even *like* milk."

They would send tractors (as they have done) and road-graders and machinery of all kinds into countries where they are unusable, where their operation would create untold misery through unemployment and where it is cheaper and more efficient to do things by hand. They have immensely confused and weakened the leadership of the greatest and most powerful nation in the world and more often than not they have immensely complicated the tragic problems of the world and cost the lives of thousands of young Americans. In their materialism, they have frequently enough joined hands with the Generals, and in an evil alliance, have promoted new troubles and complications. And yet with all their materialism, they are not realists at all and lack almost entirely the understanding and the wisdom by which man's problems are solved and civilized values continue upon this earth. Very rarely do they emphasize the values that make for civilization, such as thought and reflection, and understanding and sympathy with nature, a comprehension of the universe and its immutable laws which man can not evade or short-cut. They have lost contact with the realities and the fact that a man living in a cave without plumbing can be many times happier, more civilized and wiser than the man with five bathrooms and two cars in the garage.

Science is no more than the discovery bit by bit of patterns and universal laws that already exist, but when the results of science are put only to a materialist use—for comfort, luxury and prestige or to create threats and destruction—then man himself becomes evil, as the men in the Kremlin are materialist and evil, and in the end, like them, he becomes obsessed by fear because he has no values in which to take refuge but material ones.

Thomas Jefferson, like Voltaire and Franklin, had great faith in the common sense, the sensibility and the wisdom of simple people, and there are signs everywhere in the world today that the simple people are beginning to revolt against the "liberal," the "intellectual," the scientist of cold blood, the generals, the ambitious, demagogic politicians. It would not be the first time in the history of the world when the simple people took over and changed all history. They can be awed and browbeaten by oratory and contrived terrors and propaganda and Utopianism and demagoguery for a time—sometimes too long a time—but in the end the wisdom, which comes of living side by side with a neighbor, tilling a field or trading together, asserts itself. It is now showing signs of asserting itself in the U.S. after a long period of confusion, false gods, sentimentality and self-deception. And I do not mean by simple people the insulting term "the Common Man" who in reality does not exist; for all men are uncommon and miraculously individual, in their characters as well as their metabolisms, and to preserve that "uncommonness" is the greatest goal of civilization. I mean by the simple people the man who runs the filling station, tills his farm, sells real estate or automobiles, the skilled industrial worker—in short men who are human and unspecialized, whose wisdom and kindliness grows out of their daily lives and experience. They possess a wisdom that is somehow rooted in God and the universe. They are without vanity, without pretension or without the distorted and psychopathic ambitions which have created so much misery in the world during the past generation. The truth is that we have wandered a long way from

reason and reality during the past generation and our destinies have
been largely controlled by men with curiously distorted and mis-
shapen personalities from Hitler, through Stalin and the Communist
leaders and traitors everywhere to figures in our own immediate
history whose balance and wisdom have been dubious. It is time for
the simple people to revolt. They could scarcely provide a worse
record than that of the specialists, the "intellectuals," the "liberals,"
the Generals who have dominated and frequently distorted their
existence for so long. Believe me, my simple friends, these people
have nothing that you need hold in awe, whether it be their self-
conscious virtue which all too often is mere hypocrisy, or their
withered specialized learning or their strange psychopathic aberra-
tions. The wisdom and common sense which you possess outweigh
all of these things.

There are young people now coming of age who can scarcely
remember what life was like before World War II and the "cold
war." They are essentially the victims of the inventions imposed
upon us by the specialists and the scientists and the generals. The
physicists of bad conscience protest that their discoveries have been
put to evil use in the atom bomb, but they pass hastily over the fact
that it was the most famous of all living physicists who proposed the
construction and use of the atom bomb.

The atom bomb poses vast new problems of military strategy, of
diplomacy, of international negotiations, which may be utterly destructive or hopefully constructive according to how they are
solved. If the atom bomb makes war so terrible that it will be out-
lawed, then the world will have made a great step forward. If it is
used merely as a constant and unbelievably horrible threat, it will
not much matter whether it is actually used or not; it will have destroyed virtually all the values mentioned above. The mere threat of
it will in time corrode away all the reasons for living in terms of
civilization and human decency.

The scientists and the specialists have worked out plans for the
use of the atomic bomb and for an all-out defense against it. Although, as General Ridgway has pointed out, there is no absolute
defense, something known as the Lincoln Plan, designed to be as
effective as possible, is outlined in an article called "For a Con-
tinental Defense" in the *Atlantic Monthly* of November, 1953. It
is written by James R. Killian Jr., President of the Massachusetts

Institute of Technology, and A. G. Hill, Professor of Physics at M.I.T. and Director of the Lincoln Laboratory. It is a horrible document, for it is conceived coldly and in terms of complete materialism and is earnest in its conception and the proposals set forth. It is not impossible that the authors meant that it should shock all of us.

The picture is that of the Wellsian world which haunted my childhood, a world in which I should dread to live and in which no truly civilized man or woman would care to live. It is a world of constant peril and anxiety in which the entire population becomes merely the instrument of the military forces, in which all civilized values are destroyed and the free American people become merely an abject and terrified mass, constantly watching the skies for destruction and living at standards as low as those of Soviet Russia.

I quote from the article:

In advocating a stronger defense of our continent against atomic attack, we are mindful that this is but one part of a comprehensive military responsibility. We visualize that this total responsibility consists of five major tasks which we list without attempting to suggest relative priority:—

1. Control of the high seas
2. Defense of the North American continent
3. Capability to mount a devastating counterattack on the enemy's bases and homeland
4. Our share of the defense of Western Europe
5. Control of sudden outbreaks such as the Korean attack.

This is the perfect blueprint for the ruin of the U.S. as Lenin conceived it. It is the perfect blueprint for the ultimate victory of Fascism or Communism, identical in their evils. It is the scientist-materialist's, the General's conception of an efficient and sordid world. It is also the perfect blueprint for the creation of a world and a life that I would abandon with indifference if I were forced to choose. It is the blueprint of ruin not only for ourselves but for the world. And, together with the entire article, is as fine an example of cold-blooded, inhuman detachment and materialistic laboratory science as I have encountered in the whole of this materialistic age. If this is our only choice as against destruction by the atomic bomb, I will lie down now and take the bomb. It would be much quicker, pleasanter and easier and I should die still possessed of my self-respect as a civilized man.

Notes

I

GOVERNMENT BY PROPAGANDA AND PRESSURE

1. There is a general and dangerous misconception on the part of many citizens that the armed forces are actually a part of government to the same degree as the executive, the legislative and the judicial departments are a part of government. This is not so in any sense whatever, and the Founders of the Republic carefully excluded any such conception from the Constitution and framework of our government. The armed forces have no real powers of any sort beyond those of a police force or the duty to defend the nation in time of war. One of the most dangerous precedents established in our time was the provision passed by Congress in the case of General George Catlett Marshall, making it possible for a general rather than a civilian to head the Department of Defense. The results of the provision are today regarded by many intelligent citizens as disastrous in this particular case, and many believe that this loophole to the invasion of government by the military should be stopped up as quickly as possible. It should never be forgotten by any free people that generals and admirals are not elected by the people to represent them and are not subject to political defeat or recall when their actions are mistrusted or disapproved by the people themselves. The officers of the military forces of this or any other truly representative government are not subject to the approval or condemnation of the people as a whole and cannot be dismissed or put out of government by the direct process of free elections. The armed forces, insofar as the officers are concerned, are actually a self-perpetuating clique outside the realm of popular approval or consent and are not subject to the rules of representative government. Their presence everywhere today in our government to a degree far more extensive than in the case of any other world power, including Russia, in itself creates a danger of militarism and eventually loss of liberties, of which permanent compulsory military service is the first step. In France and England, the generals and admirals are nowhere near as prevalent in government as in the U.S. nor do they hold influence and authority to anywhere near the same degree. Nor do the military forces of any other nation in the world (again including Russia) have such an elaborate propaganda machinery, through "public relations"

officers and handouts and bulletins, paid for by the taxpayers' money, operating extravagantly in their behalf. And it should never be forgotten as a psychological point that in time of real peace, the prestige and influence of the military is greatly reduced, and that the Orwellian condition in which we now find ourselves, in which "war is peace and peace is war," is the ideal condition for infiltration of government and the assumption of unwarranted powers and influence by the military. Nor should it be forgotten that the larger the armed forces the more room there is for officers and the more room for officers the more room for generals. These are some of the considerations behind the persistent attempt of the armed forces to create the impression that compulsory military service should be and already is in fact a *permanent* affair. The propaganda in this direction is inevitably tied up with "crisis to crisis" government. It is a propaganda depending on fear and the employment of vast military "publicity" and machinery now in force. It is unlikely that we shall make much real progress in the direction of sound peace so long as the brass of the armed forces is able, through their mere presence in government, to influence and even to decide so many issues and policies, affecting not only ourselves but most of the world. Their presence and influence in our government lends constantly credence before peoples and nations everywhere in the world to the Communist accusation of "warmongering."

John M. Swomley, Jr., in *Press Agents of the Pentagon*, writes:

"The cost of maintaining such an extensive publicity and propaganda establishment [within the Armed Forces] runs into millions of dollars each year. In 1950 public relations and information had an appropriation of $9,644,143. In 1951 the amount was increased to $12,293,576. In 1952 an alert Congress reviewing a military request for $15,622,903, decided to limit the appropriation to $10,950,000.

"Unlike appropriations, which are a matter of public record, it is not so easy to determine the exact number of persons employed as the publicity staff of the Armed Forces. There is no advantage to the Military Establishment in publicizing the number employed for publicity purposes. Various Congressmen and Congressional committees have tried vainly to discover the number of public relations officials at work for the Armed Forces. A House Armed Services Subcommittee headed by Rep. F. Edward Hebert, for example, on March 7, 1952 accused the Pentagon of holding back at least 211 names from the list of public relations officials it had supplied to the subcommittee. Moreover, many military personnel who are not technically classified as publicity staff, such as chaplains, ROTC instructors, and other officers, are expected as a part of their duty to do a certain amount of public relations work, including public speaking.

"In 1947 the Navy maintained a staff of 601 public relations personnel, of whom 121 were civilians. In 1951 the Navy had 763 military personnel and 81 civilians in public relations work, in addition to those employed in the Department of Defense and paid for by Navy appropriation. In 1952 the Navy had 830 military personnel and 64 civilians in publicity activities.

"The Marine Corps reported 50 civilian public relations employees June 30, 1951 and 48 on June 30, 1952, but did not report the number of military personnel engaged in such work.

"In 1948 the Army and Air Force together employed 810 full-time and 431 part-time military men in publicity activities, in addition to 557 full-time and 197 part-time positions held by civilians in the employ of Army public relations. In the fiscal year 1951 the Air Force employed 276 civilians and 952 military personnel in publicity work.

"In 1950 Senator Homer Ferguson said there were 2,706 publicity personnel at work in the Defense Department.

"A reporter for the *Detroit Free Press* on February 18, 1951, who admitted that 'the figure is hazy' estimated that the Department of Defense employed 'approximately 1800' persons in public relations.

"A few months later, Senator Harry F. Byrd, reporting for the Joint Committee on Reduction of Nonessential Federal Expenditures, stated that the Department of Defense, including the Army, Navy and Air Force, 'this year is using 3,022 civilians and uniformed persons in advertising, publicity and public relations jobs at a payroll cost of $10,109,109.' Included in this total are 2,235 military and 787 civilians.

"Still later, Rep. Burr P. Harrison of Virginia charged that there were 4,200 payrollers working for the 'Pentagon's $10,950,000 a year publicity combine.' "

From "Press Agents of the Pentagon," John M. Swomley, Jr.

2. It should be noted that the people of European nations which have, through the necessity imposed by ancient enmities and *immediate proximity* to hostile nations, maintained compulsory military service for a century, have never regarded the practice as anything but a blight and an evil necessity from which they would free themselves immediately if it were possible. Nor should we overlook the fact that the drafted young American is drafted for a longer period of service than the young men of the great majority of countries in Europe. Moreover, we actually maintain a drafted army that, together with civilian employees, is larger than all the armies of all the free European nations put together, al-

though presumably our young men are drafted to defend a European bloc which has a total population six times as great as that of the United States. Also it becomes clearer each day that the European nations are not so eager to be defended *as our military men are eager to defend them.* What the European nations desire most—the re-establishment of trade and the free exchange of manufactured commodities, raw materials and food between the East and the West—is a development which we consistently oppose and prevent although the re-establishment of such trade would be the first and most important step toward a lasting peace on a world scale. The maintenance of huge American military installations and the "occupation" of Europe by large numbers of American troops is regarded with growing resentment by European peoples, as is our interfering foreign policy and the demands being constantly made by our State Department and military authorities. All of this lends credence and even truth to the accusation that much of our policy is a warmongering policy and that actually we are preventing the re-establishment of trade and economic stability, which are the only real foundations of peace. We are, in the opinion of many Europeans and Asiatics, merely keeping the world in an uproar. There is indeed reason and moral rightness in the growing sentiment expressed by the slogan "Ami, go home!" being chalked upon walls in cities all over Europe. Although the slogan was without doubt of Communist origin and a part of Communist tactics, it has come to have a steadily increasing meaning and validity as resentment and dislike toward the U.S. and our disrupting influence continues to mount in almost every part of the world.

3. One of the soundest and most illuminating documents of our times was the report released in September, 1953, of the World Bank. The *Wall Street Journal* in an editorial commented: "There has long been a tendency in the government to assume that if only enough American public and private capital were available, the so-called underdeveloped countries—like India, Burma, Iraq, Iran and many Latin-American countries—would bloom overnight like a rose. With this in mind, the U.S. Treasury has been made to disgorge large sums in the forms of loans and grants. And the government's foreign aid people have devised all sorts of elaborate schemes to spur private American investment, including insurance against expropriations, revolution, currency inconvertibility and other risks. But the public funds have worked no miracles, and the incentives have set up no deluge of private investments. The World Bank, though not commenting directly on American policy, tells some of the reasons why 'the availability of capital . . . cannot in itself be expected to

remove some of the most important obstacles to economic growth' its report says."

All this is, of course, an understatement in countries where illiteracy can reach as high a figure as ninety per cent, where there has been no education whatever among the people in politics or government, where tyrannical dictatorship in one form or another is the rule and where unpredictable revolution is the constant order of things. "These obstacles," continues the editorial, "which exist in the underdeveloped countries and *can only be corrected by them*, include, in the Bank's opinion, 'the lack of traditions of political responsibility; the weakness of economic initiative; low standards of education and training; insufficient understanding that economic progress requires patience, effort and self-denial.' " It is obvious that the constant and indiscriminate outpouring of vast sums of money by the U.S. government cannot correct all the difficulties and obstacles overnight, nor can they in a more sordid sense *buy* the friendship and support of these nations on any but the most illusory, temporary and shifting basis. In many cases indiscriminate grants, poured out wholesale, merely serve to maintain and perpetuate the unfortunate conditions already in existence through subsidizing the very powers that seek to maintain ignorance and political domination, and actually to suppress education. In a similar way, foreign aid to some European nations has merely served to maintain and preserve the iniquities of the European capitalist system and to block European co-operation and federation by eliminating the extreme and immediate necessity for them. If the necessary reforms of European capitalism and tax systems, especially in France and Italy, are not achieved, and present conditions are maintained up to the point where American resources can no longer afford this particular folly, the result will be a revolution, either violent as can happen in France and Italy, or gradual, as happened in Britain, in the direction of Socialism and eventually Communism. The fact remains that indiscriminate and poorly judged grants and handouts not only serve to maintain existing evils in some undeveloped nations but actually work against the interests of the U.S. (see Java, Burma, et al.). It is significant that many of the still functioning officials of the State Department and elsewhere in government who aided, either consciously or otherwise, the direction of Soviet Russian policy were the strong advocates of wholesale government and extravagant expenditures to aid foreign nations and projects. One is tempted sometimes to suspect that ardor as inspired, either directly or otherwise, by Soviet Russian agents following Lenin's wily plan of forcing the Western capitalist powers to spend themselves into ruin and from economic ruin into the arms of Communism.

4. Even so rich a nation as the U.S., with its vast natural resources and real wealth, may fall the victim of any individual, oligarchy or political party which in time of economic desperation makes big enough promises, whether grandiose and worthless or sound. The overwhelming victories of the first two Roosevelt elections indicated how willingly even the American people will turn under economic pressures to any individual or political group which promises a solution of their troubles. Regardless of individual opinions regarding Franklin D. Roosevelt, the danger might have been infinitely worse, for the American people at that time might well have fallen victim to a potential Hitler or Mussolini or, if the Communists had been well enough organized and strong enough, to the whole array of Communist doctrines. In this respect as in virtually all others, we are really no different from other peoples and are equally subject to violent economic pressures. Many or most of the changes, reforms and regulations, achieved under the New Deal were overdue and were precipitated by the Great Depression. Whether these changes were and are popular in certain quarters, they would have come about whether or not Roosevelt had ever been born. Many intelligent people regard Roosevelt, today, at least in his conduct of home affairs, not as a leader at all, but as a shrewd and sensitive improviser and follower of popular trends and plainly evident necessities. In any case, the greater part of unsound or demagogic reforms under the New Deal have long since gone into the discard and many of those which survived are today bringing stability to our economy and helping to achieve the widespread distribution (*not* *re*distribution) of wealth which is the foundation of American capitalism and high living standards. It is also what makes American capitalism completely different from the European system.

II

THE FAILURE OF A POLICY

1. Indeed, the bearing, dress, manner and presence of this Secretary of State were so thoroughly British that his appearance anywhere outside New York or Washington was actually a political liability to the Democratic Party and to President Truman who yielded the direction of our foreign policy to him and defended stubbornly his every action even when, as in the case of China and Korea, they were disastrous. It is probable that the Acheson policy and influence were one of the major elements in the crushing defeat of the Democratic Party in the national elections of 1952. In any case the Secretary was kept completely under

wraps throughout the campaign and was permitted no public appearances or statements. More than any other individual in power in our government he was responsible for the neglect and deterioration of our Latin-American relations. He, more than anyone, sacrificed the friendship and respect of Asiatic peoples by his attempt to concentrate all our aid and co-operation in bolstering and restoring the power and prestige of the disintegrating European colonial powers, in particular the waning power and prestige of the British Empire. It was a stubborn effort on the part of an Anglophile made at a terrible cost to the people of the U.S. and perhaps in the end to the world.

2. One of the most devastating reports of betrayal ever made public in American history was that of the Senatorial Investigations Committee dealing with these matters, published in 1953. The revelations coming from countless sources, including the F.B.I., disclosed a whole web of mischievous and treasonable activities by countless men and women in positions of low and high authority within the U.S. government. Much of the evidence was concrete and irrefutable and much of it was evidence merely of stupidity, of ambition, of triviality and of a petty desire for bureaucratic power and for the illusion of influencing the events of our time. The fact that in almost every case, from Alger Hiss down to the smallest horn-rimmed official, those guilty of stupidity, folly and actual treason belonged to the so-called "liberal intellectual" group, had its political repercussions in the Revolt of the Common Sense People against this element. This was indeed one of the factors in the elections of 1953 and the defeat of the Democratic candidate for President. The committee issuing this devastating report (which should be read by every American) was a bipartisan committee consisting of five Republicans and four Democrats. The report was signed by all nine members unanimously and without reservation, a fact which should put at rest any accusation that it was a partisan political report.

In its analysis of Communist infiltration into the U.S. Government, *U.S. News and World Report*, for August 28, 1953, has this to say:

"In addition to those witnesses called to the stand . . . the subcommittee also studied the records of those who appeared previously before this, or other congressional bodies. Some of these likewise invoked the Fifth Amendment. Others were persons like Alger Hiss and William Remington, who had denied the testimony of their secret Communist membership and ultimately were convicted of perjury. The employment record of Virginus Frank Coe, who denied Communist membership in 1948 and invoked the Fifth Amendment four years later, was also scrutinized. So was that of the late Harry Dexter White, who died shortly after denying the Bentley and Chambers testimony of 1948, but later was clearly implicated when notes in his own hand were found among the Chambers documents. Virtually all were graduates of American universities. Many had doctorates or similar ratings of academic or intellectual distinction. Eleven had been or still are teachers."

3. Hiss, as is well known, contributed much to the setting up of the United Nations in San Francisco and played a part in the conferences at Dumbarton Oaks and Bretton Woods, was an adviser at Yalta as well as a prominent official of the State Department to whom virtually every policy and every secret was available.

4. At the trial of Alger Hiss, Justice Frankfurter set the curious precedent of a Supreme Court Justice appearing as a voluntary character witness for a man on trial in the criminal courts. And there was Acheson's notable remark that he "would not turn his back on Alger Hiss"—a statement that has much to commend it on the score of personal loyalty and friendship, but still untactful and unwise coming from a Secretary of State who has on so many occasions found the all-covering reply "No comment" so useful.

5. It is probable that the late Senator Taft best represented the classic American liberal in the real tradition of the French Revolution as opposed to the false "liberal" whose politics and philosophy are wholly in the Marxist-Socialist-Communist pattern, which is based on the domination of the individual by the state and the bureaucracy, and the extermination of free speech and even thought. It was Senator Taft who espoused the cause of the railroad workers when a President, lacking an understanding of many principles, sought to draft them into forced service in the armed forces in order to break a railway strike. It was also Senator Taft who opposed vigorously the attempt of the same President to nullify another of man's inherent rights—that of owning property—when in a political bargain with the steelworkers' union, he attempted to seize the properties of the steel companies. In both cases President Truman failed in his reckless political attempts to infringe upon the rights of the individual over the state, and in the second case, it was the Supreme Court which declared his action unconstitutional. This is a fact which must have cheered the spirits of Jefferson, Franklin, Monroe and the other founders who were trained in the true liberalism of the French political philosophers and who designed and built the Constitution upon the principle that the individual possesses basic rights with which no bureaucracy or government may tamper.

The Orwellian idiom again comes into play in the fashion in which the "liberals in quotes" persistently label any assertion of the rights of the individual over the state as "reactionary." This utter confusion of terms has long been an avowed and practiced tactic of the Communists and in particular of the Kremlin—a tactic warmly espoused by our own "liberals in quotes" who frequently enough attempt to reverse exactly the meanings of "liberal" and "reactionary."

6. As a part of the propaganda of the Big Lie, Syngman Rhee, "President" of the Korean "Republic," has been pictured to the American people as a kind of George Washington defending the liberty of his people. Actually Rhee is like the most cantankerous old man in an old people's home who prefers and practices the methods of the totalitarian dictators. He has employed goons to control elections, has suppressed his parliament and thrown his opposition into what he chooses to call "protective custody," a term meaning exactly what it meant to the dictators Hitler, Mussolini and Stalin—merely "concentration camp." There are countless honest Koreans who look upon Rhee as a ruthless dictator on a par with the worst of the Communist satraps. These facts, however, have reached only a small portion of the American public which has access to private sources of information. They would be harmful to those in the State Department and the armed forces which brought about the whole Korean "mess" and seek to maintain and enlarge it.

7. At the time of the Bengal famine in 1945, it was a common saying in India that the famine was a failure since it did not kill off enough people. More recently a distinguished Indian friend of mine representing the Indian government came to the U.S. to purchase the equipment for manufacturing penicillin. At that time he observed, "I do not know why we are planning to manufacture penicillin for wholesale use in India. It will only serve to keep alive hundreds of thousands who would have been better off if they had never been born, who will be prevented from dying quietly only to continue lives which are no more than the apotheosis of misery and wretchedness . . . hundreds of thousands who actually would be much better off dead." At the present moment India is increasing her population at the rate of more than ten millions of people a year.

8. Actually at the moment of writing, the economy of the U.S. and the functioning of its productive facilities are *handicapped* by a lack of labor and especially of agricultural and skilled labor. Meanwhile more than three million and a half young Americans, the very cream of labor productivity, are drafted into the Army, most of them serving overseas in the forty-nine nations scattered over the face of the earth where we have troops stationed. This is not only an immense waste and drain of the productive years of these young men's lives, but also a waste and

drain upon the economy of the nation, since these young citizens, in their present capacity, are producing no wealth or commodities. Moreover, billions of dollars of taxpayers' money is being siphoned off to support them and our far-flung military installations. This drain will make itself felt economically for years after our present muddled catch-all military policy comes to an end and these young men have returned to a decent and civilized life of productivity. One cannot help suspecting that in that lofty tomb within the realms of the Kremlin, Lenin or the waxworks substituted for him, is remembering his prediction about the capacity of the Western powers to destroy themselves and is having a good chuckle.

It is notable that when President Eisenhower and some of his cabinet members suggested that we revise our military ideas and bring them up to date and in line with the realities of warfare by plane, submarine and atomic bomb, a great outcry arose from the military forces, and the demands put forth by the Chiefs of Staff for an army of nearly a million and a half foot troops and for naval equipment which was obviously obsolete remained unchanged. At the present time we have in Europe seven divisions of troops engaged in the "occupation" of Germany and presumably in the defense of other nations which have not conscripted their own manpower on the same scale or for as long periods as the U.S. has done. It is obvious that by supplying conscripted young men from among our citizenry we are not only freeing Europeans from such duty but undertaking as well a continuing burden of billions taken from the average American taxpayer in order to equip and maintain these conscripted American troops. They might properly be called mercenary troops save for the fact that it is the American taxpayer who hires them, in most cases under conscription and against their will. This burden is added to an already vast burden of foreign aid amounting in all to nearly eighty billions. The whole situation may well be described by history as "grotesque" and the direct result of military domination and influence everywhere in our government. As has been pointed out elsewhere in this book, the Orwellian condition in which "war is peace and peace is war" is the ideal soil in which militarism flourishes. As one conscript put it cynically, "You can't blame the brass for not wanting to return to insignificance in a peaceful world. The more soldiers, the more officers. The more officers the more generals and the bigger the pay and prestige and appropriations. Why should you expect military men to work sincerely for peace. . . ." Perhaps a cynical overstatement but it is supported by history itself throughout the ages.

III

A BRAVE NEW WORLD

1. Actual capital available for wholesale investment and development such as that accomplished during the growth of the United States and the world colonial developments of the nineteenth century, is rare today outside the United States save in the vague, shadowy and sometimes suspect international combines, cartels and syndicates. Most of the mass capital free for economic development exists in the United States and is held largely by the bulk of the people through their corporation investments and personal savings rather than by very small concentrated minorities as elsewhere in the world.

2. Only recently Brazil and Peru have concluded agreements which abolish frontiers and are directed toward complete economic co-operation. Part of the agreements is concerned with the development of the whole frontier area bordering the two nations along the upper Amazon. Peru is already operating on a high level of prosperity largely through earlier established agreements and co-operation with the government of the U.S. and with American capital. In such developments one is able to see the beginnings at least of the kind of co-operation that can make the Western Hemisphere the richest and most powerful combination of nations the world has ever known.

3. Even in Brazil, where the old imperialist-colonial tradition is weakest, where race and color lines have never been of great importance, and where the influence of the Roman Catholic Church is least strong in government and culture, the same intense family individualism exists. It might best be described as the subconscious feeling of families that they exist constantly within a walled fortress which they must defend against all comers. In some of the Central American countries, where government is sometimes merely a matter of which clique of families is strong enough to take over, the situation reaches a point where it would be ludicrous if the results were not frequently tragic and crippling to all progress. This feeling is destructive not only of possible progress but of such values as loyalty and patriotism. In Brazil a few families and individuals have made small or large fortunes as Brazilian citizens and then liquidated their holdings and left the country to live in Portugal. On more than one occasion I had had Brazilians consult me about the advisability of such action. This impulse reflects a lack of confidence in the economic and political stability of the nation as well as an intensely personal and selfish point of view based almost entirely upon a feudal con-

cept of family unity and security—an inheritance of most Latin-American nations.

4. Not long after the establishment of Indian independence, the writer was addressing a meeting of the Soil Conservation District Supervisors Association in Colorado when, surprisingly, he noticed an Indian among the audience of American farmers. After the meeting the Indian came forward and introduced himself as a member of one of the great Indian families which largely control the country's heavy industry and even industry in general. In answering my question as to how and why he found himself at a soil conservation meeting in Colorado, he gave the response I suspected he might give. It was this—that his family and the companies it controlled had sent him to the U.S. in order to learn as much as possible concerning soil and water conservation and modern agriculture. As he pointed out, India is mainly a huge country of farms and small villages with very few great cities, and the great bulk of purchasing power is provided by the farmers and villagers, even though this runs on an average as low as only two or three dollars a year. Indian industry in certain fields had, he observed, reached the saturation point so far as potential purchasing power at so low a level of income was concerned. His group shrewdly realized that if industry was to continue expanding in a country where agricultural purchasing power was the very base of its economy, the income, profits, savings and purchasing power of the farmer and villager upon which it was dependent, must be increased. The low purchasing power acted, as he put it, like an iron ring about future expansion of Indian industry. Therefore Indian industry had a direct and vital stake in increasing the prosperity and purchasing power of the farmer and villager. Not only private industry but the government was deeply concerned with this problem and was prepared to spend considerable sums in increasing agricultural productivity and profits. That was why he was in the U.S.—to study the most effective means of achieving this. He wanted also to study the operations of the remarkable balance between American industry and agriculture, which permits the industrial worker and the middle class to purchase at high price levels the commodities of the farmer and cattle grower, while the farmer and cattle grower at the same time provide an immense and prosperous market for the commodities manufactured by the industrial worker. This, as he realized, is a two-way process that enables both to purchase the services—all the way from those provided by filling stations to those provided by garages and motels—which are so characteristic of the American economy and capitalist system. Such a chain, he observed, not only actually distributes wealth and raises living standards but

perpetually creates and recreates wealth and more and more purchasing power.

One of the blackest handicaps to progress in India for centuries has been the absentee landlord, tax-farming system under which enormous land holdings are farmed out to jemadars or rent collectors and sub-jemadars and sub-subjemadars. In some cases there would be as many as four or five of these rent collectors at various stages between the landowner and the small farmer who rents the land, so that eventually only a fraction, although a considerable one, of the rentals finally reach the landowner after jemadars all along the way have taken their cut. Under this vicious system, the small farmer is bled to death and never escapes from debt. At the same time he is victimized by the money lenders (usually Pathans) who are the most hated class in India. Until fairly recently most of the vast agricultural areas of India were owned by a tiny minority of the huge population. In the case of many Indian states, the areas were not properly speaking states at all but only enormous estates owned outright and entirely by the princes, rajahs, et al. Land reform in India, as in most parts of the awakening world today, is one of the first and most acute problems.

5. In Brazil as in many tropical countries, real agriculture is in many areas very largely nonexistent. Farming has been principally a matter of letting things grow. The Brazilians have a classic story illustrating the point. It concerns a traveler who stopped in at a house for water. He found the proprietor lying in a hammock with bananas, guavas, manioc and other fruits and vegetables which are a part of tropical abundance, all about him. The traveler, entering into conversation, asked, "Does corn grow here?" and the proprietor answered, "No." The traveler, puzzled, continued with his questions: "Beans?" "Cotton?" Each time he received a negative answer and presently he said, "But I saw all these things growing just down the road." To which the proprietor replied, "Oh, yes. All those things will grow if you plant them!"

6. The question of corruption and privilege is always a problem in Latin-American countries where such conditions are not merely an occasional and temporary manifestation of disease as in the U.S., but are actually endemic. Under the present government in Brazil these destructive factors still operate. Virtually all imports into Brazil are managed under import license conditions. The desperate import needs of Brazil are for modern machinery, both industrial and agricultural, which would develop and increase Brazilian wealth and its distribution among the great majority of the people. Import licenses for such machinery from the U.S. are extremely difficult to obtain, yet at the same time it is a

common occurrence in Brazilian ports to see whole boatloads of American station wagons and luxury automobiles being unloaded. Import licenses were equally necessary for these automobiles which, largely speaking, contribute little or nothing toward the development of the country and the creation of wealth. The import licenses were undoubtedly issued because the importer had influence in the government. It is obvious that so long as such conditions exist, coupled with the blight of the intense nationalist-Communist reactionary trends, the growth and development of Brazil into a great, self-sufficient and dominant nation will be slow indeed.

7. It seems to me abundantly apparent that the real solution to the difficulties of Argentina—in addition to land reforms, better wages and other interior economic and social adjustments—lay always in economic understanding and co-operation with her vast and potentially rich neighbor, Brazil. Argentine capital, while controlled by a small minority of her population, was abundant, although her natural resources in almost everything but agricultural and cattle land were and are meager. If Argentina wished to bring her industry into proper balance with her agriculture, she should have arranged through economic co-operation to secure unlimited supplies of raw materials from near-by Brazil, at the same time supplying capital to make the exploitation and transportation of those raw materials easy and cheap. Through co-operation in the development of the Plata and Parana rivers, the two nations would have benefited enormously, in terms of transportation and electric power alone. Through co-operation they would in time have developed a vast and almost self-sufficient area in which the agricultural wealth would have provided the purchasing power for industrial commodities and capital for co-operation and development. Industrial development would have provided a steadily increasing market for agricultural commodities and an abundant and cheap source of tractors, farm machinery and machinery of all kinds. Such a large rich area would have proven an irresistible economic magnet for the people of the two adjoining small countries, Uruguay and Paraguay. In time it could have been enlarged to include economic co-operation with so wretchedly poor a small nation as Bolivia, even consuming, through industrial development, the total Bolivian tin supply which is virtually Bolivia's only source of wealth. Who can doubt that such economic co-operation among the five countries mentioned would not have been of the greatest benefit to *all* and have prevented such disastrous adventures as the Peron dictatorship and the economic collapse of the Argentine Republic, which affects not only Argentina but the whole of South America and indeed the world.

8. Countries such as Bolivia and Paraguay have little or no excuse for economic independence. Even political independence is purchased at a severe cost to the people in terms of education, living standards, wages and general well-being. Both nations came into existence almost accidentally as part of a kind of Chinese warlord development during the struggle of Latin-American nations for freedom from the old empires. Bolivia undoubtedly should be integrated economically into the economic and political existence of Chile, Peru or Brazil and preferably into an even larger integrated economy including all four nations. At the present time, as the sources of European capital have dried up and liquidation of foreign investments has become necessary, the resulting vacuum in Paraguay is being filled by capital from Brazil, coming largely from the immensely wealthy coffee and cattle interests. Indeed Brazil has a kind of *sub rosa* government policy of encouraging Brazilian capital simply to *buy up* Paraguay. This is the first step and will undoubtedly be a gain for the mass of people in Paraguay, whose existing economic condition and living standards are among the lowest in Latin America. Presumably Paraguay would in time become a part politically as well as economically of Brazil. The sole disadvantage (and this is a serious one) derives from the fact that the existing pattern of economic absorption is still based upon the old vast landholding, low wage, absentee landlord agricultural pattern of the Spanish and Portuguese empires. The present prosperity of Uruguay might be taken as an exception to the disadvantages which exist for any small nation persisting in the maintenance of complete economic and political independence. Actually it proves the case in the fact that Uruguay has long had a liberal policy of economic co-operation with larger and more fortunate nations and with foreign capital and has benefited far more than any South American nation by the free investment of foreign capital and the exercise of comparatively unrestricted trade. In recent years Uruguay has benefited by a virtual flood of refugee capital driven out of Argentina by the Peron Socialist government.

IV

DYNAMIC CAPITALISM VS. CAPITALISM BY INERTIA

1. The nearest approach to such conditions grew up during the "Robber Baron" period when great fortunes were amassed and later placed in trust funds for the benefit of immediate heirs. These fortunes continued

to increase through inertia and the increase was accelerated by heavy investment in tax-exempt securities, thus creating one of the serious flaws and inequities in the American capitalist system. Most of these vast and largely tax-free fortunes benefit women.

2. I remember the report made by Lord Anglesey in 1933 at a lunch party in the House of Commons on his return from a visit to the Manchester area to investigate the badly depressed conditions there. He said, "I have just seen an almost unbelievable thing. I have seen cotton machinery in some mills that was actually installed and, save for repairs, has been unchanged in nearly a hundred years."

So long as the British cotton industry had little world competition or world conditions were immensely prosperous, the money flowed in even if the machinery was antiquated or inefficient. When presently economic and world conditions changed, it was too late to achieve any effective result by changing the machinery. Behind all of this, of course, lay the principle of "wealth by inertia" and a lack of real competition within industry.

3. Here is a prime example of the destruction of potentially creative working capital under Socialist bureaucratic rule and the consequent rapid shift of tax burdens and government expense from capital and industry to the shoulders of the "people" or those in the lower income brackets. In this sense the *Labor* government, coupled with the pressures of two world wars and violently changing world conditions, was the worst thing that could have happened to Britain's general economy. Much of the capital coming from liquidated and nationalized holdings has moved out of Great Britain, which needs it sorely, into such places as Jamaica or Kenya or Tanganyika in order to avoid death duties and to benefit by the favors allowed to capital expended in developing what remains of the British colonial system. But even in these crown colonies the invasion of capital from the home islands has not in all cases been a benefit. In colonies like Jamaica, already overpopulated, and with insufficient land resources, the purchase of large tracts by British capital has created resentment and political unrest among the politically awakening people.

4. There has always been as well, throughout all history, the man of great wealth and prestige coupled with a certain congenital softness, who espoused Socialist ideas through bad conscience over the vast advantages which he himself did not earn and over his personal failure to accomplish anything real despite his advantages. This type, inclined naturally to demagoguery, began perhaps with Alcibiades and ran through the Gracchi, Engels and the Webbs into our own times where it is well repre-

sented in Communism at the one end and the New Deal and Welfare State at the other. (The reader will be able to supply easily the names of these "Liberals" with great inherited fortunes and/or advantages far in excess of those of the average citizen.) These men of bad conscience and sentimental or doctrinaire minds can be extremely dangerous to any nation or any economy until they are found out. The Anglo-Saxon countries, which abound in the missionary instinct, provide endless examples of the "Rich Liberal." Rich Latins, less emotional and more intelligent, do not seem to be so troubled by the great wealth they inherited but did not earn.

5. One of the most significant actions indicating the failure of the Socialist system was taken by the Congress of British Trades Unions at its convention on the Isle of Man in September, 1953, when the congress voted against further nationalization of industry in Britain "under existing economic conditions." Actually the phrase quoted was a face-saver to soften the full significance of the resolution—that the Trades Unions actually considered the Socialist policy of nationalization a failure in Britain and its extension a danger. This declaration, coming soon after the Russian and German Communists in East Germany shot down the workers of the "workers' Paradise," had a singular significance and indicated the general disillusionment with which Marxian doctrine is coming to be regarded throughout the world and particularly among the so-called "worker class."

6. The billions in aid furnished by the taxpayers of the U.S. prevented virtually the complete bankruptcy of the Labor government in Britain and created an illusion of success which kept it in power and postponed a real reckoning of its failures long beyond the point where the realities were obvious.

7. The idea that "shared wealth" in terms of higher wages, increased purchasing power, and constantly expanding production both of established and new commodities, creates wealth, stabilizes and improves the national economy, and raises living standards, is virtually unknown in European capitalism and industry. Again and again European industrialists have come to the United States and picked up methods which greatly cut their costs, increased their production and their profits, but only in extremely rare cases has a share of these increased profits been passed on to the worker. In a parallel situation much of the so-called "Marshall Plan" money went into modernizing plants and methods which greatly increased profits, but very little of the increased profits ever found its way into the pockets of the worker or even of the general public. Exactly this condition lies at the roots of much of the political unrest

and growth of Communism in certain European nations, notably France and Italy, where adequate tax laws and legal means of tax collections fail to force the industrialist and capitalist to bear his fair share of the expenses of national government and economy. This is the direct and accurate answer to the plaint of countless Americans who ask, "Why, when we are pouring billions into France and Italy, does Socialism and Communism continue on the increase?" The answer is that very little of the billions ever reaches the mass of the people. By far the greater part of the billions has gone into improvement and expansion of industries for the benefit of a very small minority of the people. Even in the cases where so-called "Marshall Funds" were spent directly by governments for the construction of power dams and other public utilities, American aid was rarely reflected in increased wages to the worker. In some cases, pressure from huge industrial and cartelist combinations prevented this potential distribution of American money among the government-paid workers on the grounds that any such increase would cause unrest among other workers and give rise to strikes and demands for increases in wages generally. Indeed, the humbler classes of European countries, particularly in France and Italy, have had little *direct* evidence of the billions of American money poured into their countries.

8. The repeal of the Corn Laws and the delivery of Britain over to an economy unbalanced on the side of industry brought about a large increase in wealth but at the same time a large increase in population, far beyond the capacity of Britain to provide with food. It destroyed not only the interest in the profits of agriculture but in World Wars I and II placed the nation (which could not begin to feed itself) at the mercy of any enemy which could establish an efficient blockade, something Germany very nearly accomplished in both wars. Today, it is generally estimated that Britain has more than twenty million excess population which she cannot feed out of her own agricultural activities, even at a high level of production. This condition forces her to spend very nearly a third of her budget upon the importation of food supplies. At the same time, the neglect of agriculture and its profits produced a steadily declining agricultural purchasing power for her industrial production and made her constantly more dependent on foreign areas not only for food but for markets in which to garner the foreign exchange with which to buy foods. Just before World War I both food production and agricultural purchasing power in Britain had declined to its lowest point. At the time of the repeal of the Corn Laws which protected British agriculture and in effect subsidized it, Disraeli, who bitterly opposed the repeal, observed in Parliament, "This is the beginning of the end of the British

Empire," a statement which must have sounded fantastic at the time but was perhaps the greatest example of foresight in all history. As the Empire began to develop into independent dominions and commonwealths or to disintegrate, the problems of food and overpopulation and lost markets became increasingly desperate, since England could not feed herself without vast expenditures of money outside the islands and sometimes outside the Empire and since the purchasing power of agriculture was too low to serve as a cushion to support industry. It is not well enough understood in the U.S. that agricultural price supports, parity guarantees, direct subsidies or some form of insurance of agricultural profits, are vital to the general economy and will be continued indefinitely because the American economy cannot support the sudden withdrawal of agricultural purchasing power. In the future, as the population increases rapidly, it will not be able to take any decrease in food production without finding itself in the same perilous condition that the British economy is now in. In the U.S. from 1850 onward every economic depression has begun when the farmer could not go to town with money in his pocket to buy the commodities manufactured by industry.

9. It is interesting that the trust fund, which became later the American counterpart of the British entailed fortune, was essentially an Anglo-Saxon, New England and particularly a Boston development. It produced there a series of fortunes which remained largely intact from generation to generation, increasing through inertia in the British fashion, while the inheritors lived on "the income of their incomes" and produced a static society peculiar to Boston and a static economy peculiar to New England. It is undoubtedly true that this "static" capitalism resembled very closely the British pattern and arrived presently through economic inertia at similar results in antiquated and inefficient machinery and methods of operation, which have in turn contributed to the "blight" upon New England industry. The conventration of wealth represented by the permanent and accumulating trust fund has in recent times been weakened by the increasing inroads of taxation, which have in turn tended to induce a continued dispersal of wealth through the gifts of great sums to colleges, hospitals, foundations, etc. It has also led to a more dynamic investment in common stocks and at times even in mildly speculative adventures in order to increase revenue in terms of interest.

10. Vast holdings such as the King and Waggoner ranches in Texas were anomalies and (if one excluded oil), in terms of proportional potential economy, value per acre and productive potentiality, by no means represented the accumulations of wealth involved in many of the great landholdings and concentrations of wealth existing in Britain. It

was not until the discovery and development of the oil industry that the value of such holdings reached immense proportions in terms of wealth. Before then, the aridity, the violence of the climate, the thinness of the grazing, the shortage of water, the long periodic droughts, all affecting cattle, grazing and agricultural production, cut down immensely the value per acre actually and potentially. In fact a great deal of the land included by such large holdings would not, before the advent of oil, have been accepted as a gift by many a sound farmer in the rich agricultural Middle West.

11. One constantly hears talk in Europe of the American "worship of the dollar." In the writer's experience the American respect for the dollar never has begun to approach the average Briton's worship of the pound or the Frenchman's idolatry of the franc, so clearly portrayed in the novels of Balzac and other French writers. Americans have never experienced the economic and population pressures which make hoarding so attractive in the much older European nations. Even if one grants the American's worship of the dollar, he wants it for gambling, spending and speculation rather than to invest in "the sound thing" or to hide beneath the mattress.

12. This process and the tight enclosed concentrated patterns of wealth in Britain are well illustrated not only in economic history itself but in countless British novels, especially in Galsworthy's *Forsyte Saga*, and in the British novel's peculiarly British characters who worship the "gold console." British fiction is also filled with characters of the devoted servitor type, representing men of frequently great ability who never rose, either socially or financially, above the status of servitor to the families with great concentrated fortunes. One finds a parallel in the romanticized sentimental fiction of the Southern plantation dealing with the "old and devoted servitor" but the society which produced the old servitor in the South disappeared after the War Between the States. It was never a society dominant in the American picture and it fell more from its own weakness, follies and bad management than from the abolition of slavery. It withered and died without affecting the American capitalistic pattern at all, largely because, unlike the pattern in England, only a minute minority of the plantation owners turned their land values into industrial or banking investments during the industrial revolution of the nineteenth century.

13. This was certainly not true of a few British families such as the Cecils, who generation after generation produced men of great ability who were distinguished in their own right and made great contributions to the welfare of the nation both at home and abroad. Such families as

these, however, represent a comparatively small minority. It must also be admitted that the British system produced a stability and an economic background for the special training and education of certain members of the privileged class in government, administration and politics which was of immense value to the nation. We could certainly benefit by men of special background and training and education and especially knowledge and experience in American politics and government. Fortunately more and more men of this type are beginning to play active parts in our affairs.

14. Although general conditions in the United States failed to produce the widespread British snobbery, vulgarity and sense of caste, we are not entirely innocent, as in the period of the Robber Barons when Mrs. Astor was "Queen" of New York society. And frequently, even today, ambassadorships are bestowed not on a basis of ability, experience and distinction but in return for large financial or political contributions to a political party. Oddly enough, this sort of "political" ambassador has frequently done a better job than many ambassadors of "career" State Department or military origin.

15. One of the best known is *Les Temps Difficiles* by Edouard Bourdet which the author translated and adapted for the New York stage. It concerned the sacrificial marriage of an attractive innocent young girl to a virtually imbecile young man, arranged by two families in order to unite and "cartelize" their industrial fortunes. At times fiction or the theater portrays far more significantly and vividly even the economic and political aspects of an era than does more soberly written and documented history. Just as the fiction of England in the nineteenth and early twentieth century depicted many of the characteristics and much of the significance of the economic and sociological development and the materialist philosophy of the times, so do countless French novels, and particularly those of Balzac and Zola, provide a similar picture in France. The industrialist and the rich bourgeois and the banker were more frequently than not portrayed as vulgar, common, ruthless, uncultivated and even avaricious and quite willing to sacrifice their fellow citizens and even the happiness of their own family on the altar of their own material success and the preservation and augmentation of their fortunes.

16. Wherever one goes in British possessions or "dependencies" one discovers case after case of hardship and handicaps imposed by the artificiality of the sterling bloc economy and by the licensing and cartelization of British industry. Recently in one crown colony the writer inspected an overhead irrigation system on the land of a great sugar-producing plantation. The system was British, and it provided a brilliant

example of why co-operative and competitive capitalism in the United States produces machinery and other commodities which are sought everywhere in the world over similar commodities produced by other nations. On the writer's Malabar Farm in Ohio there exists an irrigation system of the same horsepower, the same dimensions of aluminum pipe and the same potential pressures. The British-built motor and pump, constructed and mounted separately, weighed approximately three times as much as the American machine. It was clumsily mounted and subject to framework breakage under strain. The couplings on the irrigation pipes were complicated and it required sometimes several minutes of work to attach one aluminum pipe to another. Under pressure the couplings frequently gave way and parted. The cost of the aluminum pipes was three times as much as the pipe produced in the United States and the sturdiness and quality were perhaps less. The American pipes could be coupled automatically in a second or two and under pressures only sealed themselves more tightly. The inefficient and clumsy British system cost on the whole twice as much as the American system with the same horsepower, pressure and capacity, yet the purchaser in the crown colony had no choice. He was forced to buy the expensive and inefficient British system produced under the cartel licensing system which gave the manufacturing company a virtual monopoly on the manufacture of irrigation equipment. I pointed out to the grower that in the United States there were at least four great companies engaged in the production of aluminum irrigation pipe, at least twenty companies manufacturing pumps, and several companies manufacturing sprinkler heads and pipe couplings—all in competition with each other. In any open world market, unhampered by "dollar shortages," the British equipment would not have a chance of sale against the better, cheaper, more efficient American installation. Sterling bloc regulations and Empire preference operating in the crown colonies simply made a forced sale of inferior, clumsy and obsolete equipment, much as sales even of cotton goods were forced upon the conquered peoples of the old imperialist, colonial days. The profits of the *forced* sale went, of course, to the tiny minority of cartel capitalists.

17. Much of the British automobile industry is still engaged in producing extremely expensive luxury cars—Rolls-Royces, Bentleys, Jaguars, et al., for a world in which the market for luxury cars is constantly declining. The industry is aware that perhaps their biggest market is in the United States for those few individuals who want a "showy" foreign car. British automobile manufacturers could not, of course, begin to compete against American-made automobiles in the general market at home or

abroad even in this luxury field and certainly not in their more cheaply priced automobiles. In the one case the luxury car belongs in a freak market. In the lower-priced market the American car is as a rule higher powered, more convenient and far more luxurious than the British or any other foreign car within the same price range. The test of course is that in almost any country in the world the great bulk of the market wants American automobiles and is restricted from buying them only by dollar shortages and immense licensing and import taxes set up to protect the home industry or so-called "dollar exchange." The one complaint against American cars is that they consume too much gasoline and in most European and Latin-American countries gasoline costs two or three times as much as in the United States. The low cost of fuel in the United States arises from two factors, the first being the good fortune of the nation in having a very nearly inexhaustible supply of oil. The other is that American free enterprise, ingenuity and dispersed capital have reduced the costs of transportation and of processing gasoline as a rule far below the costs elsewhere, although the wages of the average oil worker in any stage of gasoline production are frequently two or three times as great as the wages paid to similar workers in parts of Europe and Latin-America. So that in the end not only is the American automobile and its universal desirability vivid proof of the working of free dispersed capitalism but its very fault (the high consumption of gasoline) arises from the cheapness of the gasoline produced by the same economic system.

18. In 1947 a young Englishman engaged to take over the horticultural operations of Malabar Farm arrived in Mansfield, Ohio, and was met by the writer at the train. On the way through this typical, prosperous industrial town (which incidentally has probably the highest average family income of any city in the world) we passed a big industrial plant and a four-acre parking lot filled with shining new, chromium-decorated cars. The young Englishman's eyes popped and he asked, "Is there a meeting of shareholders going on?" I replied, "It's very possible that some of those automobiles belong to shareholders, but all of them belong to the factory's workers." "Good Lord," replied my young friend. "In England a workingman is lucky to have a bicycle." This was, of course, an exaggeration, but not a very big one. But there was more to the story. On arriving at the farm the same young man's eyes popped again at the sight of two bushels of magnificent Hale peaches. With awe, he asked, "How much do all those cost?" and after a moment's calculation, I said, "Perhaps two or three cents apiece." This time he replied, "Just as I left England, I paid two shillings and sixpence for a single peach not

half as good as those." This anecdote I insert merely as evidence to those Americans who fail to differentiate between conditions at home and abroad that all other countries are *not* the same as the United States either in wages, costs, quality or abundance. Even in season in Europe peaches are regarded as a delicacy and a luxury and frequently are served elaborately *un*peeled on cotton in expensive restaurants. To be sure climate and soils and abundant fertility also play their part in the excellence, abundance and cheapness of the peaches in the U.S. All that too is a part of America's good fortune in possessing vast natural resources and real wealth. Nevertheless agricultural and horticultural development, research and other factors involving enterprise have made their contributions as well, contributions frequently far advanced over those of some other countries, and made possible to a large extent by the operation of free, dispersed, competitive and co-operative capitalism within the United States.

19. Sears Roebuck, in opening one of its great stores in one Latin-American country, encountered a good deal of opposition in one way or another, since the Sears ideas of merchandising, which have made the corporation one of the greatest on earth (incidentally a very great proportion of its shares is held by employees), were almost wholly new in that country. The principal source of bewilderment and even indignant opposition arose from the Sears policy of marketing a useful and popular article as rapidly, as widely and as cheaply as possible, or in other words, of extending greatly the base of demand and sale and production at low profit for the benefit of the customer while at the same time providing a constantly broader base of employment. The Latin-American reaction was that this was a foolish policy and that when a great demand developed for a given commodity, the company should immediately raise prices and make a bigger and bigger profit—with the result that the market for it would eventually be killed. The reaction was an excellent example of the difference between dynamic American capitalism, sharing profits through stockholders, maintaining a constant demand and putting its commodities within the purchasing power of almost anyone, and the primitive closed economy of an Arab merchant trying to squeeze a high profit in a quick market. Some competitors attacked such methods as "unfair." Incidentally, Sears' methods of display and merchandising have already had a considerable influence in Brazil and may eventually bring about a revolution in merchandising which could be highly beneficial to the whole nation.

V

THE WORLD FAILURE AND DECLINE OF THE MARXIAN ILLUSION

1. The foundation of the success of Belgium in dealing with her colonial empire is undoubtedly the fact that she has placed almost the whole emphasis upon the improvement of *material* conditions. The rest, the abstractions, the idealism, the political education follow logically, naturally and in good time.

2. Such cartels as that representing the Krupp, Schneider-Creusot, Comité des Forges, Vickers combinations operated even in time of war and this operation undoubtedly gave rise to the ugly rumors that their respective factories in England, France and Germany were carefully protected from damage by bombing and enemy fire throughout World War I. Similar rumors existed during World War II concerning the great I. G. Farben cartelist chemical factories in Germany. The same cartelism produced a whole string of E. Phillips Oppenheim characters of which Sir Basil Zaharoff was the most notable example.

3. The present denationalization of the steel and trucking industries in Britain would normally offer an opportunity for breaking the old European pattern of the "closed" corporation. These industries *could* be bought back from nationalization by permitting the purchase of only a small number of shares by any individual. In such a process the ownership of the wealth and sources of future wealth in terms of working money would be widely distributed. Moreover, the possibility of re-nationalization through a change back to a Socialist-Labor government would be greatly lessened, because the steel industry would be *owned* actually by *thousands* and possibly hundreds of thousands of citizens rather than by a very small group which had the capital to take it back or which under the European system are always given the first opportunity to "get in on a good thing." Actually, the process of denationalizing industries, once a nation has jumped out of the frying pan of *European* capitalism into the fire of Socialism and nationalization, is an extremely difficult one. The difficulties in Britain are greatly augmented by the fact that the high taxes born of two wars and the greatly increased costs of bureaucratic government and "welfare" benefits under the Socialist-Labor planning have consumed the greater part of the savings of the small investor who might otherwise have bought his way into fractional ownership of the steel industry on the basis of shared American capitalism. Indeed, large amounts of capital, sufficient, free

and available, to buy back nationalized industry are difficult to find anywhere in Britain in these times, especially in view of the ever present possibility that such industries may be *re*nationalized the moment a Socialist-Labor government returns to power. It should not be forgotten that great amounts of British capital have been driven by confiscatory taxes overseas into colonies and dominions in order to escape death duties and are firmly invested there in enterprises of various sorts but mostly in landholdings. It is also true that under confiscatory taxes, many Britishers have been spending their capital to live well, with houses, servants, motors and prewar luxuries, rather than have it taken over by government in the form of "Cripps" taxes and death duties. Thus the British system under the stress of war and the headlong "reforms" of a Socialist-Labor government is dispersing and destroying at a wholesale rate the limited amount of capital that still remains in the country. Of course, even though the rich spend their capital to save it from death duties, it arrives in the end in the possession of government through taxes on the incomes of servants, automobiles, rich food or whatever it is spent for. Consequently, in the present unfortunate state of British government, half-Socialist, half-capitalist, the capital needed to build up, modernize and make efficient old industry and to make sound investments overseas, is rapidly being driven out or consumed either directly or indirectly by the constantly growing expense of inefficient and costly Socialist-Labor bureaucracy and "welfare" benefits. The result will be to paralyze and eventually destroy the operations of capital even on the old closed, cartelized European basis, and in the end to raise taxes and inevitably decrease benefits for the whole British citizenry.

This economic operation in a semi-Socialized state might well be studied by those New Dealers and Welfare Staters whose hearts bleed but whose observation, mental honesty and reason are weak.

4. There has never been an openly acknowledged Communist elected to the Congress of the United States or to any state legislature. The nearest approach was Vito Marcantonio (representing a New York City district), whose loud voice and votes certainly followed the party line. Yet even he was defeated for re-election in one of the poorest slum areas of the entire nation, despite a solid political organization, the wooing of unfortunate Puerto Rican immigrants and every possible political and demagogic trick. The Communist infiltration of labor unions and the Farmers' Union reached certain proportions and even John L. Lewis dealt with the Communists at times, but in the end, once their purposes and intrigues were revealed, union leaders and dues-paying union mem-

bers turned on them in fury. It is significant that the greatest support of the congressional, state and labor union investigations of the operations of Communism in the United States comes from the people themselves, from the farmer, the well-paid, skilled industrial worker, the filling station operator, the union member, the insurance agent, the small capitalist, the druggist, the small businessman—in short the whole middle class which the Communists hate and fear.

5. This paragraph should certainly not be interpreted as a blanket endorsement of the New Deal. The enduring reforms arising out of the Great Depression would have come about if the New Deal and Franklin D. Roosevelt had never existed, and the dross of the New Deal has been very largely eliminated, either because the measures were unconstitutional or because they were unworkable or damaging. It is a remarkable evidence of the workability and other virtues of the republican form of democratic government that such changes could come about and that eventually the bad *was* eliminated and the good retained. Such a gradual transition and reform is possible under no other form of government save the limited-monarchy, parliamentarian system represented by Britain or Sweden. It simply could not occur either under a strong Socialist or a Nazi-Communist form of government, for the simple and obvious reason that such governments are fundamentally bureaucratic and extremely rigid and unflexible, and in a complete Marxian dictatorship, such as that of Hitler or Stalin, entirely a matter of the will of a single man or at best of a small, tight oligarchy.

6. One of the commonest arguments made by the Communist-Socialist zealot against capitalism is the collapse of capitalism in the United States in the thirties. They fail entirely to mention the fact that millions under Socialist or Communist governments in Russia and even in Europe, live perpetually, year in and year out, at a material level as low or lower than that of the most unfortunate unemployed citizen during the tragic years of the Great Depression. They also neglect to mention the fact that a vast amount of constructive and preventive legislation has come out of the experience with the Great Depression, legislation which will make it extremely difficult for conditions ever again to reach the economic depths of the thirties. This very fact—that the system of American government and capitalism is highly flexible and constantly capable of self-criticism, change and compromise and progress, rather than fixed and rigid as is Marxian Socialism—is in itself evidence of the advantages of a government completely controlled by the people themselves over the oligarchic, dictator, or rigid and clumsy bureaucratic systems.

7. The same confusion and cross purposes infect our whole clumsy policy with regard to Asia. The exclusion of India from the Korean conference served no valid purpose and only augmented the ill feeling against us which steadily mounts throughout Asiatic countries. It is the natural function of a large and potentially powerful Asiatic nation to speak for the other Asiatic areas and to represent them. India, for the moment at least, is the natural and real spokesman for Asia in the dispute between this nation and Red China, yet we excluded her in a manner which was tactless, to put it mildly, while, again increasing almost simultaneously the hundreds of millions of military aid extended to the French in Indo-China, where they are not wanted and have no real right to be and cannot remain without our support. All this is done on the assumption and assertion that our whole Asiatic policy is based upon the need to defend ourselves against Communism and in particular Russian aggression. The mere implication that the U.S. is to dictate conditions in Asia and Asiatic policy in general, either directly or through aid to the French or British, is offensive to every Asiatic regardless of the grounds upon which we take action. The Asiatic peoples resent, and rightly so, the interference of the U.S. and European nations in the affairs of their particular area. In our policy toward Asia as a whole—whether our militarist policy of sticking our noses in everywhere or our actions as a bargain-rate police force for the U.N.—we are following a course which is doomed to fail, and which constantly builds up a sad stockpile of dislike and resentment which can only operate against us in the future. In the end the Asiatic peoples alone can settle their problems, both as individual nations and in relation to each other. Any interference on our part only damages our own internal economy and welfare, and endangers our relations with *all* Asiatic nations in the future. The fact is that Asiatic nations would welcome friendly co-operation from this country, but they resent interference and attempted dictation. Who can doubt that any nation struggling toward independence and dignity resents most of all unasked advice or pressures of any kind? At the present time our Asiatic policy, if any, seems to be one of the worst manifestations of the megalomania which has afflicted most of our generals and a large part of our pro-British State Department. There is a vast field for leadership and guidance in Asiatic affairs, and Asiatic nations—especially India—have always been friendly toward the U.S. and toward individual Americans; but we are certainly doing our best, as rapidly as possible, to destroy their sympathy and friendliness.

8. That peoples of different customs and traditions and even different races, speaking different languages, can live together under a common

government in peace and augmented prosperity has been proven many times. Switzerland with three languages and three cultural traditions is, of course, the classic example, but within our own times we have witnessed the union and the gradual adjustment to a basis of understanding co-operation of such diverse, proud and almost tribal peoples as the Croats, Slovenes and Serbs or in Czechoslovakia, the Czechs and Slovaks. Many of the divisions of these peoples were kept alive in the past by political oppression and exploitation by the old Austro-Hungarian empire, which practiced a permanent political policy of playing one people against the other. There can be no argument whatever about the vast benefits economic union and cooperation would bring these small peoples. In a modern world complete independence and intense nationalism can yield them only a wretched and poverty-stricken existence.

It is interesting to speculate what would have been the history of the world if three hundred years ago France and Germany had begun to function under a common economy. Geographically, economically, agriculturally, in terms of population and in every possible way, France and Germany should always have been one nation. If such a union had existed, the British Empire might never have come into being at all and the old vicious balance of power tactics might never have existed. Very likely there would have been today only one great European power. This was the very heart of Napoleon's political and economic policies and of his effort to unify Europe by force, since at that time it could be unified in no other way. Indeed this philosophy of Napoleon and the pattern born of it may well be in the long run of history Napoleon's greatest single claim to fame. There has always existed a persistent impulse among some Germans and French to bring about such a union, but it has been thwarted for centuries by dynastic ambitions, by differences of culture and language which ran counter to fundamental economic interests. It is this impulse which has from time to time given rise in Bavaria and in the Rhineland to separatist movements favoring union with France and in France to those elements which have constantly favored closer economic co-operation with Germany. Indeed many perfectly honest French politicians, before World War II and even during the War, were given the contemptuous name of collaborationists because they espoused such an economic co-operation. In the broader sense of the material interests of France, they were perfectly right. Some of them were undoubtedly prompted by the hatred of Britain and her diplomatic intrigues which has always existed in both France and Germany. The whole policy of Britain for nearly two centuries has been consistently to prevent any such *entente*, economic or otherwise, between Germany and France.

9. This partition is a striking example of the economic disadvantages of fragmentation. It left agriculture largely in Pakistan and industry in India, thus creating stresses, shortages and limitations crippling to both nations. A united India and Pakistan would solve many of the difficulties plaguing both nations and make India without question the soundest and most powerful nation in Asia and a nucleus about which Asiatic peoples and nations might gather in mutual co-operation for the benefit of all.

VI

SUMMARY

1. The use of the name Selective Service to soften the honest if ugly meaning of the word conscription has been part of a general program of deception. The purpose of the original Selective Service law was ostensibly what it said—that in time of total warfare, young men and even citizens of all kinds, should be drafted to the task or job in which they could make the greatest possible contribution to the total war effort. This meaning and intent has long since been cynically tossed into the discard and the policy in general has been to conscript *all young* men indiscriminately. Now and then this policy has been violently and successfully disputed, but the only other exception has been the case of the "college deferments." This is a somewhat fantastic interpretation of the Selective Service Act, which in some hundreds or perhaps thousands of cases permitted students who secured deferments to escape service altogether by marrying and producing dependents while still in college. Only a decision by President Eisenhower as Commander-in-Chief closed this loophole. The Armed Forces, and in particular the Army, are constantly complaining that they are "scraping the bottom of the barrel" for conscript material. This is another piece of deception and a situation, if true, that is created by the army itself through its refusal to lower the physical and mental standards of acceptable conscripts. These standards are fantastic compared to those of any other nation in the world. They require almost physical perfection and a high intelligence even for clerks, typists and the thousands of soldiers engaged in purely menial tasks. If the Armed Forces abided by the standards that all other nations have found acceptable and workable, there would be no shortage at all of potential conscript material. Furthermore I have never been able to uncover the least evidence of any attempt by the Armed Forces to check on draft registration or registration cards. I think it reasonable to suppose that there are in this country upward of at least 200,000

potential draftees who have never taken the trouble to register at all. Much of this group, which is escaping military service, belongs to what might be called the "floating population;" it is an element that would probably benefit by army training and experience. These people could be found in beer parlors and dancehalls in every part of the U.S. but apparently no effort whatever is made to round them up. As a result, the legitimate cases for deferment are denied while this more undesirable element runs entirely free (and is frequently the cause of much petty crime), largely because the Armed Forces and in particular the Army want only "the cream." Owing to this negligence, the penalty of conscription is imposed entirely upon the honest and conscientious elements of our society. The truth is that the original Selective Service Act left far too large a margin for "interpretation" to the brass of the Armed Forces and that in general the administration of the law has been capricious and muddled and unfair. Since it was passed the Selective Service Act has undergone so many amendments that it is difficult today to discover what it really does mean. If conscription is to be continued Congress has an obligation to enact a new law in which the purpose and administration are clarified and severe limitations put upon the "interpretation" now employed so loosely by the Armed Forces. No other nation tolerates such a situation, and the reform can only be brought about by pressure of American citizens upon their representatives in Congress.

2. Part of the necessary revaluation and reorganization now taking place should be, it seems to me, extended still further into the field of the future. An article by General Carl Spaatz in *Newsweek* of September 21 should cause a lot of thinking. General Spaatz points out that the atomic-propelled submarine is a reality and that atomic propulsion permits a submarine to go anywhere in the world without refueling and that it can operate almost indefinitely anywhere without the necessity of emerging to the surface. General Spaatz questions seriously the value of the super-aircraft carriers which are planned at a cost running into billions. It is clear that an atomic submarine could do away with any carrier in a second. Or one could be vaporized by a single atomic bomb or a suicide plane in the same length of time. Yet the Navy has been feuding with Air Force and Army for years to construct these antique engines of warfare which the atomic bomb and atomic-propelled submarine have made as obsolete a weapon as the Roman catapult.

In the same fashion the Army continues to clamor for more conscripts in order to carry on the kind of warfare which in the atomic era is comparable to the cross-bow battle of Agincourt. The Army is pushing a hugely expensive "atomic cannon" (presumably just to get its oar in) which is so clumsy, heavy and unmaneuverable that special bridges and special trains would have to be built to transport it from one area to another. It could be vaporized by a single bomb. It cannot be moved forward quickly in ground battle nor can it be withdrawn quickly in time of retreat. And the cost of a single atomic cannon represents the lifetime earnings of a dozen prosperous American citizens.

What has become overnight of the fabulously expensive old dreadnaughts? You know the answer. The best use for the Big Mo would be to tie her up in the Hudson River and charge admission to see her. She is virtually in the class with the old flagship *Constitution*.

Set in Linotype Janson
Format by Robert Cheney
Manufactured by The Haddon Craftsmen, Inc.
Published by HARPER & BROTHERS, *New York*